DEFENDING HERTFORDSHIRE

DEFENDING HERTFORDSHIRE

The Military Landscape from Prehistory to the Present

MIKE OSBORNE

FONTHILL

First published in Great Britain in 2026 by
Fonthill
An imprint of
Pen & Sword Books Ltd
Yorkshire – Philadelphia
www.fonthill.media

ISBN 978-1-03615-681-7

A CIP catalogue record for this book
is available from the British Library.

Typeset in SabonLTStd 10/13 by
SJmagic DESIGN SERVICES, India.
Printed and bound in the UK by CPI Group (UK) Ltd, Croydon, CR0 4YY

FSC
www.fsc.org
MIX
Paper | Supporting responsible forestry
FSC® C013604

The Publisher's authorised representative in the EU for product
safety is Authorised Rep Compliance Ltd., Ground Floor,
71 Lower Baggot Street, Dublin D02 P593, Ireland.
www.arccompliance.com

For a complete list of Pen & Sword titles please contact
PEN & SWORD BOOKS LIMITED
George House, Units 12 & 13, Beevor Street, Off Pontefract Road,
Barnsley, South Yorkshire, S71 1HN, England
E-mail: enquiries@pen-and-sword.co.uk
Website: www.pen-and-sword.co.uk

or

PEN AND SWORD BOOKS
1950 Lawrence Rd, Havertown, PA 19083, USA
E-mail: uspen-and-sword@casematepublishers.com
Website: www.penandswordbooks.com

Acknowledgements

I am indebted to Fred Nash who surveyed the Outer London Defence Line 'A' in Hertfordshire for the County Council and made his collated results available for Colin Alexander and myself to walk the Line back in the 1990s as part of the Defence of Britain Project. William Foot, with whom I was fortunate to collaborate on that project, includes a detailed description of the Cheshunt section of the Outer London defence-line 'A' in his detailed study of the anti-invasion landscape of 1940.

Amongst those to whom thanks are due for providing information, for permission to reproduce illustrations or for facilitating access to sites are: Paul Francis; Mike Bardell; Bonnie West and Florence Dahlberg at Hertfordshire Archives and Local Studies; Lawrence Lucas of Bell Farm, Nuthampstead; Gabriel and colleagues at The Grove, Watford; kind people with long memories at Ganwick Farm; the current occupants of Bricket Wood; the manager at A10 Timber at Barwick; and the Bishops Stortford Tourist Information Centre; and Linda Dixon, Nick Catford and Keith Ward at Subterranea Britannica.

As ever I am indebted to my wife, Pam, who has helped with fieldwork and general encouragement. I must, once again, acknowledge the professionalism of those at Fonthill.

Mike Osborne, Market Deeping

Contents

Abbreviations

AA	anti-aircraft
AA	Automobile Association
ACF	army cadet force
ADGB	Air Defence Great Britain
AFS	Auxiliary Fire Service
AI	airborne interception (radar)
AM	Air Ministry
ARC	Army Reserve centre (formerly TA centre)
ARG	Airfield Research Group
ARP	air raid precautions
ARS	air raid shelter
A/T	anti-tank
ATA	Air Transport Auxiliary (civilian ferry pilots)
ATC	air traffic control (tower)
ATC	Air Training Corps
ATS	Auxiliary Territorial Service (1938–49, then WRAC)
BAT	beam approach training
BEF	British Expeditionary Force
BHQ	battle headquarters
BL	breech-loading (artillery piece)
CBA	Council for British Archaeology
CCF	Combined Cadet Force (successor to JOTC)
CD	Civil Defence
C-in-C	commander-in-chief
CO	commanding officer
CRO	Civilian Repair Organisation (Second World War aircraft)
CTA	county territorial association
DFW3	Directorate of Fortifications and Works, Department 3
DH	de Havilland
DL	defended locality

DMV	deserted medieval village
DPs	displaced persons (post-Second World War)
DORA	Defence of the Realm Act (emergency legislation)
EFTS	Elementary Flying Training School
EMS	emergency medical service
E&R FTS	Elementary and Reserve Flying Training School
ETOUSA	European Theatre of Operations United States Army
FTS	Flying Training School
GC&CS	Government Code and Cipher School
GCHQ	Government Communications HQ (successor to GC&CS)
GCI	Ground Control Interception (radar system starting from Second World War)
GDA	gun-defended area (AA defences)
GHQ	General Headquarters (GHQ Line, GHQ Reserve, etc.)
GL	gun-laying (radar)
GPO	General Post Office
GS	grammar school
GWR	Great Western Railway
ha	hectare (2.5 acres)
HAA	heavy anti-aircraft
HCC	Hertfordshire County Council
HD	Home Defence (First World War RFC squadrons)
HER	Heritage Environment Records (ex-Sites and Monuments Record)
HG	Home Guard
ICI	Imperial Chemical Industries
KRRC	King's Royal Rifle Corps
LAA	light anti-aircraft
LDV	Local Defence Volunteers (later Home Guard) (Second World War)
LG	landing ground
LMS	London Midland Scottish (railway)
LNER	London North-Eastern Railway
MAFF	Ministry of Agriculture, Fisheries and Food (post-Second World War)
MAP	Ministry of Aircraft Production (Second World War)
MI5, MI6, etc.	military intelligence departments
MOS	Ministry of Supply
MP	military police
MRRS	military road route system
MT	motor transport
MU	Maintenance Unit (RAF)
NAAFI	Navy, Army, and Air Force Institutes

NATO	North Atlantic Treaty Organisation
NCO	non-commissioned officer—corporal, sergeant, warrant officer, etc.
NFS	National Fire Service (Second World War)
NRA	National Rifle Association
OTC	Officer Training Corps (school or university cadet corps)
OTU	Operational Training Unit (RAF Bomber/Training commands)
(P)AFU	(Pilot) Advanced Flying Unit
POW	prisoner of war
QF	quick firing (artillery piece)
QAIMNS	Queen Alexandra's Imperial Military Nursing Service
QM	quartermaster (logistics organisation and personnel)
RA	Royal Artillery
R & D	research and development
RAuxAF	Royal Auxiliary Air Force (until 1957)
RAF	Royal Air Force (from 1 April 1918)
RAFVR	Royal Air Force Volunteer Reserve
RAMC	Royal Army Medical Corps
(R)AOC	(Royal from 1918) Army Ordnance Corps (until 1993)
(R)ASC	(Royal from 1918) Army Service Corps (until 1993)
RCM	radio countermeasures (the beam-benders)
RE	Royal Engineers
REME	Royal Electrical and Mechanical Engineers (formed 1942)
RFA	Royal Field Artillery
RFC	Royal Flying Corps (up to 31 March 1918)
RFCA	Reserve Forces and Cadets Association (successor to CTAs)
RGA	Royal Garrison Artillery
RHA	Royal Horse Artillery
RHQ	Regimental Headquarters
RLG	relief landing ground
RN	Royal Navy
RNAS	Royal Naval Air Service (until 31 March 1918)
(R)OC	(Royal from 1941) Observer Corps
RSG	regional seat of government
RSM	regimental sergeant major—the most senior NCO
RSS	Radio Security Service
RTR	Royal Tank Regiment—mechanized cavalry units
RVC	Rifle Volunteer Corps (1859–81)
SAA	small arms ammunition
SAC	Strategic Air Command (USAF, post-Second World War)
SAM	surface-to-air missile

SAS	Special Air Service
SF	Special Fires (bombing decoy—aka 'Starfish')
SFTS	Service Flying Training School
SIS	Secret Intelligence Service (also known as MI6)
S/L	searchlight
SLG	satellite landing-ground
SOC	Sector Operations Centre
SOE	Special Operations Executive
SOS	Service of Supply (US army logistics organisation)
SP	self-propelled (artillery piece mounted on armoured vehicle)
STS	Special Training School (SOE)
TA	Territorial Army (from 1920–39 and 1947–2014)
TAC	Territorial Army Centre (Drill Hall 1947–2014) (see ARC)
tb	temporary brick (single brick with buttresses in RAF buildings)
TDS	training depot station
TF	Territorial Force (from 1908–18)
TNA	The National Archive (formerly Public Record Office, Kew)
u/g	underground
UHF	ultra high frequency (radio wavelength)
UKWMO	United Kingdom Warning and Monitoring Organisation
UP	unrotated projectile (see ZAA)
USAAC	United States Army Air Corps (until 1941)
USAAF	United States Army Air Forces (1941–47)
USAF(E)	United States air force (Europe) (1947–present)
VAD	Voluntary Aid Detachment (First World War)
VB	volunteer battalion (volunteer elements of line regiments)
VHF	very high frequency (radio wavelength)
VTC	Volunteer Training Corps (First World War)
WAAF	Women's Auxiliary Air Force
WOSB	War Office Selection Board
YMCA	Young Men's Christian Association

Introduction

Straddling three of the major northern approaches into London, and traversed by prehistoric trackways and Roman roads, the county of Hertfordshire has always enjoyed strategic importance. Defensive structures of national, regional, or merely local significance have always been prominent in the landscape across the centuries. These include Iron Age and Roman forts; early medieval *burhs* and earthwork castles; the stone castles and strong houses of kings, prelates, and nobles; right through to the last-ditch anti-invasion defences of the Second World War.

The manoeuvres of armies through numerous civil conflicts, most rooted in the possession and domination of territory, have sometimes culminated in pitched battles such as those at Barnet and the two at St Albans during the Wars of the Roses. The threat of foreign invasion, real or delusory, whether at the instigation of disaffected sections of society or as a product of the paranoia of kings and politicians has resulted in widespread defensive measures being undertaken. These have taken the form of both physical structures and the raising of volunteer defence forces.

In the twentieth century, two world wars produced a militarised landscape of extensive airfields and training camps; industries intensively adapted to a focus on munitions production; anti-invasion defences; and the infrastructure to support these developments. Much of the detail of these circumstances resides in local memory and opportunities to tap into this are fast disappearing, so every opportunity must be taken to record the field where aircraft chasing the Zeppelins landed to refuel in 1915, the house which served as a military HQ in 1940 when invasion was expected, where air raid shelters were located and where a bomb landed in 1941.

Much of our rich heritage is still visible and this book, the thirteenth in the series which began with *Defending Lincolnshire* in 2010, sets out to show what once was and what remains. But there are still mysteries to be solved. The eight earthwork mounds so closely adjacent to the outer ditch of Great

Berkhamsted Castle were surely built for the purposes of the defenders, rather than as artillery platforms for the besiegers, but only their excavation might give us an answer. Nevertheless, discoveries of heritage survivals or their original existence continue to be made by fieldwork, oral evidence and documentary research, and readers are urged to report any such happy event to the relevant Heritage Environment Record.

For the purposes of this book, Hertfordshire is defined as the Hundreds of Braughing; Broadwater; Cashio, including Chipping Barnet and East Barnet—the Liberty of St Albans; Dacorum (Tring & Danais); Edwintree; Hertford; Hitchin; and Odsey. It will take in East Barnet and Barnet, the two urban districts which were hived off to the Greater London Council (GLC) in 1965 to form part of the outer London Borough of Barnet. In 1993, Elstree and Borehamwood, parts of which had once resided in the former county of Middlesex and parts in the Liberty of St Albans, were wholly incorporated into Hertfordshire. The spellings of Great Berkhamsted, Little Berkhamsted, Nuthampstead and Wheathampstead conform to that adopted by the Ordnance Survey as do those of South Mimms and North Mymms.

1

Defensive Structures and Military Activity Prior to the Norman Conquest

This chapter covers eras which, to some extent, overlap but nevertheless may conveniently be split three ways: the Bronze and Iron Ages; the Roman occupation; and the period of migration or early medieval period, lasting from the departure of the Romans until the Norman Conquest, during which time the county's main occupants were Anglo-Saxons.

Prehistoric Hertfordshire

According to the list of scheduled ancient monuments published by what was to become English Heritage, there are six monuments in Hertfordshire which appear to fall into the category of 'hillfort'.

One, Arbury Banks, however, cannot ever have represented a serious fortification. On the other hand, the impressive position and defences of Ravensburgh Castle has caused it to be put forward as a possible candidate for a sometime stronghold of Cassivelaunus, the leader of the Catuvellauni, who resisted the first Roman invasion led by Julius Caesar in 54 BC.

Both Ravensburgh and Wilbury Hill, outside Letchworth, have been associated with a chain of hillforts along the line of the Chilterns, which may have related to the Icknield Way, the prehistoric trackway which enters the county to the north of Luton, proceeds through Letchworth and Baldock, and exits the county at Ashwell. Prehistoric sites along this trajectory are still appearing and recent LiDAR surveys have revealed a newly discovered hillfort, 'somewhere in the Chilterns', whose precise location remains secret.

Arbury Banks, in Ashwell, is a settlement standing 295ft (90m) above sea level and measuring 315x265yds (290x245m) in the shape of an elongated horseshoe, dated to the Late Bronze Age (1,000–700 BC). It was surrounded by a weak rampart and ditch, both of which have largely disappeared, only surviving as buried features. The ditch was originally 20ft (6m) across and

15ft (4.5m) deep, but the internal rampart measures an inconsequential height at the south-western end of the site. There were entrances on the north-west and the south-east where causeways crossed the ditch. Aerial photographs have enabled the identification of hut circles and several square enclosures. It is possible that livestock were kept in the enclosures for safety and that the huts were permanent dwellings with pits for storing surplus crops. The discovery of Roman coins may offer evidence of continued occupation.

Ravensburgh Castle, in Hexton, on the other hand, is an imposing rectangular hillfort enclosing an area of 22 acres (9ha). Now masked by the trees, initially planted in 1908, it occupies a site of exceptional natural strength, but its steep, formerly treeless slopes were revealed in a photograph of c. 1900, demonstrating its dominant position in the landscape. While finds and the footprint of a larger-than-normal roundhouse indicated occupation of the site in much earlier times, the fort was built around 400 BC. Two further distinct building periods followed, before a significant refortification in about 50 BC. Surveys on two sides revealed double ramparts and ditches with less well-defined defences on the eastern side. The entrance in the north-west corner, with in-turned and out-turned banks, accessed by a hollow way across a neck of land from the main hill, belongs to the original construction, whilst that on the south-east was added in c. 50 BC and may have been given additional defences. The north-western gate defences incorporate an apparent tumulus which may have had special significance beyond the functional but would have still contributed height to the defenders and has been consciously integrated into the defences.

In places the ditch measures 40–60ft (12–18m) across, and the rampart is 16–18ft (5–5.5m) high. On all sides, but to a lesser extent on the east, the ground falls away steeply. Evidence of burning on that more vulnerable,

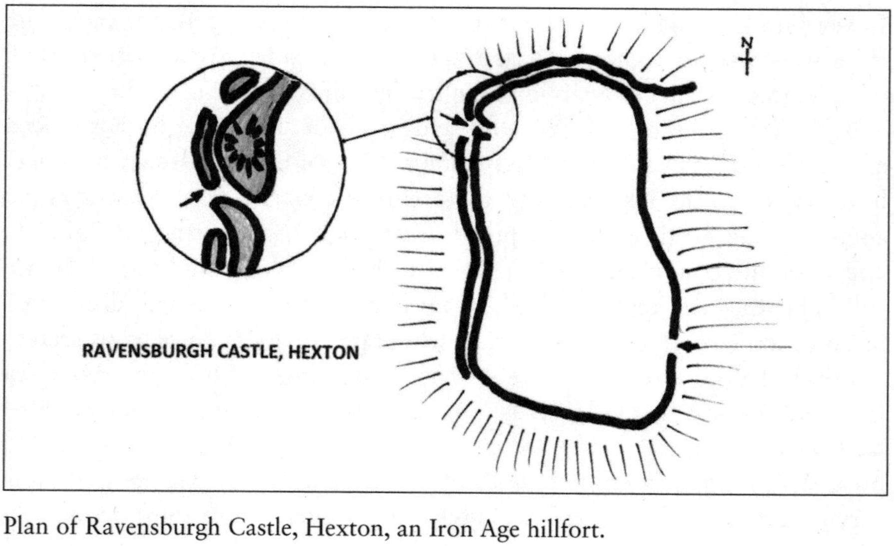

Plan of Ravensburgh Castle, Hexton, an Iron Age hillfort.

eastern rampart may point to the site's involvement in conflict, possibly around the time of its refortification. It was still in occupation at the time of the Claudian invasion in AD 43. Material for the ramparts appears to have been extracted from the interior of the fort where the pits of chalk quarries have been traced.

Wilbury Hill, outside Letchworth, covering an area of 14 acres (5.5ha), was built around 700 BC, toward the end of the Bronze Age. An eastern enclosure surrounded by a bank and ditch, and 650ft (200m) across, abuts a larger, semi-circular enclosure, similarly banked and ditched, which extends towards the west. Excavations have shown that the eastern enclosure dates from the late Bronze Age when a weak bank supported a palisade within a shallow ditch which was subsumed by later works. Around 400 BC, stronger defences were constructed within ditches measuring 25ft (8m) across and 9ft (2.7m) deep. The southern entrance was across a causeway and through a sequence of timber gateways signified by postholes.

The adjacent rampart contained timber frameworks to bind the earth and rubble infill, and revetments to limit slide. Indications of a causeway on the western side suggest a connection between the two enclosures. The interior of the eastern enclosure contains remains of hearths, flint-cobbled surfaces, storage pits and huts. No signs of habitation were uncovered in the western enclosure, suggesting its use was mainly for agriculture and livestock. Quarrying for railway ballast in the northern corner of the western enclosure yielded Roman coins, which prompted a claim, never to be substantiated, for the site as a Roman fort, although occupation by Romano-British farmers may well have continued.

The Aubreys, in Redbourn, described by Historic England as a plateau fort, on a flat area overlooked by higher ground on all sides, is an oval enclosure dating from the Iron Age with a double bank and ditch on three sides but a stretch of single bank and ditch on the north-west. It covers an area of 20 acres (8ha), and its original main entrance, described as of the 'passage' type, with in-turned ramparts, was on the west. There is no evidence for permanent occupation and the camp appears to have been abandoned soon after the start of the Roman occupation.

As well as these hillforts, there are other related sites in the county which may or may not have been defensive. One such site is the trapezoidal, univallate, embanked enclosure in Brickkiln Wood, Cockernhoe, near Offley. This has been identified as a possible late-Iron Age or Romano-British settlement site, most likely related to stock control. The area enclosed is around 3.75 acres (1.5ha), which is slightly larger, and may be slightly older, than many of the 100-plus analogous sites in the county. It occupies an elevated site and has an entrance formed of parallel in-turned banks forming a funnel. As an indication of its future use, there is evidence for historic clay extraction dating back to, at least, Roman times.

Given the discrepancies in the criteria for *oppida*, or tribal centres, between Continental Europe and England, the status of Wheathampstead has been called into question. What has long been traditionally accepted as the Belgic *oppidum* of Wheathampstead, generally thought to have been the capital of the Catuvellauni, is represented by the Devils Dyke and The Slad, two parallel lengths of rampart and ditch, roughly 1,100yds (1km) apart, forming two sides of a large enclosure of around 100 acres (40ha). The western Devil's Dyke, running for 430yds (400m), 130ft (40m) across and up to 40ft (12m) deep, ran along the base of the hill which, rising to a height of 360ft (111m), provided a secure base for the Iron Age camp.

The Devil's Dyke part of Wheathampstead's Iron Age defences appears to line up with the Beech Bottom Dyke, which stretches for nearly a mile (1,500m) in the north of modern-day St Albans and extends as far as Gorhambury, where a further section remains. It is of impressive proportions, being as much as over 30ft (10m) deep and up to 95ft (30m) wide. This last section terminates at the bottom of the hill which demarcates the forested clay-land to the west.

These three lengths of dyke share building techniques and dimensions, and it would appear that this dyke could have been constructed to mark a territorial boundary between the rivers Ver and Lea as well as a defence against cattle raiders. A hoard of coins, deposited in the partially infilled dyke, point to a date prior to AD 120. It must be noted, however, that the recent study by Bryant has shown scepticism over Wheathampstead's status as an *oppidum*, citing lack of evidence for sufficient occupation, ritual and burials. It is also possible that The Slad is actually a natural feature.

Excavations in Prae Wood, to the west of the later Roman city, uncovered a settlement site which extended for around half a mile (800m) along the hilltop and as far south as the Hemel Hempstead road (A4147). Its construction suggests parallels with Wheathampstead, and it may represent its first successor, being occupied between the end of the first century BC and the Roman invasion of AD 43. In AD 50 the Catevellauni of Verlamion were granted self-government as a *municipium*, and it is likely that it was this tribal capital, a collection of huts with no defensive works, probably the settlement in Prae Wood, which was destroyed by Boudica in AD 60. A rebuilt Verlamion, characterised by the earthwork known as the Fosse, was established in the second half of the first century AD as the new *oppidum*, or fortified capital, of the Catevellauni under the leadership of Tasciovanus, apparently assuming the status of any earlier Belgic *oppidum* such as Wheathampstead and on a site exhibiting no evidence of earlier occupation.

Additionally, there are several Iron Age settlements recorded in the county, including that related to the very significant cremation cemetery at Welwyn, but most of them seem to have been at most ditched and lacking anything approaching substantial defences. Such enclosures as that excavated at

Panshanger Golf Complex, would have been effective in protecting livestock from predators but were unlikely to have been intended as serious defences against human aggressors.

Gorhambury was a late-Iron Age settlement, abutting the imposing New Dyke. It had an aisled timber barn, a granary, a roundhouse, and other structures within a ditched enclosure. It later developed into a Roman villa with masonry buildings being added to the earlier farmstead. Dating from the first century BC, the complex straddling the river Rib and centred on Braughing-Puckeridge, has many of the attributes of other supposed *oppida*, including a wealth of imported wares, but lacks defences.

Only the undated Gatesbury earthwork on the east bank of the Rib shows evidence of any attempt at fortification, and then only of a small area within a much larger complex. Here, a double-ditched oval enclosure of 7.5 acres (3ha) accessed via a flint causeway, contained an inner ditch and a bank supporting a timber palisade. The wider settlement as a whole appears to have lost status early in the next century.

Baldock, dating from the later first century BC, and seen as an important late-Iron Age site, was defended by neither its Iron Age nor its Romano-British inhabitants. Bryant's study of the major Iron Age locations within the St Albans area and the Rib and Gade valleys has concluded that strategic military considerations in their selection were secondary to other factors such as communications and access to agriculture and trade. However, there was no evident attempt to exert control over those trade routes by implanting fortified settlements.

As we have seen at Wheathampstead, he also questions the criteria by which *oppida* have historically been defined, referencing the differences between those of the English south-east and the monumental fortresses of the Gauls. The best known of those was Alesia, most probably in Burgundy, but its location remains the subject of many alternative suggestions. It was the capital of Vercingetorix, stormed by the Romans under Julius Caesar in 52 BC. In neither form nor function would sites identified as English *oppida* compare with such places.

An extremely thorough exploration of early British history by Miles Russell, drawing on the writings of Gildas, Nennius, Bede and Geoffrey of Monmouth, and taking the kings as its primary focus, sheds light on personalities, events, and locations. Cassivelaunus appears to have occupied a position of overlordship amongst the tribes of the region: the Catuvellauni, the Trinovanti, the Iceni of Norfolk/Suffolk, and the Cantiaci of Kent. While the Catuvellauni were centred on Verlamion, the Trinovantes were based in Camulodunum, later Colchester, but it is likely that the two tribes were combined under a single leader, possibly Tasciovanus, by the first century AD when his coins bore the stamps of both centres: VER and CAM.

Further evidence provided by coinage, predominantly emanating from Hertfordshire, and bearing the name Addedomarus, appears to point to another authenticated ruler of the Catuvellauni, following Cassivelaunus, whose death one writer dates to 48 BC, but predating the time of Tasciovanus. The various historic accounts which Russell interrogates, compiled between 600 and 1,100 years after the events described, are inevitably garbled, with some even recording three Roman incursions under Julius Caesar. Contemporary or earlier accounts are cut and pasted by the later writers, attempting to make sense of a plethora of contradictory statements; confusions over names and places; and all parcelled up within a mix of oral tradition, myth and legend, not to mention pure fantasy.

LINEAR DYKES

As well as the dyke connecting Wheathampstead and Verlamion, there are several other such lengths of dyke, dated to the Iron Age, which may denote tribal or clan boundaries, or they may simply have been dug to control progress along the Icknield Way, where they parallel similar such blocking earthworks in Bedfordshire to the west and Cambridgeshire to the east. They include Telegraph Hill, near Ravensburgh Castle; Deadman's Hill, near Arbury Banks; and Mile Ditches, west of Royston, which originally comprised three ditches and four banks.

Much discussion surrounds the generically named 'Grims Ditch' in the vicinity of Berkhamsted and Tring, which appears to be part of a longer, but discontinuous, dyke system extending into Buckinghamshire. Although sometimes presented as a Saxon boundary, its origins in the Iron Age, revealed by excavation, do not preclude its later reuse. It took the form of a bank of upcast earth with a turf core, separated from a ditch by a berm. The ditch was always downslope from the bank and had a timber fence or palisade supported by a trench along its outer rim.

A surviving stretch of Grim's Ditch, west of Chesham Road at Wigginton Bottom, extends for 1,460yds (1,350m). It has been pointed out that this length of dyke, 10–12ft (3–4m) in height and 20ft (6m) across, does not follow the contours of the land, and overlooks the southern end of the Bulbourne valley close to where it joins the valley of the Gade. It would thus have presented a dominant feature on the skyline to the traveller approaching from the south, possibly acting as much as a political statement as a functional barrier.

Roman Hertfordshire

The Romans under Julius Caesar were more ambitious in their second invasion of England in 54 BC. Constantly harassed by local tribes, Caesar's five legions with a strong force of attendant cavalry, chose a route which took them from their landing place on the east Kent coast and across Surrey to a point west of London, where it would be possible to cross the Thames. This would be the first point at which serious opposition would be encountered, as the crossing would be contested by forces under Cassivelaunus, who, despite other tribes choosing to submit to Caesar, chose to fight.

The Romans overcame the makeshift defences of the Thames crossing, consisting of iron-shod and lead-sheathed sharpened stakes, and advanced northwards. The Roman advance was informed by those they encountered, who directed them to the stronghold of Cassivelaunus, traditionally accepted as being at Wheathampstead. The Romans laid siege to the fortress, but, lacking siege engines, and labouring under a rain of missiles hurled down from the high ramparts, the Roman legionaries would have resorted to attempts to storm the gate under the protection of their interlocking shields, forming the *testudo* or 'tortoise'.

Although Cassius Dio, writing a century after the events in question, states that the Britons were driven from their fortress, such an assault may never have taken place, as the Romans' tactic of laying waste the surrounding lands of the Catuvellauni persuaded Cassivelaunus to come to terms. Caesar admitted to learning little from the fighting tactics of the Britons beyond their use of light chariots, whose operation in the hit-and-run raids had been a constant irritation, although the Romans' counter-tactics, perfected only with great difficulty, would ultimately prove effective.

It must be noted that those tactics employed against the Romans in 54 BC—the deployment of chariots; the preference for open or loose formations; and the complementary use of infantry and cavalry as a tightly-packed shock force, making oblique attacks on enemy advances, or advancing themselves—all re-appear in Geofrey of Monmouth's fanciful accounts of the campaigns of Arthur, five centuries after the fighting choreographed by Cassivellaunus. So closely aligned are the parallels between the characters, locations and events related by Geoffrey of Monmouth in his versions of the twin stories of Cassivellaunus and King Arthur, that Russell sees one as the source of inspiration for the other, extrapolating from the time and place of Hertfordshire in the first century BC to the whole of Britain in the sixth century AD.

It is significant that while Julius Caesar achieved his, albeit limited, ambition to impose Roman order on the British by extracting tribute and acquiring hostages, his hurried exit from Britain was hailed by later patriotic writers as a great victory for Cassivellaunus.

Although Julius Caesar never returned to Britain, there were three occasions when Augustus made tentative plans to invade: in 34, 27 and 26 BC. The motivation for such an expedition may have been connected with the sojourn in Rome of Dubnovellaunus, apparently a king or tribal leader whose name appears on coins minted in the region, who was seeking military aid from Rome to effect his reinstatement, having been ousted by Cassivelaunus or one of his successors.

The rule of Cassivelaunus was followed, not necessarily immediately, by that of his nephew Tasciovanus, one of whose sons was Cunobelin, who may have been raised in Rome, held as a hostage, but exposed to the benefits, and infused with the values of Roman civilisation. He ruled both the Catuvellauni and the Trinovanti for around thirty years before AD 40 and was adopted by Shakespeare as Cymbeline and described by the Roman historian Suetonius as 'king of the Britons'. His brother and three sons expanded their influence into Kent and the territory of the Atrebates, south of the Thames.

Cunobelin's coins were stamped either CAM or VER and a hoard of over forty of his gold staters, dated to the period AD 8–41, was found as far away as Borden in Kent in 2019. Such finds demonstrate the spread of Catuvellaunian influence, but the accompanying physical acquisition of territory carried out by Cunobelin's brother Epaticcus and son Caratacus caused renewed interest in a Roman invasion when a defeated chief, Verica, fled to Rome to seek military aid. While both Cunobelin's sons led the resistance to the subsequent invasion of Claudius in AD 43, their resistance crumbled following two decisive defeats in battles where they failed to prevent the Roman legions crossing first the Medway and then the Thames.

It was Caratacus who would continue the British resistance, carrying out guerrilla warfare for ten years. But ultimately, he would be defeated in a set-piece battle, betrayed in his refuge and taken as a captive to Rome. Meanwhile, Cunobelin's other son, Togidubnus, had proved acceptable to the Romans as a client king, ruling from the civil *municipium* of Verulamium, Camulodunum having been appropriated by the Romans, initially for use as a military base and subsequently as a veterans' *colonia*.

As befits its strategic location, Hertfordshire is criss-crossed by Roman roads both south to north and east to west. Watling Street runs from London to the north-west of the country, passing through St Albans. Just to the north of St Albans, Akeman Street branches off from Watling Street to run west through Hemel Hempstead, Berkhamsted and Tring, terminating in Cirencester in Gloucestershire, where it meets the Fosse Way. Ermine Street, running north from London, enters the county at Cheshunt and leaves it at Royston, heading, ultimately, for Lincoln and York via Godmanchester. Stane Street, following the course of an ancient Belgic trackway, runs north-east from St Albans to Braughing, meeting another Roman road at Old Welwyn, which fords the river Mimram and runs north to Baldock, continuing to the Roman settlement of Sandy in Bedfordshire. Meanwhile, Stane Street, having crossed Ermine Street, runs eastwards from Braughing through Little Hadham and Bishops Stortford to Colchester. A further road runs north-west from Braughing to Baldock through Clothall.

These all represent key routes for moving troops and materials across the province and many of them attracted roadside settlements. Several such Roman stations have been located, including those at Baldock, Bishops

Stortford and Braughing on the road network, as well as other smaller settlements at Reed, Therfield, Clothall, Cow Roast, and at Wilbury Hill, which sits full-square on the ancient Icknield Way.

Baldock, designated as a nameless *vicus*, and representing an important crossroads, despite references to a possible Roman fort, was apparently undefended. However, the vestiges of earthworks near where Ermine Street, coming up from Braughing, enters the town may suggest an attempt to monitor or control traffic. Amongst traditional circular houses, two rectangular buildings stand out, one of which may have been a *mansio* or government resthouse for official travellers. Braughing, standing where Stane Street takes off from Ermine Street, and the start of roads to St Albans and Baldock, demonstrates more of the physical characteristics of a small Roman town, including a planned street grid and substantial stone, civic buildings, but was never fortified.

Traces of a further substantial Roman settlement have been found at Bishop's Stortford, where Stane Street crosses the river, not at the established ford which would have introduced a kink into the new road, but at a point where a timber bridge might have been necessary, though no bridge piers have ever been found. Sections of the Roman Stane Street had previously been excavated in 1976 at Legions Way, but recent excavations have uncovered a fresh section and revealed obvious signs of extensive commercial and industrial activity spanning the entire period of Roman occupation. This would suggest a trade hub with road and river links.

Whilst there is as yet no evidence for a permanent fort, a *mansio* probably stood near the ford, affirming the settlement officially as a posting station, but its status beyond that are only now being established. Despite the lack of evidence for a permanent fort, archaeologists have, however, found significant numbers of weapons and other military-related objects, suggesting either a settlement for veterans or a military presence, either permanent or intermittent. All this points to Bishop's Stortford being a destination in its own right, as well as the location for what has previously been described as a site analogous to motorway services.

Cow Roast, a Romano-British settlement near the source of the river Bulbourne on the other side of the county, has been designated a Roman town, and identified as the centre of the iron-working industry, continuing in operation into the fifth century. The preponderance of well-shafts and evidence of timber and flint structures point to its importance lying, well positioned, just off Akeman Street and on a drove road.

Following Boudica's destruction of the Belgic Verlamion, its Roman successor, Verulamium, was initially enclosed by a bank and ditch, the Fosse. The ditch, 50ft (15m) wide and 18ft (5.5m) deep, produced the gravel which formed the rampart which was then faced with turf to consolidate it. This first Roman-era enclosure, delineated by the Fosse, would, in turn, be replaced by a far larger urban area. Excavations in the 1930s found that where the new walls intersected the Fosse, it was flattened to produce a level compacted surface for the walls of the new town.

The Fosse was found to underlie this second Roman city wall which crossed it at an oblique angle near the Fosse's southern angle and just to the north of the later South-west Gate. The Fosse had then made a sharp eastward turn toward what would become the new North Gate. These new, third-century defences comprised a 2-mile circuit of walls of brick, tile and stone, with internal earthwork strengthening, and external, V-shaped ditches enclosing the expanding Roman city.

The North-east and South Gates through which Watling Street, on its way to Chester and London respectively, traversed the city, were monumental constructions each with a pair of D-shaped, four-storey towers flanking two pedestrian passages and two central archways for wheeled transport. The South-west gate opening onto the Silchester road was less ambitious and narrower, with two square-fronted towers, two pedestrian passageways and a single central archway over a carriageway of rammed gravel. This gate was contemporary with the third-century build and was later repaired.

At intervals between the gates, towers, solid to first-floor level, straddled the wall, presenting a sheer, semi-circular face to the field but affording storage to the rear. One of these towers was found to have fallen out of use by the late third century, suggesting that, unlike many Romano-British town defences, they had not been added to the original walls as artillery platforms. The walls were 16ft (5m) high and carried a wall walk protected by a parapet 5.5ft (1.8m) high with merlons. These allowed the defenders to fire bows and arrows or even small, wall-mounted, bolt-firing catapults such as the *manuballistra*. The internal face of the wall was backed by earth banks, sloping up to the rampart walk. The outer ditch was up to nearly 97.5ft (30m) wide and over 19ft (6m) deep. Foundations of the two D-shaped towers and entrance passageways of the Londinium or South-west Gate remain visible. A length of upstanding wall lies to its east, and a longer, lower length of wall with vestiges of one of those projecting turrets lies to its west.

Over the years there has been much speculation regarding the site of Boudica's defeat by Suetonius Paulinus, the governor of Britannia, as he travelled south from his campaign against the druids in Anglesey. Suggestions have ranged from sites on Watling Street, either close to Dunstable or further north at Mancetter, to Arbury Banks, and even to a site to the west of Silchester. The most recent proposal, from William Foot, is put forward on the basis of a supposed homeward retreat by the Iceni, eastwards along the Icknield Way, following the sack of St Albans. He suggests that Boudica transited Hertfordshire before she was caught by the Roman army in the Heydon Valley, a little way into western Cambridgeshire.

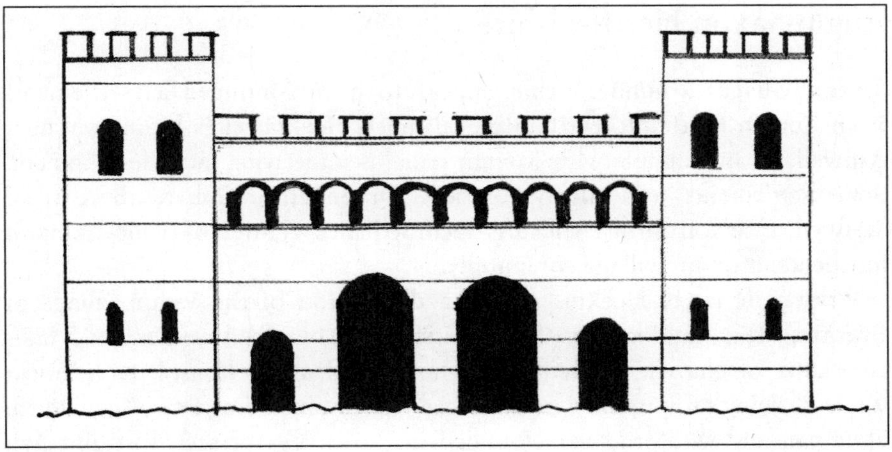

St Albans, reconstruction drawing of the Londinium Gate of Verulamium Roman town.

St Albans, the bases of the drum-shaped gate-towers of Verulamium's Londinium Gate.

St Albans, a short length of upstanding town wall at Verulamium Roman town.

Anglo-Saxon Hertfordshire

Several villages around Hitchin appear to have continued as settlements from Roman times into early medieval times. Hoskins cites Litlington, near Ashwell, as an example with Roman remains underlying later development. Some settlements were always outliers. Queen Hoo Hall, to the east of Welwyn, a Saxon farm enclosure, recorded in a charter of 1060, remains independent of any village community.

Writing in 1950, Hoskins quotes a description of the Saxon village of Bygrave, near Baldock, as 'a primitive self-contained settlement', later consisting of church, moated manor-house and a few houses, with 'not a single outlying farm in the parish'. Saxon villages, including Sawbridgeworth, Hadham, and Widford, were founded in the valleys of the Stort and Ash below the forested uplands. These would survive, but others such as Thorley, in a forest clearing, disappeared as a village, now represented only by a church and a hall and a scattering of dispersed farmsteads. Priors Hill in Pirton has been found to consist of three or even four rectangular enclosures, still partly represented by earthworks, which were occupied from the fifth to the ninth centuries by well-off families.

King Offa of Mercia founded the monastery of St Albans in 793. Unlike other monastic sites which exploited surviving Roman enclosures, Offa's monastery of St Albans was located outside the Roman town and surrounded by its own Anglo-Saxon boundary ditch, later built over and encroached on by a monks' cemetery. The monastery was plundered by the Danes in the time of Abbot Wulnoth in the early 900s.

Close by, but on a separate site, was the royal palace and associated township of Kingsbury. Conflict existed between this Kingsbury settlement and the dependency surrounding the abbey, and this may have been a further factor in Abbot Wulsin's decision to lay out a new town with a market in 948, offering greater security to the monastery. His successor, Abott Alfric, then purchased Kingsbury's fish-pool from King Ethelred and then destroyed the dam which controlled it, thereby taking away the townspeople's livings. The last vestiges were ploughed up in the reign of Stephen when a bastion, the last standing remnant of the borough's fortifications, was demolished. Only slight traces of the rampart remain, represented by the raised pavement on the north side of Fishpool Street. Building works have also uncovered evidence for the timber palisade which surrounded the town.

The recovery of the original charter, issued by Offa and subsequently lost, would represent one of the major goals for the townsfolk during the conflict in 1381. Even in 1100, St Alban's still had no more than 200 inhabitants. The manor of Hatfield, an area of woodland, was given by King Edgar to the monks of Ely in Cambridgeshire, at some time between 959 and 975, to provide them with timber for their building operations.

At the time of the Danish incursions of the eighth century, seaborne raiders sailed their shallow-draught longships far inland using navigable rivers such as the Cam, the Great Ouse and the Lea. The Danish 'Great Host' would over-winter by enclosing a semi-circular area of flat land backing onto the river with a palisaded rampart and ditch. The boats would be drawn up on land, timber huts would be built, and the crews would sit out the bad weather until the next season's campaigning could commence. Such a Danish camp is likely to have stood alongside the Lea and may possibly be represented by the outer earthworks of the later Norman castle.

Once demarcation lines had been drawn between the Saxon kingdoms and the Danelaw, the boundary would run along the course of the River Lea and Watling Street. Attempts by Alfred to make the river impassable to raiding longships by diverting the waters into numerous channels created problems once the river serving as the traditional boundary between Cheshunt (Hertfordshire) and Waltham Abbey (Essex) became obscured, each town, as might be expected, claiming the maximum territory. Alfred had also instituted a string of defended towns, known as *burhs*, to defend the border of his kingdom, and he began the construction of two such enclosures on opposite banks of the Lea at Hertford but abandoned them when the Danes retreated.

Alfred's policy of building *burhs* was continued by his daughter in Mercia and his son, Edward the Elder, in Wessex. Each *burh* consisted of a planned settlement on a grid system enclosed by ramparts and ditches. There were robust timber walls strengthened with towers, and the gates sat between towers with the continuous wall walk extending over the gateway itself. The circuit of the walls would be determined by the manpower available to defend them. This assessment was based on the number of hides of land in the *burh*'s hinterland. Depending on the quality of the land, each hide could be anywhere between 60 and 120 acres (24 and 48ha), enough to support one man and his family. Each hide would produce, therefore, one defender, responsible for 4 linear feet (1.25m) of *burh* wall. Applying this measure, a mile of wall would require around 1,300 defenders.

Following an earlier Frankish approach, further developed by his father, Edward adopted the practice of building his fortified enclosures on opposite riverbanks linked by bridges, thus controlling the movement of shipping. He first did this in Buckingham and then at Hertford, where his northern *burh* was built first, in 912 or 913, and the southern *burh* a year later.

The northern *burh* lay between the rivers Lea, Mimram and Beane and was protected by marshy land. It formed a bridgehead into Danish territory, protecting the river crossing. The southern *burh*, possibly utilising elements of the former Danish camp, would later become the site of the Norman castle. This double *burh* arrangement would be repeated at Bedford, Nottingham, Stamford and elsewhere.

The Anglo-Saxon Chronicle describes the speedy construction of these fortifications, which would have meant a large concentration of labour being assembled along with the appropriate engineering expertise. Between 975 and 1035, the reigns of three kings from Edward the Martyr to Knut, coins were produced by the Hertford Mint.

Hertfordshire is packed with 'bury' names, understood to refer to Anglo-Saxon thegnal residences. To qualify as a thegn, it was necessary to have a hall, a bell tower and a *burhgeat*, implying a defended enclosure, sometimes referred to, at the time, as a 'hedge'. Often a church tower would be incorporated into the complex, usually as the bell tower. Several sites in the county exhibiting some of the qualifying features have been proposed as possible thegnal manors.

At Northchurch, a church containing Saxon masonry, there is evidence for a square, thick-walled chamber at the west end of the church thought to represent the stump of a Saxon tower. Both the words '*burh*' and 'belfry' derive from European roots of words relating to protection or fortification. At Caldecote—a village of fourteen households at Domesday time, but whose deserted medieval village remains were excavated in 1973–77—there is an enclosure dating from c. 1050 which contained halls, with an adjacent church containing late-eleventh century masonry.

It has been proposed that the Anglo-Saxon ditched enclosure at Pirton, with an area of 10 acres (4ha), provided the basis for the later Norman earthwork castle. The royal manor of Little Berkhamsted was the site of a timber hall and ancillary buildings, in existence long before 1066. These were still standing in 1225, when they were confiscated and taken down for re-erection at Hertford Castle. Benington would become the centre of a barony held by Peter de Valognes, sheriff of Hertfordshire in 1086. The greater part of these lands had formerly comprised the estate of Aelmer of Benington, a thegn of Edward the Confessor. It is likely that his manor was the predecessor of Benington's Norman castle and that its defences may have formed the basis of the later castle.

It was not unknown for sites of strength from earlier times to be brought back into use, if only temporarily. Ravensburgh Castle, the Iron Age hillfort, was reoccupied by Ealdorman Wigmund, of Cambridge, during the revolt of AD 873, but then quickly taken by Birna's Danish troops. Grims Ditch is an Anglo-Saxon boundary ditch which curves from Berkhamsted north-west to pass south of Tring and thence into Buckinghamshire, running roughly parallel to The Ridgeway. Extant stretches of the dyke measure 35ft (10.75m) across and may have served as a means of directing travellers into prescribed channels: an attempt at controlling movement, if not an overt offensive/defensive feature. Other, earlier linear dykes may have been adopted as boundaries by Anglo-Saxon thegns.

The St Brice's Day massacre of the Norse in England, initiated by King Aethelred the Unrede on 13 November 1002, appears to have been centred

Northchurch, St Mary's Church, the later structure of which conceals Saxon walling and traces of a square, thick-walled western chamber possibly representing a Saxon tower.

on the borderlands of Danish territory, taking place in towns with small Danish populations such as Oxford. It is said to have started in Welwyn, itself located on the very edge of the Danelaw. The victims, men, women, and children, may have included the sister of Svein Forkbeard, king of Denmark.

Given such an excuse by the actions of the ill-advised Aethelred, Svein retaliated by invading and pursuing a policy of conquest over the next ten years. Occupying the English throne for only a few weeks, he was succeeded by his son Knut, who gave the royal manor of Hitchin to his second-in-command, Earl Tovi, 'the Proud', and the benefactor of Waltham Abbey. After his death, the manor reverted to King Edward the Confessor, who granted it to Earl Harold Godwinson.

2

Hertfordshire in the Middle Ages 1050–1500

Following Harold Godwinson's defeat at Hastings, his putative successor, Edgar the Atheling, accompanied by Aldred, the Archbishop of York, the earls Edwin and Morcar, and all the chief men of the City of London gathered to surrender to William the Conqueror, almost certainly, at the royal manor of Little Berkhamsted.

After this Saxon capitulation, the Conqueror's primary task was to secure his new kingdom. This involved placing his most loyal vassals in key strategic locations, particularly in relation to the routes from the Channel crossings to Normandy, but also to the northern approaches to London. This ambition would account for the location of the castles of Great Berkhamsted, Hertford and Bishop's Stortford (Waytemore). These castles covered the approaches via the Roman roads: Great Berkhamsted through the Chiltern Gap via Akeman Street; Hertford with the Ermine Street ford of the Lea; and Waytemore, the causeway carrying Stane Street over the marshes of the river Stort.

Although castles were limited in their ability to exert control over more than a small area of land, their judicious positioning could only make the task easier in strategic as well as tactical terms. Castles, of course, though fulfilling the role of barracks, storehouse, arsenal and jumping-off point for rapid response forces, had much greater significance than these military functions. They were also administrative, judicial, and domestic centres and, located at those nodal points, were able to influence and facilitate settlement, trade and commerce.

On the eve of the Great Plague, six of the county's nine towns: Baldock, Chipping Barnet, Buntingford, Royston, St Albans and Watford had been consciously planted by either clerical or secular landowners. Five of them had clerical foundation in the cases of Chipping Barnet, St Albans and Watford by the abbot of St Albans; by the templars at Baldock; and by the Austin Friars' priory at Royston. Only in Buntingford's case was the foundation secular.

The three organically grown towns were Hertford, Standon and Ashwell, which had been founded by Westminster Abbey as a borough between 1066 and Domesday, when only fourteen burgesses were recorded. Both St Albans and Baldock stand in the top sixteen planted towns, nationally, for tax assessment purposes in 1334, with St Albans eleventh in the table for all English towns, but Stanstead Abbots was so small it had soon faded away.

In medieval times, Hatfield Park and Ashridge were enclosed by banks and ditches as hunting reserves. After his wife's death, Edward I took up residence at Ashridge, holding Parliaments there in 1290 and 1291. St Albans Abbey was the base for a succession of the country's most prominent chroniclers of the medieval period from the thirteenth century into the fifteenth: Roger of Wendover, Matthew Paris, the astronomer and mathematician Abbot John of Wallingford, Thomas of Walsingham and Abbot John Whethamstede, some of whom were fond of straying from the parochial annals of the abbey into world history and commentary.

Early castles, 1066–1300

Norman castles, including those constructed in Hertfordshire, generally conformed to one of two basic models. The motte was an earthen mound produced by the spoil of a surrounding ditch. It might be the development of an existing feature or built from scratch. The level top would have a timber tower, surrounded, if space permitted, by a palisade around the lip of the motte. The motte might occupy a corner of a court, or bailey, which would contain the castle's domestic and service structures, and be enclosed by palisaded ramparts and ditches.

The alternative form was the ringwork, little different from pre-Conquest thegnal-defended sites. Here, the spoil from a surrounding ditch would be heaped into a large and low raised platform, on which stood the castle's buildings. This platform would be defended by a rampart and palisade with a timber tower defending the gate. The motte was clearly more dominant and was often built in an urban situation to cow the populace, its dominance often reinforced by the need to demolish dwellings in order to accommodate it. The ringwork provided more living space but had less impact on the landscape. The motte might be built up in layers, capped with clay or reinforced with stone or timber. After having been given time to settle, it might take the weight of stonework either in the form of a tower or a shell-wall around its lip.

Despite the lack of documentary evidence before 1171, the consensus is that Hertford Castle was one of those castles commissioned by William I in shire towns. It consists of a motte beside the River Lea and a bailey, originally enclosed within a rampart and palisade, which was later replaced by a stone wall with polygonal and semi-circular towers by Henry II. The motte-top, around 30ft (9m) across, reveals traces of what may have been either a tower or a stone shell-wall. A lead-roofed timber tower is recorded as being dismantled in 1237, but this may not necessarily have stood on the motte.

The motte-and-bailey castle at Great Berkhamsted, a royal manor, was handed by William I to Count Robert of Mortain, his half-brother, who began the construction of the castle. The 45ft (14m)-high motte has been dated to post-1066 by the Round Mounds Project. There is a circular stone wall, around 50ft (15m) in diameter, on the motte's top, suggesting a shell wall with lean-to buildings against its interior, presenting as a shell keep. Wing walls, one of them 12ft (3.7m) thick, descend from a forebuilding to cross the ditch. Three semi-circular towers have been added to the oval bailey which was accessed by timber bridges across the moat and simple gate passages.

In 1254, Richard, Earl of Cornwall, king Henry III's younger brother, built a three-storey, solar tower. This has generally been accepted as the existing three-storey rectangular tower, but this appears too early to be Richard's, having been inserted into the bailey's western rampart, possibly during the twelfth century. Like another of Richard's constructions at Launceston in Cornwall, he may have erected his tower on the motte top, employing the existing shell wall as a *chemise*, or he may have simply roofed over the central court and heightened the shell wall to create a tall cylindrical tower. The base of an octagonal pillar and evidence of vaulting may point to such a circular tower, which would match contemporary references to an elaborate tower on the motte.

Richard is credited with enlarging the palace complex, integrating the western tower and adding a chapel and apartments, replicating an arrangement he also employed at Wallingford, in Oxfordshire, where the solar tower is inserted into the side of the motte. Within the bailey, the foundations of domestic buildings can be seen adjacent to the motte. There is a well-shaft down through the motte, lined with chalk blocks. On two sides there is an additional outer-earthwork bank with eight projecting bastions. These might have been added as platforms for stone-throwing artillery prior to the siege of 1216 or may even have been thrown up by the French besiegers for their mangonels, although any defender prepared to let the enemy get that close without let or hindrance must deserve to be swiftly subdued.

Benington, the *caput* of a barony, is a ringwork with a small, square stone keep inside the embanked enclosure, and a small outer bailey. Stylistically, the 40ft (12.5m) square keep with its herringbone masonry and pilaster buttresses, appears to belong to the first half of the twelfth century. The earthworks were raised by Peter de Valognes who was sheriff of Hertfordshire at the time of the Domesday Book, and his son, a supporter of Stephen, built the keep in 1136. It was one of twenty castles ordered to be destroyed in 1177 by Henry II in the aftermath of the Young King's rebellion against his father. Waytemore Castle in Bishop's Stortford has an oval 40ft (12.5m)-high motte carrying a rhomboidal tower in one corner of a rectangular court, walled in stone. The motte was constructed in stages by adding a layer of soil and compressing it prior to adding the next layer, allowing consolidation and settlement. The manor was purchased from William I by the diocese of London, which clung onto it in the face of Matilda's unsuccessful attempts to use it as bait to entice de Mandeville to change sides. It was destroyed in 1211 but restored to the bishop with compensation in 1214, and the present walls on their deep foundations may represent the rebuild. The motte sits inside a pentagonal bailey marked by ditches.

The castle at South Mimms illustrates quite a different style. It takes the form of a motte and bailey, but the arrangement of the motte is unusual. A low ditched mound provides the base for the stone footings on which was erected a timber tower with further layers of soil heaped up around its lower storey. It is entered through a passage carved through this skirt. This passage may have been covered over or remained an open trench. If it were effectively to fulfil its role as a watchtower, it is possible that the timber tower could have risen to a height approaching 100ft (30m) in order to gain a view over intervening high ground. Obtaining timber of the necessary length would have presented problems so a height of around half that is more likely and still gives a reasonable sight of approaching attackers or the manoeuvres of hostile forces. The existing footings show that the tower tapered 10 degrees from the vertical for stability. It would have been surrounded by a timber palisade around the lip of the motte, with a timber bridge on stone footings crossing the ditch. A kidney-shaped inner bailey and a rectangular outer bailey lay to the south.

South Mimms Castle is likely to have had a short life, as, regardless of whether it was actively demolished in the mid-1140s as an illegal construction, dereliction had already set in fairly quickly in the ten years after its build. Anstey Castle was built by Count Eustace of Boulogne, whose granddaughter Matilda married King Stephen. It passed into the hands of Geoffrey de Mandeville and then to the de Anstey family. The large motte, 27ft (8m) in height and measuring 246×213ft (75×65m), carries the buried shallow flint foundations of a structure which may have been analogous to that at South Mimms. The motte is surrounded by a wide, wet moat crossed by a causeway. External to the castle is a village enclosure marked by rampart and ditch.

Pirton Toot Hill is a motte-and-bailey castle probably raised by the de Limesy family during the Anarchy, and possibly unfinished. A large bailey to the east encloses the twelfth-century church, suggested as a former chapel for the castle, and there was also, formerly, a bailey to the west. Medieval house plots and a hollow way represent the shrunken medieval village which was planned in tandem with the castle.

The motte-and-bailey castle at Great Wymondeley, held by the Argentein family, occupies one corner of a village enclosure measuring 570×325ft

Bishops Stortford, the motte of Waytemore Castle.

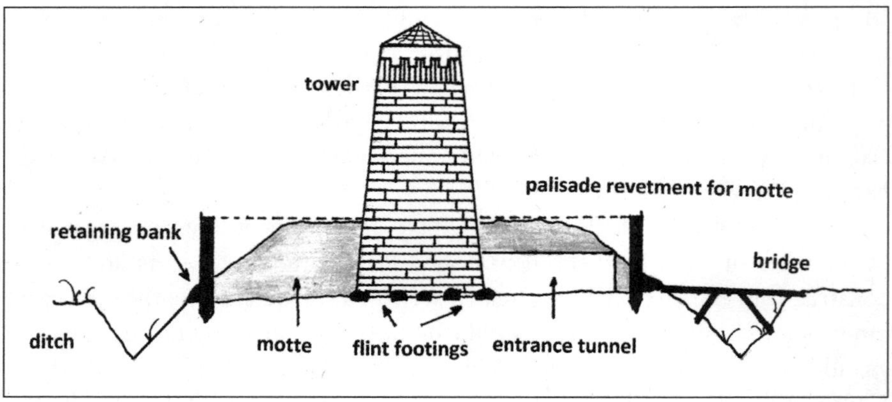

Above: A conjectural reconstruction of South Mimms Castle based on reported excavations.

Left: Berkhamsted Castle, the motte and the wing-wall.

(175x100m). The low motte, surrounded by a dry ditch, has a diameter of 91ft (28m) at its base. Therfield Castle, whose tiny motte sits in a village enclosure once defended by a palisaded rampart with timber revetments, is thought to have been begun by the abbey of Ramsey in Cambridgeshire. When Geoffrey de Mandeville forfeited his castles and fled to the Fens, he famously seized Ramsey Abbey, turned out the monks and converted the buildings into a fortress. It is wholly reasonable that the monks would attempt to defend their possessions elsewhere, and although suspected to be unfinished, there is evidence for its deliberate destruction.

Walkern Bury, built by Hamo de St Clare, a confederate of Geoffrey de Mandeville, as the *caput* of his Honour, is an oval ringwork measuring 420x325ft (130x100m) constructed around a natural knoll with an outer bank and ditch. A gap in the rampart on the south is accessed by a causeway across the moat. The presence of medieval building materials, including flint nodules, points to the site having contained masonry structures, but many elements of the site were changed by nineteenth-century landscaping.

Other castle-like earthworks of the period include Periwinkle Hill, a ploughed-out possible motte at Barkway; Sandon, an oval-banked and ditched ringwork at the Mount; and presumed mottes at Hales Farm, in Anstey; Cole Green, in Brent Pelham; Hadham; and Barrow Hill, in Widford, where a possible motte measures 140ft (43m) in diameter across the base and is conical with a flat top. There is evidence for a ditch, possibly water-filled, but no bailey. Many of these ephemeral structures had been abandoned or put to other uses: the possible motte at Sandon serving as a mill-mound by the 1300s.

The conflict known as The Anarchy, 1135–54

When Henry I died in 1135, leaving no male heir, many of those barons who had sworn to acknowledge his daughter Matilda, widow of the Holy Roman Emperor, reneged on their oaths and supported her cousin Stephen, and the struggle between these two factions would dominate much of English life for the best part of the next twenty years. The absence of strong leadership, which allowed lawlessness and brigandage to flourish, led to the period being dubbed the Anarchy.

Local barons took every opportunity to exploit the power vacuum and to play off one party against the other. Typical of these warlords was Geoffrey de Mandeville, who played the power game with more commitment than most. Both contenders for the throne used royal appointments to secure their supporters' loyalty. Gilbert Fitzrichard of Clare, one of his most loyal adherents, was granted the newly created earldom of Hertford by Stephen in 1138. Originally supporting Stephen, who created him Earl of Essex in 1140, de Mandeville transferred his allegiance to Matilda when her fortunes rose with the capture of Stephen.

Empress Matilda exerted pressure on de Mandeville to continue to support her against Stephen, promising him Waytemore Castle at Bishops Stortford. This was the residence of the bishop of London, a supporter of Stephen, but an army led by Queen Matilda of Boulogne, Stephen's consort, prevented him from taking it. De Mandeville was subsequently granted numerous appointments, including those of sheriff of Hertfordshire, Essex, Middlesex and London, becoming so powerful in East Anglia that he came to believe himself unassailable, gathering a number of local barons around him who benefitted from his protection.

At one point, Stephen had been kept in captivity by his cousin, but, on his release, de Mandeville re-joined him, abandoning Matilda and fighting alongside his troops. Stephen held his 1143 Court at St Albans, where four of his most prominent supporters had to be bribed not to fire the town as revenge for previous perceived betrayals. Instead, resentful of his favoured position, they took out their anger on de Mandeville, arresting him as a turncoat and depriving him of his castles. Unhappy with this treatment, for which he held Stephen responsible, by 1143 de Mandeville was in open revolt as an outlaw in the Fen country, and in 1144 he was killed attacking Burwell, one of the castles that Stephen was in process of building in Cambridgeshire to blockade the Fens.

One of de Mandeville's confederates was Hamo de St Clare, sometime sheriff of Essex, whose ringwork at Walkern Bury is thought to have been one of several contemporary fortresses built during the Anarchy. Other similar castles were thrown up in similar circumstances at Pirton, Great Wymondley, Benington, Anstey and Therfield. The castle at South Mimms, one of de Mandeville's own manors, most likely also dates from these unsettled times and has been linked to charters from both Stephen and Matilda entitling him to build a castle 'wherever he may wish on his land'. Some of these examples may be counted amongst the numerous unlicensed or adulterine castles regarded as endemic to the period, centres of the infamy so vociferously described by the monastic chroniclers. Most would be abandoned or destroyed during the latter years of Stephen's reign or the early years of Henry II's. In 1177 the cost of 100 picks is recorded for the purpose of throwing down the keep at Benington, and Anstey was ordered to be demolished in 1218 by Henry III.

Richard of Anstey's recorded expenditure included loans at 100 per cent interest *per annum,* so the king's demand had costly implications for him. The abbot of St Albans petitioned Stephen to demolish the last vestiges of Kingsbury in 1143, as it was being used as a base for brigands. The resumption of strong kingship did not, however, solve all disputes. The inhabitants of Hertford objected strongly to the presence of a bridge and a ford at Ware and took the appropriate action to ensure that tolls for crossing the River Lea came to Hertford. In 1191, the bridge was sealed with a bar and the ford impeded by a chain. Although the Ware crossing was opened to traffic during the Barons' wars around 1216, it was once more closed in 1258, when the men of Hertford broke down the bridge and dug a deep trench across the ford.

Baronial conflicts

Rob Liddiard has pointed out that, throughout their active lives, most castles were exposed to neither siege nor assault. Whilst there are no surviving records of any of Hertfordshire's castles seeing action during The Anarchy, they nevertheless played their part in holding territory, threatening the lands of adversaries, controlling communications and acting as bases for raiding expeditions.

Work was being carried out at Hertford Castle from 1171, and in 1173 it was considered to be in a fit enough state to be provisioned, garrisoned, and prepared for action during the crisis of the rebellion of Henry, the Young King, against his father, Henry II, in 1173–74. The royal castles of Berkhamsted and Hertford were similarly readied for action during his subsequent insurrection against his younger brother, Richard (the Lionheart), in 1183, over ownership of lands in France. Shortly after this, however, both those Hertfordshire castles would undergo actual sieges during the conflict between King John's forces and those of the barons with their French allies. Liddiard suggests that the county's sixteen castles saw only four actions in the whole of the period beginning in 1066 and ending with the Civil Wars in 1652, but castles did not have to be involved in action to have an existential impact on the course of campaigns.

John, contemptuously known as 'Softsword', was never going to be a popular king after his illustrious but perennially absent brother Richard. He became even less popular following the disasters of his military campaigns across the Channel. By losing Normandy and failing to consolidate much of his territory south of the Loire, he had failed to live up to his father's achievements and, more importantly, deprived many of his barons of their Continental lands and the consequent income.

Magna Carta, whose first draft was drawn up in St Albans Abbey in 1213, was an attempt by the barons to restore rights which John had eroded, and to control the king by imposing a council of twenty-five barons on him. John found himself forced to sign the document agreeing to its provisions but soon reneged, pushing the barons into revolt. The battle of Bouvines had summarily brought John's Continental campaign to an end, when his potential Continental allies were routed by Philip of France.

By May 1215, the majority of the barons appeared, though not openly, to have taken sides, but over the next year, more and more defected to the rebels, many of them coming from the eastern counties. Both Gilbert de Montfitchet and his brother Richard, who held the manor of Letchworth, were barons who imposed Magna Carta on John, and Richard was among those who were subsequently excommunicated in 1216 for their impertinence in forcing the hand of the Lord's anointed. John increased the garrisons of his castles and provisioned them for a siege.

As royal castles, both Hertford and Berkhamsted were expected to be defended by their Royalist garrisons against the barons, and appropriate preparations were undertaken to resist the coming attack. John held a conference with those barons loyal to him at St Albans in the December before setting off with his mercenaries to ravage the rebels' lands, while his troops in the castles of Hertford and Berkhamsted endeavoured to keep the rebels penned in their London stronghold.

Hertford Castle had been held by Robert Fitzwalter, one of the rebel barons' leaders, but he had been forced out by King John and had fled to France, where he was among those who incited the Dauphin, the future Louis VIII, to invade England with an army and to seize the English crown. Two other leading barons in the rebels' faction instrumental in bringing the Dauphin of France to England were Gilbert de Clare, born in Hertford in 1180 to Richard, 3rd Earl of Hertford, and the former Justiciar of England, a guarantor of Magna Carta and joint commander of the rebel army, Saer de Quincy, lord of Ware.

Close behind the cohorts of French troops who had been landing in England since the beginning of the year, Louis arrived in England in May 1216, making straight for the rebels in London and gathering support all the while along the way. Still on his mission to subjugate the country, John was unexpectedly taken ill and died in Newark in October 1216, removing the barons' *casus bellum* at a stroke. Louis and the rebels, however, would make one last attempt to increase their territory by seeking to expand north and west from London.

In November, the French army began a siege of Hertford Castle. Hoping to avoid a protracted siege intended to starve out the garrison, Louis chose, rather, to apply brute force, using mangonels to batter the walls. The garrison, under the command of Walter de Godardville, held out for twenty-five days before coming to terms. These permitted the garrison to march out, armed and unmolested. The next month it was the turn of Berkhamsted to face an anticipated siege, an eventuality for which some preparation had been made, when, in 1215, timber had been taken from the surrounding woods to strengthen the defences. The rebel force's siege of the castle was initiated by William de Mandeville, an enthusiastic champion of baronial rights as enshrined in Magna Carta who had recently inherited the title of Earl of Essex from his brother.

From the start, however, the garrison, under Waleran the German, one of King John's mercenaries, carried out several successful sallies, capturing baggage and even William de Mandeville's standard, which it used in another such sally to confuse the enemy. These early successes, though, could not last once Louis had brought up his siege engines and started hurling large rocks at the castle walls, and the tide soon turned in the besiegers' favour. It may have been at this time that the earthwork bastions beyond the castle's counterscarp were thrown up to mount those mangonels. Waleran managed to hold out for a fortnight but was then ordered to surrender by the Regent, William Marshall, who had also been entrusted with the care of the 9-year-old Henry III and may have negotiated a truce in the young boy's name. St Albans was visited by Louis, who demanded that the Abbot William de Trumpington pay homage and, on his refusal, extorted money from the local populace.

Although the town, having purchased some degree of immunity, avoided trouble the next time the French army approached, within the month it was again raided. This time it was the Royalists, under the robber baron de Breaute, who took hostages, pillaged the town and threatened to torch the abbey, as retribution for previously capitulating to French demands. Only by making a payment of £100 in silver, an enormous sum, would St Albans avoid being burned.

After John's death, the appeal of a French king gradually dissipated and those barons who remained with the French were heavily defeated at Lincoln, as were French reinforcements at sea off Sandwich on the Kent coast. The English barons returned to the royal fold under their new king, some of them being held to account for their disloyalty. Nicholas de Anstey was one of those barons who had fought against King John, and in 1218 he was required

Berkhamsted Castle, a panoramic view of the bailey from the motte.

Above: Berkhamsted Castle, the tower in the bailey.

Left: Hertford Castle, the octagonal tower and the adjacent postern gate.

by the Regent to return his castle to the state it was in prior to the start of the wars, contributing any excess masonry to the repair of the parish church.

Hertford Castle was turned over to Fawkes de Breaute who had also acquired the manor of Little Berkhamsted. After the death of his protector, King John, de Breaute had become vulnerable to those he had antagonised and mistreated over the years. He was brought to trial, his estates were confiscated, and he was sentenced to be banished from England for life. The timber structures from his Little Berkhamsted manor were dismantled and installed in Hertford Castle. Over the years, parts of these timber buildings must have been renewed. but it is possible that those structures still standing in the sixteenth century, though having been continuously repaired, may well have been, essentially, those which, having originated in Saxon times, may have witnessed the surrender to William I after the Battle of Hastings.

Still smarting from the disappointments of John's reign, England's barons, led by Simon de Montfort, Earl of Leicester, continued their dispute with the new king, Henry III, and war broke out in 1263. In April 1264, de Montfort gathered his army together at St Albans in an unsuccessful attempt to raise the siege of Northampton. Gilbert de Clare, 6th Earl of Hertford was initially a supporter of the rebel barons but having fallen out with de Montfort in 1265, he changed sides and contributed to the rebels' defeat by Henry III and his son, the future Edward I, at Evesham.

Even when warlike activity at home diminished, there were still military obligations to fulfil. In 1282–83, Edward I impressed fifty diggers and twenty carpenters from Hertfordshire for work on his Welsh castles. As part of a concerted campaign against the Welsh, de Clare led a force into mid-Wales in 1282. After initial success, they were ambushed at the Battle of Llandeilo Fawr, after which de Clare was relieved of his command.

Knights were expected to maintain their distinctive warrior skills, and tournaments are recorded as being held on Therfield Heath, outside Royston, during the reign of Edward I, possibly as part of his drive to encourage the development of martial skills in the face of Welsh and Scottish aggression. Royston, however, appears not to have been among the five officially permitted tournament venues chartered by Richard I and may have been the intended location for tournaments banned in 1234 and 1331. Most kings sought to limit tournaments, as important figures were sometimes killed when they should have been available for the king's wars. Matthew Paris, chronicler and monk of St Albans, recounts the death of a knight in 1252. He was killed in a tournament by an illegally sharpened lance, wielded by an adversary who had been severely injured by his victim in a previous encounter.

However proficient individual knights might become, if the leadership was incompetent then there was no guarantee of victory, and Gilbert de Clare, the 7th Earl of Hertford was among those of the English nobility killed at Bannockburn in 1314, in a battle mismanaged by the incompetent Edward II.

In 1335, Edward III called up over fifty Hertfordshire archers for service in his Scottish campaign. Property was still held on the basis of military service, and the manor of Watton-at-Stone was required to supply one fully equipped archer to the king for forty days' service in Wales and, later, for fifteen days in Scotland. Other royal demands were more peaceful. At the same time that the Welsh castles were being built, work was being carried out on the royal palace of Kings Langley and elsewhere, under masters of the works appointed by the king.

Under Edward III, several clerks of the works were responsible for Kings Langley: William of Wykeham, until his promotion as bishop of Winchester and lord chancellor; William de Strete; Adam of Hartington; and Henry of

Mansfield in 1366–74. Sometime around 1390, Geoffrey Chaucer, Richard II's clerk of the works, visited Kings Langley to inspect progress. Painters in royal service included Master John of St Albans, working for Edward II at Westminster Palace and apparently doubling as a court clown, and Master Hugh, also of St Albans, carrying out further commissions for Edward II.

Later castles and strong houses, 1300–1500

In 1299, Edward I spent Christmas at the palace of Kings Langley in the company of John of Berkhamsted, abbot of St Albans. Kings Langley first appears as a royal palace when held by Edward I's Queen Eleanor. It would appear that there was a busy building operation going on in 1279–81 when £400 was spent on chambers for the royal couple and their children. The filling in of a moat and the digging of a new one suggests the expansion of an earlier moated manor and a new gateway in the surrounding stone wall was built the next year.

In 1292 the hall was decorated with paintings of knights at a tournament. It was granted to Edward II as Prince of Wales and remained a favoured residence. He built a new friary nearby and it was there that Piers Gaveston's body was brought for re-burial in 1315. By this time, the palace had expanded to three courtyards, with a third outer gateway. Queen Isabella granted the palace to herself, but her son, Edward III, bought it back from her, and it became his favourite residence with the installation of increasingly luxurious facilities.

His fifth son, Edmund of Langley was born there in 1341. In 1415, Henry V exchanged the palace with Queen Joan of Navarre, widow of Henry IV, for Hertford Castle, only resuming ownership after her death. Along with Berkhamsted Castle, it was later given to his mother by Edward IV in exchange for his father's birthplace, the castle of Fotheringhay in Northamptonshire. After periods of ownership but not occupation by Henry VIII and his wives, the palace fell into decay and was demolished in the 1600s. Only fragments now survive.

The castles of Hertford and Berkhamsted both remained in royal hands and were used as both residences and prisons. Edward III imprisoned his mother in Hertford Castle in 1330 and other royal captives included David II of Scotland and his queen, and King John II of France, after the slaughter of the French aristocracy at the battle of Crecy. Both castles were given to members of the royal family at regular intervals. In 1299, Edward I gave them both to his new wife, Margaret of France, and Edward III's son, the Black Prince, as Duke of Cornwall, was granted the castle which became one of his favourite residences.

A survey carried out in 1327 had revealed multiple defects in the fabric of the castle over which little action could have been taken, since the deterioration was allowed to continue unchecked. Minor repairs had been carried out in 1360 for the reception of John of France as a prisoner. But nobody was in residence after 1495 and the ruins became a quarry.

Hertford had been kept in good repair until the early 1300s, when it began to be neglected prior to repairs begun in the reign of Henry VI. A new brick gatehouse, with fireplaces of local Ashwell stone, was built by Edward IV in 1463–65 prior to the castle becoming part of the queen's jointure. In the bailey, the castle hall of three and a half bays and all the domestic buildings around it were of timber construction on dwarf walls. The whole complex accommodated the law courts, evacuated from Westminster in plague years in the sixteenth century. By

Right: Hertford Castle, external view of Edward IV's gatehouse.

Below: Hertford Castle, internal view of the gatehouse.

1600 the buildings of the bailey had totally disappeared, leaving only the gatehouse, the octagonal tower and postern, and an outline of the half-moon tower, 60ft (18.5m) in diameter.

Brick as a building material was becoming fashionable at this time, being employed by magnates and prelates alike as well as veterans of the French wars who had observed its use in Flanders. Bishop Morton of Ely was one of a clique of bishops, including Wolsey, as abbot of St Albans, who all built extensively in brick during the latter part of the fifteenth century. Morton chose brick for his palace at Hatfield, which was built in 1480–90 around a quadrangle with a hall, accessed by a robust tower porch, an attached gatehouse, which survives, and a further gatehouse range fronting onto the old High Street. Other brick buildings of the period include the Manor of the More, where the brickwork was faced with stone, Hunsdon House, Salisbury Hall, the Lordship at Standon, and Rye House, in Hoddesdon.

Sir William Oldhall had been one of the Duke of York's most active supporters early on in his career. He had pursued that career in France as a diplomat and an administrator, particularly in areas where he held lands as in Normandy. His work had helped him amass such wealth that, after the fall of England's French possessions, he was able to return home and to complete Hunsdon House, the grand, castellated mansion licensed to York in 1443. Using the newly fashionable material—brick—the works cost him 7,000 marks, something approaching half a million pounds in today's money.

His dealings with York had brought him the office of Lord Chamberlain in 1440, and returning to England in 1450, York again used his influence to enable him to become MP for Hertfordshire and, very quickly, speaker of the commons. In 1452, he was implicated both in Jack Cade's Rebellion and in York's abortive bid for the throne. It was, very likely, Oldhall who was one of those who pushed the Commons into proposing York as the rightful heir to Henry VI, thereby ending the dynastic aspirations of the Lancastrian usurpers. Such a suggestion got him indicted for his complicity in treasonous activities and he was arrested. He fled into sanctuary and was then held under royal supervision, fortunate to escape execution, the fate of so many others found guilty of such crimes.

With York's victory at the First Battle of St Albans, Oldhall was rehabilitated. The only known representation of Hunsdon House is indistinctly glimpsed through a window in a portrait of Edward VI. It would seem to be a typical early-Tudor moated, quadrangular house entered through a gatehouse, with what appears to be a solid, high brick tower standing at one corner. This is likely to represent the structure put up by York and Oldhall, and now only partly visible under the Georgian remodel of 1805. The lower storey, an embattled gate tower, diagonal corner buttresses, and part of one side wall survive, and other features such as stone-and-brick cross-loops can be seen around the walls of the building.

Oldhall was also named on Sir Andrew Ogard's 1443 licence to crenellate Rye House, in Hoddesdon. They had fought together in France, along with Sir Robert Whittingham, former Captain of Caen, and owner of Pendley Manor in Tring, who was also named on the licence. Whittingham fought on the Lancastrian side, was implicated in plots against Edward IV and was killed at Tewkesbury in 1471. The licence included permission to empark a large area of meadow and pasture, and the house would have served as a convenient hunting lodge for a group of comrades in arms, even if sometimes on opposing sides politically.

Right: Hatfield Palace, the tower porch to the Great Hall of Bishop Morton's palace.

Below left: Hatfield Palace, the inner gatehouse to the palace, leading from the end of the hall-block to the kitchen court.

Below right: Hoddesdon, the gatehouse of Rye House.

There may have already been a moated house there, visited by Edward I, and Ogard may have simply added to it. There was a square inner wet moat, three sides of which remain, within an outer, pentagonal ditched enclosure, but the surviving evidence is for not only an insignificant outer enclosure but a stronger inner one. The surviving two-storey brick gatehouse is entered across a bridge over a wet moat and through a vaulted gate passage. It is richly decorated with brick diapering and is fronted by two, first-floor oriel windows, but the wall heads are topped by merlons, giving it a more military aspect. There is a spiral staircase in one corner which ascends to a turret at roof level. A chamber adjoining the north elevation was demolished as recently as 1972.

Sir John Thornbury (aka Wenlock, recorded on his licence as a knight of Totnes, in Devon) was granted licence to crenellate two houses in Bygrave in 1386. Thornbury had served in France in the Hundred Years War, gaining considerable military experience. This enabled him to raise and lead a mercenary company under contract to the schismatic Avignon pope in his ongoing conflict with the Visconti family of Milan. By 1373 he was leading the English forces in Italy but struggling to extract his company's pay from Pope Gregory XI. In 1377 he returned to England, and, having secured a royal pardon as indemnity for his exploits abroad, as well as much of the money owed him by the pope, he bought lands in Hertfordshire, adding Bygrave in 1383. He became a retainer of John of Gaunt, a knight of the body to Richard II, and served as MP and commissioner of array for the shire and as a royal adviser on matters military. Aided by his Italian wife he continued to conduct business in the Italian courts. He died in 1396, and nothing remains of either of his fortified mansions beyond some moats near the church.

The manor in Shenley, which came to be known as Salisbury Hall, has been owned by a succession of illustrious occupants, including lord mayors of London. John Montagu, a supporter of Richard II and, later, heir to the earldom of Salisbury, married Maud Francis, daughter of one of the richest men in London. When her father died, she inherited Salisbury Hall. Their daughter Alice, his sole heiress, married Sir Richard Neville, later earl of Warwick, whose two sons were killed at the battle of Barnet in 1471. The owner in the reign of Henry VII was Sir John Cutte(s), the treasurer of the royal household. A new man with no identified pedigree, he amassed lands in Hertfordshire, Essex and elsewhere. He acquired Salisbury Hall on the marriage of his son to one of the sisters to whom it had been left and carried out building works in 1507, possibly renovating the existing moat. The site is still moated and accessed via a bridge with original features, but any house that Cutte might have built was replaced in the late 1600s by the building that largely survives today.

On a site first recorded as a manor in 1346, Knebworth House was a quadrangular brick house with a gatehouse in its front face built by John

Hotoft. A local man, Sir John had come to the notice of the future Henry V when on campaign with him in Wales and may have accompanied him to France for the Agincourt campaign. He would become treasurer to the prince's household from 1411; MP for Hertfordshire 1413–22; sheriff of Hertfordshire and Essex in 1428; and treasurer of the household of Henry VI in 1430. Adding to his many properties in the county, he acquired the Knebworth site in 1428. Sir John died in 1443 and his daughter married Sir Robert Lytton, under-treasurer to the household of Henry VII, a favourite of the king and governor of the castle of Boulogne.

Lytton built a new quadrangular brick house attached to the original gatehouse. Following the demolition of most of this Tudor house in 1811, to be rebuilt in a Victorian Gothick style preserving but a single, much embellished wing, the slim three-storey tower, formerly attached to the east wall of a strong single-storey brick gatehouse with stone crenellations, was re-erected as part of Tower (or West) Lodge. A deer park was in operation by 1472.

Outside Rickmansworth, the Manor of the More was a house dating to the thirteenth century. A double-island moated site was in existence by 1250–1300, enclosing a structure of timber and thatch identified as a kitchen within a palisade. The islands were combined by 1350, and a house with a timber superstructure mounted on stone-and-tile dwarf walls and a tiled roof was constructed. It contained a hall and was apparently of two storeys. An outer moat may have been a compound for cattle.

In 1426, the London merchant William Flete, supported by Henry Beaufort, cardinal bishop of Winchester and others, obtained licence to crenellate a new house of brick and stone around three sides of a courtyard. On the south, a gatehouse with a pair of half-octagonal towers and a drawbridge and corner

Knebworth House, this turret, now transplanted to the tower or West Lodge, was part of the original gatehouse built in the 1430s and then incorporated in the later house of *c.* 1575.

turrets fronted a 55ft-wide moat. On the other three sides there was a 32ft-wide berm between house and moat. The lower walls were built of chalk blocks with a string course of tile surmounted by brick walls. The moat was crossed by a timber bridge on brick piers. This new house sat in a hunting park of 600 acres (240ha).

By 1456, the house had passed to Sir Ralph Boteler, or Butler, Lord Sudeley, who also received a fresh licence to crenellate, and may have been responsible for much of the new work. His son, Sir Thomas Butler, possibly knighted soon after the first battle of St Albans, at which his father fought on the side of Henry VI, died after a later battle. With no male heir to whom to leave the manor, Lord Sudeley then conveyed ownership of The Manor of the More back to St Albans Abbey, where his wife's cousin, John Whethamstede, served two spells as abbot. This transfer of ownership would fund the prayers which Sudeley would want said for the souls of himself and his family. Sir Thomas had been married to Eleanor Talbot, who was subsequently secretly married to Edward IV, a complication which would render illegitimate the several children of the king's bigamous marriage to Elizabeth Woodville, including Edward V and, embarrassingly for Henry VII, Elizabeth of York, his queen. The Manor of the More then passed through the hands of George Neville, Archbishop of York and brother to Warwick the Kingmaker.

Neville was so desperate for a cardinal's hat, that he placed his loyalty to the pope over that due to his king. Having previously, like his brother Warwick, sided with both Yorkists and Lancastrians, his involvement in the power struggle between Edward and his brothers, rendered him unworthy of the king's trust. Expecting a social visit from Edward, for which he had made extravagant preparations, Neville was waiting to welcome his royal visitor to The More, when armed members of the royal household forced their way

Hadham Hall, the fifteenth-century gatehouse incorporated into Sir William Capel's later mansion.

in through the defences and arrested him on a charge of treason. He was swiftly bundled off to imprisonment in the fortress of Calais, and The More was stripped of upwards of £20,000 worth of jewels, books and furnishings, and his household turned out.

All these goods were handed over to the household of Prince Edward but the manor reverted first to the crown and then back again to St Albans Abbey in 1515. It then remained in the abbey's hands under the abbacy of Thomas Wolsey, who is reputed to have created there a palace which surpassed even Hampton Court for grandeur. The Gloucestershire-based Butlers of Sudeley are also associated with another Hertfordshire manor. Juvenellesburg, now Jenningsbury, was a fortified house on the south-eastern outskirts of Hertford, whose moat survives.

Other Tudor houses include Tyttenhanger House, a property of St Albans Abbey, which came into the possession of Henry VIII at the Dissolution and was utilised by him as a sanctuary from the plague. The house was demolished and replaced with the current mansion in 1654. The west range of Hadham Hall, at Little Hadham, contains an altered brick gatehouse with semi-octagonal towers. It was added to the west range of the current house in c. 1575, but its basic structure dates from the fifteenth century.

In 1507, Sir William Capel, Hadham Hall's owner and Lord Mayor of London, was hounded by the king's tax collectors, falling foul of Edmund Dudley and his enforcers, and may well have felt that having a secure bolthole in the country was advisable. The Lordship in Standon, a Tudor house of 1546, retains only vestiges of the courtyard house built by Sir Ralph Sadleir. The west range—with a four-centred gateway arch, formerly flanked by four octagonal turrets each containing a newel staircase—part of the south range—which contained the hall—and the reconstructed north-west corner turret all remain. Sir Ralph, knighted on the battlefield of Pinkie in 1547, was a member of Henry VIII's Privy Council, lord lieutenant of Hertfordshire, seven times the shire's MP and also served Edward VI.

TOWN DEFENCES

St Albans was never walled, but in the second half of the thirteenth century, Abbot Roger de Norton installed bars across the major roads into town designed to control trade and to keep out undesirables. These bars were recorded in a charter of Edward VI as being in Sopwell Lane, Kingsbury Lane and Sandridge Road, and at the bottom of Holywell Street.

The Tonman Ditch or Dyke, marking the borough's boundaries, was in existence by 1142 and described in a document of 1327. It was not intended as a defensive work though it may have figured in the Second Battle of St Albans in 1461 and was exploited as the basis for a defensive line in 1648 during the Second Civil War when the town was threatened by resurgent Royalists. There exist references to a defensive ditch, rampart and palisade

St Albans' town belfry of 1405 played its part in the two Battles of St Albans and served as an Admiralty signal station in the chain stretching from London to Norwich during the Napoleonic Wars.

being constructed in c. 1265 in the Second Barons' War and a further such dyke in the fifteenth century running parallel with and to the west of Tonman Ditch between Sopwell Lane and what is now the Hatfield road. The town belfry was built in 1405 to sound the curfew at eight o'clock each evening and to alert the townsfolk to danger or emergency.

ECCLESIASTICAL DEFENSIBLE SITES

Bearing in mind the tribulations of St Albans Abbey in the armed conflicts of the thirteenth century, it is unsurprising that the monastic authorities sought to defend themselves. Most monasteries at this time were surrounded by sturdy stone walls pierced by gatehouses.

The Great Gate at St Albans is a massive structure licensed to abbot Thomas de la Mare in 1357. It was the main entrance to the abbey precinct and consists of a three-storey fortress-like block with vaults at ground level. It has two separate arches for wheeled and pedestrian traffic on the exterior, northern front, but a single arch on the inside. There are semi-octagonal stair turrets each side of the inner archway entered by doors at ground level, and a third spiral stair in the thickness of its north-west wall. It is built of flint with stone dressings, a rag-stone base and brick patchings. Windows are minimal and narrow, and the embattled parapet was rebuilt in 1396–1401.

The entire precinct was strongly walled with a gate onto Holywell Hill and a Water Gate, which consisted of an embattled, three-storey tower. Other walled monastic communities include Wymondley Priory moated site; the twelfth-century house of the Austin canons at Royston; and the fourteenth-century Dominican priory of Kings Langley. At Ashridge, the monastic college

St Albans, the exterior face of the Abbey's Great Gate, licensed in 1357.

St Albans, the Great Gate from inside the abbey precinct, showing the two archways.

was walled with a gatehouse large enough to include apartments. Parts of its precinct wall and external ditch have been reported as surviving in the stableyard.

Templar preceptories were farms managed by a templar knight-brother or sergeant (man-at-arms) and worked by lay-brothers. The intention was for the produce to finance the operations of the templars on crusade in the Holy Land. A preceptory, endowed by Bernard de Baliol in 1147, was established at Temple Dinnesley, in Hitchin, with another at Temple Chelsin, in Bengeo. The Templars were given lands in the north of the county by Gilbert de Clare in 1148. They established the planted town of Baldock (named for Baghdad) at the crossing of the Icknield Way and Ermine Street and encouraged trade and commerce by encouraging merchants to rent plots in the town and then exempting them from market tolls. Reginald de Argentein of Great Wymondley became a knight Templar and was killed fighting in Antioch around 1240. When the Templars were suppressed, their wealth went to the crown and their property to the knights hospitaller of St John. The hospitallers held the manor of Standon Friars, granted them by Gilbert de Clare, as well as half of Letchworth. The Templars are popularly, but mistakenly, associated with the artificial Royston Cave, mysteriously decorated with medieval carvings.

At Watton at Stone, there are extensive earthworks regarded as dating back to the twelfth century. The earthwork in Well Wood is an irregular rectangular moated site measuring 570x290ft (175x90m) with an inner bank and an entrance causeway. Those in Chapel Wood form a triangular double enclosure, its longest side measuring 880ft (270m), surrounded by a dry ditch 16ft (5m) wide and an internal bank, with a partly excavated chapel in its centre. The inner enclosure is rectangular, measuring 160x210ft (50x65m), with an in-turned entrance. The presence of high-quality Caen stone points to an important, possibly ecclesiastical defended site.

The disastrous fourteenth century: famine, plague and rebellion

The fourteenth century began with a climate emergency, with sustained freezing temperatures followed by incessant rainfall causing widespread crop failure and famine, lawlessness, civil upheaval and rebellion, plague, and the beginnings of a drawn-out dynastic struggle. Representative of the climate of insecurity, in 1309, the tenant of Holwell in Hatfield complained of 'certain men' breaking into his house, carrying away his goods, felling his trees and snaring his rabbits, the implication being that no action was taken against them for this blatant and protracted outrage.

In the 1340s, the de Ludwicks, father and sons, were indicted for stealing their Woodhall neighbours' property and assaulting their servant. One of these sons then went on to serve for many years as a JP for Hertfordshire. Homicides in most rural areas, at this time, ran at around eighteen to twenty-two per 100,000, in contrast to the current figure of about two. Whereas murderers are usually familiar and often related to their victims nowadays, in medieval times, conversely, murders tended to be random and carried out by strangers.

In St Albans, the seeds of later conflicts were sown in 1326 when the burgesses took advantage of the chaotic conditions created by the weak leadership of Edward II, to enter into a dispute with the Abbey over their rights. While the townspeople were officially granted representation in Parliament, the monastic authorities took every opportunity to reverse these gains with extreme violence apparent on both sides, the abbey being besieged on one occasion and townsfolk killed by the abbot's marshals. By 1332, the townsfolk, accused of conspiracy and undermined by the abbey, had found themselves back where they started.

Although the priors of Royston had been granted powers to enforce law and order, their shortcomings led to the town being seen as violent and lawless. Thus, in 1337, owing to its ambiguous location astride the county boundary, it became necessary to create a separate commission of the peace. This was intended to counteract the failures of different jurisdictions to apprehend those criminals, guilty of numerous assaults and robberies in the town, who escaped justice by crossing from one shire to the other.

By this time, Waytemore Castle survived mainly as the Bishop of London's gaol, the inmates of which, by and large, were convicted clergy. The regime must have been both harsh and lax, as in some years half the fifty or so prisoners died, while, conversely, a fair number managed to escape.

THE GREAT PLAGUE OR BLACK DEATH

Across the country, this particularly virulent outbreak of bubonic plague in 1348–49 would reduce the general population by 30–50 per cent. Due to their either closeted lifestyle or ministering to the sick, the proportion for the monks of St Albans was even higher. Forty-seven of the sixty-odd monks died, a mortality rate approaching 80 per cent. The county contains many deserted medieval villages, some of them owing their demise directly to the effects of the Great Plague. Caldecote in the previous two centuries comprised a dozen crofts around the manor house. Two generations after the plague, there were fewer than ten households and the settlement became unviable.

A study of the county's deserted medieval villages (DMV) has concluded that, unlike other midland counties, where desertion was caused by the proliferation of pasturage in the sixteenth century, it was overpopulation and the consequent impact of starvation and vulnerability to pestilence which cleared out Hertfordshire villages in the fourteenth century. The combination of the Little Ice Age at the beginning of the century, followed by the incessant rains of the second decade, which caused widespread famine, had so weakened the population that people had little resistance when the plague arrived. Whilst most had little choice but to stay put, Edward III removed the court from London to Kings Langley in an attempt to avoid the worst of the plague in 1349.

Between 2008 and 2018, 115 archaeological test pits were dug in the medieval village of Pirton. They revealed a high density of potsherds in 60 per cent of the pits, but this figure fell by 75 per cent after 1350. Additionally, three distinct areas of the village showed up as being depopulated after 1350, contributing to a critical overall reduction down to 25 per cent of the pre-1350 population.

At the same time, there were also those who managed to prosper. Explorations at other villages revealed through the number and size of their barns how a village could prosper in the years following the Great Plague. In the immediate aftermath of the pestilence, when the Statute of Labourers sought to limit wages in a labour shortage by implementing a return to pre-Plague levels, royal building projects found it difficult to secure labourers as other employers were ignoring the law and paying over the odds, affecting the development of royal sites such as Kings Langley.

THE GREAT REVOLT OF 1381

Despite its significant losses in the plague years, Hertfordshire was comparatively densely populated and was a county amply endowed with markets, giving its inhabitants opportunities for combining agricultural work with a craft. For many, living within easy reach of several market towns, trade would supplement income from the land. However, it was the comparative wealth of these people which the Poll Tax targeted, thus causing the general discontent which would lead to rebellion. Although the beginnings of the revolt are generally located in Essex, the determined gathering of opponents to the tax included men from neighbouring counties, including Hertfordshire, represented by a delegate from Benington, a Flemish weaver.

One of the fomenters of revolt was a cleric called John Ball, who would be arrested and imprisoned in the Bishop of London's prison in his castle at Bishops Stortford. He would be freed by rebels who stormed the prison and destroyed the records of the sheriff. The diocesan prison, in buildings close to the castle's gatehouse, would see mass breakouts of convicted clerks later in the century. A longstanding dispute between the men of Ware and John of Gaunt's manor of Hertford led to an assault on the castle causing a large amount of damage to the structure and theft of property. It was lead, salvaged from Gaunt's destroyed Savoy Palace, which would later be used to repair the roof of Hertford Castle.

Gaunt was particularly unpopular for his demands for ever more taxes to be raised to finance his costly and largely unsuccessful adventures in Spain. This action by the men of Ware was followed by the decision of fifty of them, including their vicar, to march on London with the other East Anglian contingents to petition the young Richard II. Under pressure, the king agreed to the petitioners' demands to abolish serfdom and to curb the powers of lords. Largely satisfied by these royal promises, the rebels naively dispersed to their homes to ensure that the king's declared wishes were carried out and recorded in legal documents.

A clearly biased contemporary account of the rebels' action in St Albans by the abbey's chronicler, Thomas of Walsingham, nevertheless provides a plausible narrative for what happened there. A tradesman, William Grindecobbe, who had been consistently ill-used by the abbot, was one of several townsmen who had been in London and had taken the king at his word. Upon returning, he pressured the abbot into restoring ancient rights to the town, including its former borough status and the right to use alternatives to the abbey's mills.

Grindecobbe and his colleagues made a thorough job of implementing all the implications of the king's proclamation, much to the anger of abbot Thomas de la Mare and his chronicler. Limited concessions, forced by the king's wishes, included granting freedom from villeinage to the abbey's tenants in South Mimms, Rickmansworth and Barnet, and liberties, relating to hunting and fishing, to tenants in Cashio and Watford. The abbot's concessions, however, delivered through gritted teeth, would neither continue nor endure. Despite the achievement of all these transactions by non-violent means, the abbot would respond with main force.

Following the eventual abrogation of the king's undertaking to abolish serfdom and his apparent encouragement of the rebels, a large troop of men-at-arms and archers arrived in St Albans. Its leader appears to have given himself the task of settling the local dispute and made a start by arresting and jailing Grindecobbe and two of his fellow townsmen. The arrival of Chief Justice Tresilian, determined to make an example of the town's wealthiest men, sealed their fate. Although successive juries refused to indict them, Grindecobbe, his two main supporters and a dozen other prominent citizens were tried, found guilty, and hanged in St Albans, their bodies displayed and the burial of what remained of them only permitted over a year later. Eighty other citizens were imprisoned, predominantly for inflammatory speech rather than deeds.

Abbey tenants in Watford and Rickmansworth who had temporarily obtained rights made themselves scarce, affecting the harvest that year. John Ball, who had been recaptured, was delivered to St Albans and tried before Tresilian and the king. On the flimsiest of evidence—preaching his radical views on social equality was apparently sufficient to prove his treason—he was sentenced to be hanged, drawn and quartered in the presence of Richard II.

Whilst the abbey of St Albans was the main focus of Hertfordshire's rebels, men from Watford, Digswell and Puttenham also made attacks on the persons and property of the sheriff and justices of the peace. Local worthies such as Sir Thomas Hoo of Offley and the JP John Lodewyk put enough faith in the authenticity of the king's concessions to stand as witnesses to documents recording charters and liberties. So trusting in the legitimacy of their new status were many, such that, in the aftermath of the rebellion, writs had to be issued requiring all tenants of whatever status to fulfil the tasks demanded of them by their lords. As the king pointed out: they were neither free of their commitment to labour for their lords, nor would they ever be. These writs were mainly issued by abbeys such as St Albans, but, leaving nothing to chance, the king also issued a writ for his own manor of Kings Langley.

Right at the beginning of the new century, there were attempts to unsettle the new king, Henry Bolingbroke, regarded by many of his subjects as a Lancastrian usurper, interrupting the Yorkist dynasty founded by the Plantagenets. Although the body of Richard II had been exposed to view and buried at Kings Langley, rumours of his survival were, nevertheless, circulating. One John Bernard of Offley was persuaded by a friar and sent by his kinsman to gather friends and assemble at Atherstone in Warwickshire to join the movement to restore Richard to his throne. Henry IV moved quickly to arrest the dozens of friars who were recruiting for the pseudo-Richard, many of whom were imprisoned. Bernard was arrested and tried, but, fortunately for small fry such as him, only those at the very centre of the conspiracy were executed.

Ironically, any gains accruing from these revolts were largely wiped out by landowners, who abandoned arable farming as being too labour-intensive and costly in terms of wages, preferring pastoral farming, which required far less labour, thereby putting many out of work. Both this conversion of arable land into pasture for sheep and the enclosure of common land would have a significant impact on the life of the peasant farmer. In 1426, an area of 600 acres (240ha) was enclosed to create Moor Park, and two years later further appreciative acreage was taken for Bushey Hall Park. Around 1440, Robert Whittingham built a new mansion at Pendley, near Tring, destroying what was described at the time as 'a great town' with over thirteen ploughs as well as artisans such as potters, cobblers and blacksmiths.

The Wars of the Roses: three battles and a loveday

The received wisdom regarding the wars of the second half of the fifteenth century has mainly stemmed from Shakespeare's history plays and Sir Walter Scott's imagined rose garden. These have presented what we now call the Wars of the Roses as a succession of flare-ups in an ongoing dynastic struggle, but this romantic approach has concealed much of the underlying reality.

England in 1450 was in the throes of an economic depression: the English armies had been defeated and, notwithstanding Henry VI's coronation as king of France, the French possessions had been lost; English exports to its major trading partners on the Continent, mainly large quantities of wool and cloth, were crippled by trade embargoes with a consequent catastrophic fall in customs revenues; there was a dearth of bullion, perceived as being diverted out of the country by foreign merchants, which was seen as a cause of restricted investment; shortages of skills and labour remained as a hangover from the Great Plague; hundreds of discharged soldiers roamed the country; taking advantage of the collapse of law and order, powerful noble families were pursuing their vendettas and rivalries, not in the courts, but on the battlefield; a significant and already out-of-control national debt continued to grow; a weak king, apparently unaware of his limitations, refused to curb the expenses of his household and continued to grant lands from whose income his personal circumstances might have recovered; and to crown it all, since nobody had any money, Parliament refused to levy the taxes which might restore some health to the public purse.

Public opinion held that the cause of all these problems lay not with the king, who must be entirely above reproach, but with his evil counsellors. Chief amongst these was Suffolk, who was murdered in 1450, and Somerset, who, following his defeat in France, returned not in deserved disgrace, but well on the way to becoming the king's favourite. Prominent among the vocal critics of these dire circumstances was Richard, Duke of York, a direct descendant of Edward III's fourth son through the male line, and on his mother's side, from his second son.

When Henry VI and his queen had failed to produce an heir after nearly ten years of marriage, York saw an opportunity to restore the line of succession interrupted by the usurpation of the Lancastrian Henry IV, son of John of Gaunt, Duke of Lancaster and third son of Edward III. The reigns of Henry IV, V and VI were thus seen by York as invalid, an unlawful intrusion into the undeniably legitimate Yorkist succession. Moreover, he regarded Somerset's dominant position as particularly abhorrent given his descent from the retroactively legitimated Beauforts, descended from John of Gaunt and his mistress. The wars, therefore, resulted primarily out of issues of ineffective governance, evolving into the dynastic struggle for which the conflict is chiefly remembered. Abbot Whethamstede of St Albans is one of the chroniclers of the wars, but as an avowed Yorkist, he, it has been suggested, cannot always be regarded as giving an entirely impartial account.

When York failed to persuade Henry VI to nominate him as heir, he resorted to firmer measures. An attempted *coup d'état* failed in 1452, and the next year Margaret of Anjou, Henry's queen, was successfully delivered, somewhat unexpectedly, of a legitimate male heir, the Prince Edward. Unaccountably unpunished for his rebellion by a conciliatory king, York continued to gather support, all the while professing his loyalty and even seeking the queen's intercession at Hitchin in 1453.

By May 1455, however, such petitions had been abandoned, and he was leading a 3,000-strong army of his retainers and those of the Nevilles—Salisbury, the father, and Warwick, the son—towards the capital, intending to put on a show of force. Declarations of loyalty were sent to the king from Royston and from Ware, but in the meantime, the king and his court were proceeding to Leicester to convene a council at which Somerset, restored to favour, was expected to impeach York for his treasonous activities.

While these letters were sent to the Earl of Devon at Watford, the king apparently never received York's missives and altered course to intercept him at St Albans, hoping to find a peaceful outcome. York's army was prepared for battle, whilst much of the king's company was made up of administrators and household servants, totally unprepared for war.

Buckingham, commanding the royal army attempted to construct a defensive position in the town, but under cover of York's ultimately unsuccessful frontal attack, Warwick contrived to break through house plots and outflank the Royalist defenders. Any fighting that took place in the confined spaces of the town was over very quickly. Somerset was deliberately sought out and killed, along with others of the nobility. The king's troops had been anticipating a repeat of the peaceful resolution they had witnessed previously, so many of them were caught without their armour. Surprised by Warwick's attack and seeing their leaders cut down, most fled.

The king was wounded and was taken into York's control. Medieval battles usually resulted in the deaths of common soldiers, archers, and men-at-arms, while their leaders would be rescued and held for ransom. The targeted killing of Somerset, Northumberland and others, however, would set the scene for a reversal of this practice, as throughout the wars the winning side would systematically eliminate the elite amongst their defeated opposition.

One attempt by the king to draw a line was the 'loveday' held in 1458, where mediators committed the warring parties to enormous sureties. The event was held at St Paul's Cathedral, but its misleadingly successful outcomes were reported to the king at Hertford Castle. One of the forfeits the Yorkists were obliged to pay to atone for the killing of Somerset and his confederates was the endowment of a chantry at St Albans Abbey. Whilst the event may have gone some way to addressing the warring factions as the straightforward result of private quarrels amongst the nobility, the elephant in the room remained the king's inability to rule, the main cause of disquiet amongst both nobility and commons.

Attempts by York to rule in the place of Henry VI were largely unsuccessful, failing to cure any of the nation's failings. A further rising in support of York in 1459 was initially successful but the battle of Wakefield saw Yorkist forces facing a superior Lancastrian force under the queen. York and his younger son, Rutland, were killed, and Salisbury was captured and executed after the battle. The Lancastrian army then began a destructive march southward, aiming to enter London, the Yorkist powerbase, and to re-establish the kingship of Henry VI. Warwick led an army in an attempt to intercept the royal army.

The Second Battle of St Albans in February 1461 was fought in the streets of the town, just outside the town at Bernards Heath, at Sandridge, and as far to the north as Nomansland Common. Despite his archers' early success in staving off the Lancastrian attack down Watling Street and into the town centre, Warwick's poor generalship, his failure to support his brother, and a desertion by part of his army contributed to a Yorkist defeat. Those Yorkist leaders who fell into the hands of the queen were despatched, it is said, on the instructions of her 8-year-old son, Edward, the Prince of Wales. Lancastrian success was short-lived, as, at the end of March, they were routed at Towton and York's son became Edward IV, ending the first war.

War broke out again in 1469 when Warwick, now Prince Edward's father-in-law, changed sides, wrong-footing Edward IV, who fled the kingdom. He returned six months later in March 1471, landing in east Yorkshire, and marched south, gathering troops along the way. Warwick, now leading the Lancastrian forces, reacted by bringing his army first to St Albans and then south to Barnet. The Battle of Barnet was fought on a foggy Easter Sunday, with both armies drawn up on the high ground which extended to either side of Monken Hadley church. The poor visibility had two significant results. Not being able to see each other, the armies overlapped their lines, thereby producing unequal opposing forces. And the Yorkists were drawn up much closer to the Lancastrian lines than had been realised, thus nullifying the effects of the Lancastrian gunfire, which went harmlessly over their heads.

While the Yorkist left wing under Hastings was driven from the field by the enveloping Lancastrian right wing and chased toward London, the Yorkist centre and right held firm against the assaults of Prince Edward, Edmund Beaufort, styled Duke of Somerset, and Exeter. A suggestion, ever-present in so many of these internecine battles, that treachery was about triggered a panic in Warwick's army, leading to a mass exodus of his troops from the field. Warwick was caught while attempting to escape and despatched, as were many of his troops, being pursued as far as Deadman's Bottom, now on the A1000 Potters Bar road.

A month later, Edward IV's follow-up demolition of the Lancastrian army at Tewkesbury, in Gloucestershire, saw the young Prince Edward among the dead. His father, the king, was absent from the battlefield but held effectively a prisoner in the Tower of London, dying under suspicious circumstances three weeks later. This marked the end of the second war, with the Lancastrian line temporarily terminated, leaving Edward IV in the ascendant, but his death in 1483 would mark the start of the third war.

There had long been speculation over the legitimacy of Edward IV himself, but his secret marriage pre-contract with Eleanor Butler sometime in the early 1460s rendered his marriage to Elizabeth Woodville bigamous and their children illegitimate and hence barred from inheriting the throne. Edward had earned a reputation for dalliances with maidens, and one, Alice Farwell of Ware, is thought to have numbered amongst his sometime paramours in

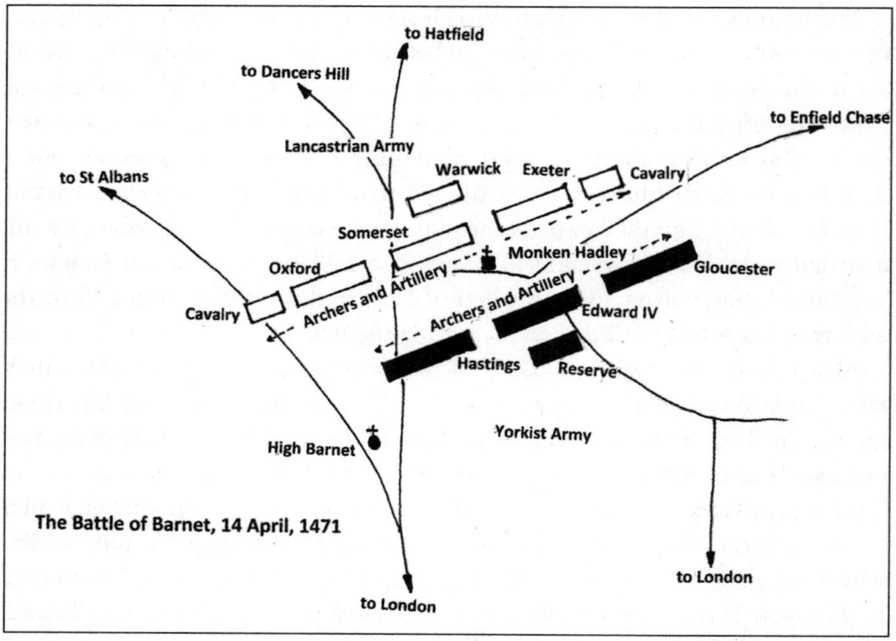

The Battle of Barnet showing the initial dispositions of the two armies (after Seymour).

1464. These ambiguities would pave the way for Richard III to claim the throne and to dispose of his inconvenient nephews, alienating public opinion and shedding the support of many previously staunch Yorkists, pushing them into Henry Tudor's camp.

Whilst Tudor gathered support in France, the Earl of Oxford was fanning the flames of discontent in his home patch of Essex and Hertfordshire, energising former servants of Edward IV who had looked forward to seeing Edward V's coronation and enthronement. Matters came to a head in spring 1485, when Henry Tudor landed in south Wales and made his way across the country to the Midlands, forcing Richard to confront him. As Richard made his way northwards in May 1485, stopping en route at Berkhamsted Castle, he assembled an army, the loyalty of certain elements of which was doubtful. Many of those supporters whose loyalty he had managed to retain, such as Lord Ferrers, who had been granted the manor of Cheshunt in 1484, would suffer defeat and death with Richard at Bosworth in Leicestershire. Victorious on the battlefield, the Lancastrian Henry VII, began a reign scarred by continual uprisings and conspiracies, with this third stage of the wars, in effect, dragging on until the end of the century.

Even after their resounding defeat at the Battle of Stoke, Yorkist opposition to Henry VII continued. Aspenden, the Hertfordshire home of Sir Robert Clifford, became a focus for continuing Yorkist discontent. Clifford was a former supporter of Edward IV, having fought against Richard III and then been pardoned by Henry VII, and appointed as Master of the Ordnance. One of those attracted to the developing conspiracy was one of Clifford's neighbours, his father-in-law, William Barley. As a boy he had served the old Duke of York; later he would become a yeoman in Edward IV's guard and a halberdier in Richard III's and ended up fighting in numerous battles, culminating in Bosworth Field and Stoke. These two were deputed by the assembled Yorkists to decamp to the court of Richard III's sister, Margaret of Burgundy, which was the focus of Yorkist resistance, at Malines in Flanders.

Their mission was to forge a link between hitherto uncommitted Yorkists in England and the retinue of a new pretender. Perkin Warbeck, having apparently avoided his brother's fate and escaped from the Tower of London was masquerading as the young Richard of Shrewsbury, Duke of York. Enjoying the patronage of Margaret of Burgundy, he awaited his opportunity to invade England and 'reclaim' his rightful throne.

Barley and Clifford were welcomed and sought to ascertain his plans, worming their way into his confidence, with Clifford even acting as his chancellor. Having confirmed that Warbeck was, indeed, an imposter and, furthermore, having found out the sources of his support in England, Clifford was ostensibly enticed home by the promise of another royal 'pardon' and made a dash for Calais and safety. But Barley stayed on longer in Burgundy, attempting to gain more information regarding the Yorkists' intentions and expected timings.

News of an assassination plot and a likely Yorkist invasion, placing Warbeck on the throne, forced Henry's hand and arrests were made. Included in those tried for treason was Thomas Powis, Prior of Kings Langley, who, pleading benefit of clergy, was pardoned. In 1494, prior to his eventual invasion, Margaret of Burgundy drew up a document committing Warbeck to the reimbursement of her expenses and bestowing upon her the formerly Yorkist manor of Hunsdon.

Barley, who had remained with Warbeck's party in Flanders, sailed in June 1495, with the advance guard of Warbeck's invasion force. Although blown away from their intended landing in East Anglia, they still expected to be met by friendly Yorkists. However, when they landed at Deal, they were routed by locals, who killed over 150 of them, and captured a further 150, and saw only a handful, including Barley, safely rejoin Warbeck on board ship and sail away to fight another day. There remain doubts around the commitment of both Clifford and Barley to Warbeck's mission.

Violent times in Merrie England

As had occurred during previous reigns, the weakness of monarchs would again be exploited by the unscrupulous and the criminal.

Henry VI appears to have been reluctant to take decisive action against rebellious or unruly members of the nobility. Exploiting the context of the dynastic struggle, a number of ongoing feuds resulted in the short-term gaoling of protagonists followed by general pardons, often without conditions or sureties to be forfeited for recidivism. The Earl of Wiltshire and Lord Bonville were gaoled in Berkhamsted Castle in 1451 for continuing a feud after the expression of royal displeasure. From 1454, Lord Cobham also spent two years incarcerated there for similar misdemeanours, as did Exeter a few years later. Repeat offences incurred repeat punishments. Only York, for whatever reason, had escaped this treatment.

It has been suggested that the contemporary chronicles of John Hardyng, who was employed by both Henry VI and Edward IV, overstated the occurrence of endemic violence. Nevertheless, apart from the battles and skirmishes, which were part of the ongoing war, other incidents, often involving families sustaining prolonged feuds across generations, point to a consistently violent and lawless society. Additionally, there was outright criminality made possible by the distractions of war and the constant political manoeuvring of local factions who should have been maintaining the peace.

In 1428, an outlaw named William Wawe broke into the nunnery at Sopwell in St Albans and ransacked the place until a local hue and cry was raised, forcing him to flee, chased by a posse of townsfolk. In April 1459, the lawyers of London's Fleet Street burst from their chambers to attack the neighbours who had been goading them. In the ensuing street fight, nine of the lawyers and five of their citizen neighbours were killed. After the post-mortem, three of the lawyers' main ringleaders were imprisoned in Hertford Castle. Such events encouraged copycat behaviour in those who needed little encouragement to grab what they could in such chaotic times. It is difficult not to see royal behaviour as a model for some of this lawlessness.

Edward IV's avarice was plain for all to see and was typified by his seizure of George Neville' goods at the Manor of the More. Richard III shared his brother's cavalier attitude to wealth and inheritance, which can be seen in his acquisition of the lucrative stewardship of St Alban's Abbey from one of the queen's officials and the brutal treatment of his own loyal follower and once best mate Hastings, confined to the Tower and soon to be dragged out of a meeting and summarily beheaded for his support of Edward V.

MOATED SITES

Given the insecurities of the age, those who had something to protect took the appropriate steps to secure their lives and property from marauding soldiers discharged from the French wars, manoeuvring armies living off the land and bands of local brigands. Usually, these precautions took the form of a moat surrounding an island on which would stand a manor house and its associated farm buildings, produce stores and workshops. As well as affording protection against both human and animal aggressors, the moat would provide drainage, a water supply and the fish which constituted the nation's diet on getting on for a third of the days of the year. There are at least 187 moated sites in Hertfordshire, of which ten are scheduled as ancient monuments and five have been excavated: the Manor of the More, Ashwell, Essendon, Nuthampstead and Welham Green.

The parish of Reed contains half a dozen confirmed moats with possibly others now marked only by ponds. Moats came in different shapes and sizes and were representative of a range of their occupiers' status. A moat at Owles Hall near Buntingford, of which only faint traces remain, was circular. At Dixon's Hill Close, in Welham Green, the Pancake Hall moat is an irregular quadrilateral with sides measuring 95–135ft (30–40m) with water-filled moats on three sides, 20ft (6m) wide but three times as wide on the fourth. Excavations uncovered evidence of timber buildings, originally thatched but re-roofed in tiles. Water for the shallow moat came from a pond and overflowed into a stream.

Penn's Place moated site, in Aldenham, consists of two rectangular islands formerly surrounded by water-filled moats. The eastern enclosure is a platform measuring 97×325ft (30×100m) surrounded by greatly modified water features. The western platform measures 195×340ft (60×105m) and is also much altered. On the outside of the eastern arm of the eastern platform there stands a slight external bank.

At High Wych, the platform in Mathams Wood rises above the surrounding land and is thought to have carried a building. Its dry moat measures 325×245ft (100×75m), with three sides, 5ft (1.5m) deep and 26ft (8m) across, crossed by a causeway. The missing side was filled in when the perimeter track of RAF Sawbridgeworth was laid in 1941. Documentary evidence points to the site being occupied in the mid-thirteenth century by the de Matham family.

Even larger in size is Thundridgebury, a D-shaped moated site measuring 630×650ft (195×200m). The dry moat varies in width between 23 and 65ft (7 and 20m) and encloses the remains of a Tudor house, the west tower of St Mary and All Saints medieval church, and former cultivation plots. Moated sites may also carry a variety of structures.

Home Wood, the moated site at Eastwick, is a rectangular enclosure 325×230ft (100×70m) with a dry moat 20ft (6m) across. Remains of a substantial building thought to be Eastwick Hall have been excavated on a platform within the moated area. Another similar moat exists just 160yds (150m) across the valley. Little London at Kings Langley measures 390×195ft (120×60m) with a largely dry moat, which is 39ft (12m) across, and 6ft (1.5m) deep. It is thought to have held a hunting lodge which was part of the neighbouring royal estate.

Depending on the underlying geology and the elevation of the land, not all moats were water-filled. The majority of moated sites lay on water-retaining clay-lands, but some moats required additional methods for holding water, either relying on dams and other earthworks, or construction methods such as revetments to retain the water.

Reed Hall includes the west wing of a manor-house dated to 1430 standing on a platform 130×245ft (40×75m) within a water-filled moat measuring 39ft (12m) across, parts of which remain with an external bank up to 6ft (1.5m) high. An outer enclosure, 325×146ft (100×45m), is defined by ditches on three sides and a steep scarp on the fourth. Throcking Hall is a moated platform containing traces of brick foundations, with brick revetments, like those at Cheshunt Great House.

One of at least six moated sites in The Lordship, Much Hadham, is a dry moat 39ft (12m) across and 6ft (1.5m) deep, surrounding a platform measuring 340×275ft (105×85m) externally. The outer bank of the moat's south arm is shored up with large timbers, but there are no traces of structures on the platform. Ardeley Bury is a square moat measuring 455×375ft (140×115m). Its currently dry ditch, 30–45ft (10–15m) wide and 7ft (2m) deep, may have once held water, though nineteenth-century landscaping has created the present lake in front of the house. Chamberlains Moat at Brent Pelham is a large rectangular platform, 420×290ft (130×90m), with three seasonally waterlogged arms and a fourth abutting the Roman road and two adjacent wet fishponds.

Access, whether across a bridge or a causeway, and entry, through a porch or gateway, were always points of vulnerability. Whilst the solidly built medieval bridge at Ardeley Bury has been replaced by a modern timber bridge, and the brick arches of Cheshunt Manor's bridge are long collapsed, High Wych, Little London, at Kings Langley, and The Lordship have causeways crossing their moats, the latter's being 7ft (2m) wide. Drawbridges are not unknown at moated sites, while The Grange, at Pirton, has a timber-framed gatehouse with a portcullis. At Welham Green, a gravelled area close to a possible causeway site, coupled with an iron-bound door, suggest some form of formal entranceway, and a gatehouse dating to c. 1300 but abandoned a century later was indeed excavated there.

Three sites in Cheshunt could be imagined as once displaying the grandeur of those such as The More. The original Theobalds Palace, of which only fragmentary remains stand in Cedars Park, was a moated manor consisting of two quadrangular inner courts with corner turrets and an eastern base court within the moated area, all accessed through gatehouses, with outer walled gardens beyond. By 1571, William Cecil, the queen's chief adviser, and about to be appointed lord high treasurer, had built a new palace on a different site, in readiness for the visit of Elizabeth I in 1575. This house was itself replaced in the nineteenth century on an adjacent site and is now a hotel.

Cheshunt Great House was a fifteenth-century moated manor house with a Great Hall, recorded by Pevsner in 1955, but it burned down ten years later.

An octagonal staircase tower had survived at the south-west angle of the house, when it was remodelled in the 1750s. It was excavated in 1969 and the foundations can be seen on the north side of Goffs Lane. Half Moat Manor, in the angle of Goffs Lane and Dark Lane, is the original site of Cheshunt Manor and is marked by a 245ft (75m) square moat, water-filled and 23ft (7m) across. The sides of the moat are revetted in brick and the brick arch abutments of the original bridge are visible on the east side. The outline of buildings can be discerned in the interior. The moat is linked to ditches, leats and ponds.

In contrast to those moats, which enclosed veritable palaces, many moated sites were very simple, and some, so-called 'empty moats', enclosed only cash crops such as orchards or beehives. Not all moats were ever completed. The Warren, in Nuthampstead, proved to have been an unfinished moated site with a central platform around a quarter of an acre (1,000 square metres) in area comprising a jumble of mounds and platforms, some 10ft (3m) in height, with hollows in between. The moat, 10–25ft (3–7.5m) across, was filled with black boggy silt when excavated in 1946.

Cheshunt, the scant remains of the original Theobalds marooned in Cedars Park.

3

Hertfordshire in Tudor, Stuart and Georgian Times 1500–1840

Whilst the Wars of the Roses had, for the most part, not involved sieges, the practice of incorporating defensive features in the houses of the gentry, the aristocracy, and royalty continued well into the sixteenth century.

As Simon Thurley has emphasised, 'Early Tudor royal buildings self-consciously revived features of genuinely defensive buildings from the Middle Ages.' This observation extends to the houses of gentry, aristocrats, and prelates. Many of the grand houses of the period were based on a quadrangle, with ranges of buildings around a central courtyard, often moated and accessed by a strong gatehouse. Domestic or service buildings might occupy a second courtyard, securely walled and with its own gatehouse. Bishop Morton's palace at Hatfield retains two gatehouses and the porch of the great hall is contained in a tower.

As the arrangement, juxtaposition, and purpose of the various elements of the royal houses evolved, it may be significant that the only room whose function and location remained a constant was the watching chamber, or guardroom. As the events of the next century would demonstrate, any such building was easily defensible given the difficulty of transporting the artillery necessary for the reduction of such structures.

The Manor of The More was adopted as a residence by Wolsey, by now abbot of St Albans, in 1522. He added an outer walled base court with gatehouse and corner turrets within a rectangular moat on the south side and a further similar moat on the north. On Wolsey's fall from grace in 1531, the abbey of St Albans formally ceded the house to Henry VIII that year. It gradually became apparent that the house stood on inadequate foundations in the valley of the Colne, and by 1574 the unsustainable costs of repair forced its decay and demolition. Henry VIII acquired Morton's palace of Hatfield with its Chase in 1538, adding it to the other houses he owned in the county: Ashridge, which was intended as a nursery, Hertford Castle, Tyttenhanger and Hunsdon.

With over a hundred such residences spread across the country, each one might only seldom be occupied but together they formed a useful pool of accommodation. It would appear that Henry VIII took on most of his Hertfordshire properties without initiating significant building works, but given his intense interest in the fine detail of fortification, particularly in Flanders and on the English coast, he would have satisfied himself as to the secure nature of these houses. From 1525, he spent £3,000 turning Hunsdon House into a palace but appears to have retained its embattled tower. It also achieved the status of Honour, the centre of a group of local royal land holdings, in 1531.

Queen Katherine was given Hitchin; his daughters both spent time at Hatfield; and Edward, his precious heir, spent time at both Hatfield and Ashridge. After Katherine of Aragon was put aside, she spent the best part of the next twenty years at the Manor of the More. Elizabeth kept her head down at Ashridge during the reign of her big sister, Mary. It would be from Hunsdon that Mary Tudor decamped for the more distant Norfolk when avoiding arrest on the accession of Lady Jane Grey, the designated, but doomed successor to Edward VI in 1553.

There were other grand early-Tudor houses in the county. Cecil bought the moated manor of Theobalds in 1564, rebuilding it to be fit for a queen. Sopwell Nunnery, alongside the river Ver, was founded in the twelfth century by the abbot of St Albans. After the Dissolution it was granted to Sir Richard Lee, a renowned military engineer who had implemented Henry VIII's fortification designs in France and Flanders and would design the new bastioned works at Berwick-upon-Tweed. He adapted the medieval buildings at Sopwell to produce a Tudor manor house ranged around the former cloisters entered through a gatehouse.

Sir Nicholas Bacon, keeper of the Great Seal, built his manor at Gorhambury in 1568 on land formerly held by St Albans Abbey, and the location of three previous houses each built on a new site. The last of these has revealed itself by parch marks to have incorporated a large tower. The main front of Bacon's new house was flanked by octagonal towers, but the entrance porch was designed in the new Renaissance style with classical motifs. The medieval and Tudor heart of Royston was taken over by James I as a base for his hunting activities. The timber-and-tile lodging known as 'The Greyhound' was converted into a guard-chamber for when the king or his son, the future Charles I, were in residence, and the lanes which served the royal lodgings were secured by gatehouses.

When Elizabeth came to the throne, she inherited around fifty palaces but soon reduced this number to a dozen. Some of her properties, including the Manor of the More were left to decay and collapse, whilst others, such as Ashridge, were given away, sold or otherwise disposed of. Sir Edward Cary, a half-brother to the queen's spymaster, Sir Francis Walsingham, was Master of the Jewels, and the queen leased Berkhamsted Castle to him with a nominal annual rent of one red

Sopley Nunnery, St Albans, was converted into a semi-fortified house by Sir Richard Lee, Henry VIII's principal military engineer. The gatehouse is visible on the left of this view.

rose. Cary demolished the already ruinous castle to use the stone for the mansion, which, known as Berkhamsted Place, was itself demolished in 1967.

The queen retained the old palace of Hatfield but, away from London, generally preferred to lodge with others on her progresses. In 1572 she visited Sir Nicholas Bacon at Gorhambury, which she deemed too small, and in 1575, she stayed at Hatfield and Theobalds. Two years later she returned to a greatly extended Gorhambury. The reign of Elizabeth was characterised by insecurity, parsimony and legalised piracy. This last was such a dominant feature of life that even landlocked Hertfordshire might get involved.

A state of almost constant warfare with Spain (1585–1604), punctuated by deniable assaults on Spanish treasure ships, attracted investors. Henry Carey of Hunsdon was the queen's cousin and Lord Chamberlain of the Household, and with Mary Boleyn as his mother, was, almost certainly wrongly, suspected of being an illegitimate son of Henry VIII. Together with his son, Sir George, he joined with others to back a voyage which turned a good profit but arrived home in the middle of the celebrations following the defeat of the Armada, which rather stole their thunder.

Edward Seymour, Earl of Hertford from 1559, was part of a coterie in which his brother was a sea captain. His step-uncle was hereditary Lord Admiral, raking in his 10 per cent of all profits from privateering. And various cousins had entered the family business, benefitting from the presence of the professionals: Drake, Hawkins, Newport and Frobisher.

John Watts, once described by the Spanish ambassador as 'the greatest pirate that has ever been in this kingdom', found his Hertfordshire birth no impediment to a life on the ocean wave. Having married the daughter of a Lord Mayor of London, he quickly joined the city merchants who fitted out and commissioned ships as privateers. Watts contributed vessels to Drake's expedition to Cadiz and is recorded on one of his ships, the *Margaret and John*, as being the owner/captain sailing against the Armada and successfully attacking a Spanish galleass in Calais harbour. Throughout the 1590s, deprived by Philip II of the chance to trade legally, he despatched his ever-expanding fleet of corsairs across the Atlantic and on into the Pacific to seize Spanish prizes. He was knighted by James I, became Lord Mayor of London and was appointed the second governor of the East India Company.

Musters and home defence

Butts Close Park in Hitchin and Butts Meadow in Berkhamsted are but two amongst the many similarly named locations which memorialise compulsory archery practice. Townsfolk and their country cousins were required not only to hone their military skills but to own some of the necessary equipment themselves.

In the Muster of Easter 1539, there were eighty-six archers and billmen recorded in the town of Hertford. These would be joined, if called out, by varying numbers across the county's towns and villages, ranging in numbers from sixty-eight in Hodesdon to just ten in Stansted Thele but altogether mustering a total of 601 men. In April 1588, with the Spanish Armada poised to invade, the Hertfordshire Militia, commanded by Sir Rowland Lytton of Knebworth, numbered 3,000 ablemen, of whom half were considered trained. Further details listed an additional 200 pioners (pioneers), twenty launces (lances) or heavy cavalry, and sixty lightors or light horsemen. These were among the troops which mustered at Tilbury to be inspired by Queen Elizabeth I.

In 1591, England was again threatened by the efforts of the Catholic League led by Spain to exploit the civil war in France. Spanish forces under Parma invaded France through Flanders, while others came in from the west through Brittany. The intention was to seize French ports both in Brittany and on the Channel coast to threaten England. Henry of Navarre, the Protestant king of France, was resisting these Spanish incursions, and a force of 6,000 men, mainly levied from the county militias, under Robert Devereux, Earl of Essex, was sent to his aid. Hertfordshire provided a levy of 150 men under Captain Grymston.

Lord Burghley's papers in Hatfield House contain details of payments for the supply of munitions supplied to French garrisons holding back the Spanish invaders through Brittany, and for the export of beer for the English troops, as well as correspondence between Elizabeth, Navarre and Essex. Essex joined Navarre in the siege of Rouen, the key to Normandy, but meeting with stiff resistance from the defenders, he brought his men home within a few weeks. Ironically, some of those same men may have been members of the

Hertfordshire Trained Bands who turned out to keep the peace in London in 1601 whilst Essex was being tried for treason and executed.

Chains of beacons, the use of which dates back to Saxon times, were maintained to warn of foreign invasion. Hilltops were not always available and church towers often took over the function. The towers of Cheshunt and Monken Hadley churches both carried beacons: at the former a cresset at one angle of the parapet, and at the latter a copper beacon, renewed in the eighteenth century.

The landed gentry were expected to play their part in safeguarding their country. In 1569, Sir Henry Carey of Hunsdon, who had been knighted, created a baron and also a garter knight by Elizabeth I, and whose later participation in privateering we have just encountered, was appointed lieutenant general of the force sent to deal with the rebellion of the Catholic northern earls: Howard, Percy and Neville. Though greatly outnumbered, he managed to defeat the rebels comprehensively. A grateful monarch rewarded his success with further appointments as principal captain and governor of the army at the time of the Armada.

His son, George, was knighted in the field and appointed governor of Carisbrooke Castle on the Isle of Wight, a key stronghold in the defences of the south coast. His second son, Sir John, served as marshal of the principal border fortress of Berwick-upon-Tweed during the latter years of Elizabeth's reign. A third son, Sir Edmund, served with Dudley's expedition to the Netherlands and was appointed vice-admiral of Lincolnshire before serving as a colonel in the army raised against the threat of foreign invasion.

The youngest of Sir Henry's sons, Sir Robert, served with the Earl of Essex in Normandy, commanding a regiment at the siege of Rouen. As warden of the middle march, he successfully carried out a campaign to suppress the local reivers. Bearer of the news of Elizabeth's death to James VI at Holyrood, he later benefitted from the king's patronage, becoming Earl of Monmouth. His son, another Henry, chose the life of a reclusive academic, and his death at Rickmansworth in 1661 saw his title become extinct, as, of his two sons, amongst eight daughters, one had been killed fighting on the Royalist side at Marston Moor in 1644, and the other, also an ardent Royalist, had died childless in 1649.

'Commotion times'—civil disturbances

Following the dissolution of the monasteries, many landowners seized the opportunity to exploit the potential of their lands by increasing their productivity, thereby feeding an ever-increasing population. In 1532, Sir William Cavendish had entered the service of Thomas Cromwell, and, when the Abbey of St Albans was dissolved in 1540, he was using his connections as an auditor of the Court of Augmentations to acquire land for himself, leasing the manor of Northaw from the abbot in 1535, then purchasing it outright, along with the abbot's house in St Albans. In 1544, he enclosed 120 acres (48ha) of common land at Northaw, provoking the commoners to riot, and four years later, he was in the process of obtaining a royal licence to enclose a much larger area of common land in North Mymms, Northaw and Cheshunt to farm rabbits for fur. Rumours of this plan, possibly initiated by his own household, began to circulate, and resistance was quickly mobilised.

Aware that the commissioners were in Sir William's house in Northaw, 500 armed villagers laid siege, on 21–25 May, threatening to burn the manor down and refusing to budge until he agreed to speak with them. They then proceeded to slaughter 1,000 of Sir William's rabbits, blew up their burrows with gunpowder and returned the next day to kill 300 more of the poor beasts. Confronted by the local rioters, by now augmented by sympathisers from further afield, and numbering around 700 men, the commissioners were forced to flee.

Disturbances continued for several more days with vocal harassment of Sir William in his house, further brutal killings of rabbits and the release of half a dozen of his horses. Sir William brought charges against ninety-five of his riotous neighbours, some of which resulted in prosecutions. The commoners claimed to be protecting their rights, arguing that he was using legislation deemed to be invalid during the king's minority and exploiting his position as an official, thereby revealing a conflict of interest and laying himself open to accusations of misappropriation. His bid to enclose a further 500 acres (200ha) of common land was regarded by the commoners as excessive and would leave them with far from sufficient land to avoid overgrazing. Sir William countered by accusing the commoners of the serious crime of riot and rebellion.

Unfortunately, no evidence has yet emerged as to the resolution of this matter, but going by what was to happen elsewhere, it is difficult to be confident that the ringleaders, especially such men of substance and official position—they included yeomen and constables—would have escaped severe punishment. It seems that they were imprisoned rather than being hanged, as might have been warranted by a proven charge of treason. Whatever the rights and wrongs—and they would subsequently occupy much court time—the violence of the protest was significant. These enclosure riots at Northaw and Cheshunt, referred to at the time as 'commotion times', were the spark which ignited a much wider rebellion across twenty-five southern, East Anglian, and Midland counties, even reaching up into Lincolnshire and Yorkshire.

The best known of these was Kett's Rebellion, in Norfolk, the following year, which, being better documented, has tended to put other events in the shade. Sir William went on to hold senior positions at court, becoming, with his third wife, Bess of Hardwick, a member of the Protestant elite. Mary I's accession, coupled with close connections to Lady Jane Grey and her relatives, rendered the exposed location of Northaw uncomfortably close to London. Sir William therefore disposed of his southern properties to concentrate on amassing property in Derbyshire and developing Chatsworth. When he died in 1557, the official records of his financial affairs were in disorder, and he came under suspicion of embezzlement arising from his position from 1546–53 as Henry VIII's treasurer of the chamber. The unpopular Protector Somerset, governing for the young Edward VI, was judged to have been incompetent in dealing with the frequency and intensity of these and other riots across the country and was deposed.

Hertfordshire and the Civil Wars

The religious inclinations of the people of Hertfordshire leant largely toward Puritanism, meaning that, James I, perceived as a closet Catholic with a Catholic wife, consequently enjoyed little support in the county, despite the town of Royston being dominated by one of his favourite residences. However, it was Lord Mounteagle, a resident of Royston, who had passed on to the authorities the tip which led to the foiling of the Gunpowder Plot to blow up the king in 1605.

In 1627, Sir John Heveningham of Bygrave was one of several squires imprisoned by Charles I for refusing him a forced loan, one action amongst several that prompted Parliament's Petition of Right. In 1638, the proud borough of Great Berkhamsted had neglected to pay its ship money, and other neighbours had their possessions seized or were even imprisoned for defying Thomas Coningsby, the sheriff who attempted to collect what the king saw as his due.

Another tax which raised objections was that which paid for soldiers' clothing and transport. Charles had other less law-driven means of raising cash too. Sir Charles Caesar of Benington was appointed master of the rolls when his winning bid of £5,000 secured the role in a royal auction of state offices. Several local churches had their altar rails, symbolic of 'high church' popery, torn down by anonymous soldiers. Although ordered to take action, the county's JPs, among them Sir John Jennings of St Albans, were unaccountably unable to glean any information whatsoever from the eyewitnesses, so were consequently unable to come down hard on the perpetrators, even had they been so inclined. When one of the guilty soldiers was caught and imprisoned in Hemel Hempstead, he was forcibly released by his compatriots. The county's MPs joined others from across the country in presenting petitions outlining their constituents' grievances to the Long Parliament. The drawing up of battle lines was accelerating.

In 1638, the county's trained bands consisted of 750 musketeers and a similar number of pikemen. In 1640 some 650 of these men were ordered to take ship from Harwich to Newcastle to fight in Charles I's vain attempt to impose the organisation of the English church onto the Scots, as Scottish Presbyterians preferred to elect their own leaders rather than having bishops thrust upon them. This, the second instalment of the so-called Bishops' Wars, like its predecessor, ended in stalemate after only minimal and inconclusive action. In 1641, the 2nd Earl of Salisbury, resident in Hatfield, who would support Parliament throughout the wars, was appointed as a fit person to be entrusted with the organisation of Hertfordshire's militia. However, he found himself conflicted, and his reluctance to abandon the king, coupled with his consequent inactivity, saw him replaced as Lord Lieutenant by his son, Lord Cranborne, more amenable to the wishes of Parliament. At the commencement of hostilities, the race was on between the two sides to secure control of the trained bands themselves and their armouries.

At Hadham, Arthur Capel's armoury, sufficient to arm a thousand men, was seized by the Parliamentarian authorities, and the magazines in Hertford and St Albans were also secured for Parliament. Recruitment for Parliament's army was in full swing, and Watford contributed a troop of sixty cavalry to the force being assembled in London. Guards were mounted in Hertford to ensure that local Royalists would be unable to take the town. Should the Parliamentarian army now gathering in London need to deploy northwards, Watling Street, through St Albans, and the Great North Road, through Ware and Baldock, were made secure. This enabled the Earl of Essex at the head of an army of 20,000 men to counter the king's southward march from Nottingham. Torn between traditional loyalty to the king and the need to reform government, the county's people were still finding it difficult to decide where their loyalties would ultimately lie.

Sir Marmaduke Rawdon of Hoddesdon, a successful merchant in the city of London, where he was a militia captain, dropped everything, raised a regiment of infantry and a troop of horse, and joined the king in Oxford, where he was promptly knighted. His regiment would hold Basing House in Hampshire for the king through successive sieges, once being relieved by a force which included his own son. On the eve of the final siege, he was asked, as a Protestant, to leave its final doomed defence to the Marquess of Winchester's Catholic troops. He became governor of Faringdon in Berkshire, where he died having held out to the bitter end.

Lucius, 2nd Lord Falkland, succeeded to the title on the death of his father, the Royalist MP, Sir Edward Car(e)y of Aldenham, who never recovered from a broken leg sustained in an accident whilst hunting with Charles I at Theobalds in 1633. Having fought in the Bishops' Wars in 1639, Lucius was elected to Parliament and, although opposed to the way Charles regarded Parliament and its members, chose to accept high command in the king's army when war broke out in 1642. He would be killed at the Battle of Newbury in September of the following year.

After the stalemate at Edgehill, the Royalist Army had finally advanced on London, heading for defeat at Brentford. In November 1642, some from the Royalist forces managed to reach Watford, clashing with troops of the Earl of

Essex, the proud owner of Cassiobury, after its sequestration from Arthur Capel. The Watford men held out and the town was afterwards garrisoned with 500 cavalry. This skirmish, though relatively minor, drew attention to the vulnerability of the county, which lay on the exposed western flank of the Parliamentarians' Eastern Association, revealing the need to make it secure. In January 1643, as the High Sheriff, Sir Thomas Coningsby, was in St Albans market square reading a royal proclamation regarding the raising of trained bands for the king, he was interrupted and arrested by Cromwell with a cavalry force. A Parliamentarian garrison was installed, and the town was put in a state of defence.

St Albans, lying on the route by which a Royalist march on London might be taken from Oxford, quickly became a military stronghold, being garrisoned and serving as Parliamentarian HQ under the Earl of Essex and Sir Thomas Fairfax. Fortifications were constructed with ramparts across the northern face of the town, with the medieval Tonman Ditch being re-dug, and redoubts for cannon being constructed in the vicinity of St Peter's Church. Harpenden, too, was perceived as vulnerable to attack and garrisoned.

Hertfordshire would quickly settle into its role as recruiting ground, arsenal and victualler for the parliamentarian armies fighting across the land, while accepting that the army of the king in his Oxford fastness was only a few days' march away and, even more sobering, that Prince Rupert and his cavalry were but a few hours' ride away. A party of Parliamentarians returning from London to Cambridge was attacked by Royalists near Buntingford in 1643. Although much of the baggage they were escorting was pillaged, Cromwell's new helmet, commissioned from an armourer close to the Tower of London, escaped notice and made it to Cambridge.

Salisbury's son, Charles, Viscount Cranborne, now Lord Lieutenant of Hertfordshire and the county's MP, had appointed Sir John Wittewronge as captain of the Trained Bands in West Hertfordshire and then as colonel of the county's volunteer regiment. Taxation to support the army was organised by the Hertfordshire Committee under such as the merchant Gabriel Barbour of Hertford, who operated as a goldsmith in the City of London.

In May 1643, the county was assessed at £3,000 to pay the costs of the volunteer regiment raised in the county. This was stationed in Aylesbury and Leighton Buzzard in spring 1643 and provided troops for the garrison of the strategically important Newport Pagnell, which had been fortuitously vacated as the result of garbled communications in the Royalist leadership. Such exactions prompted petitions describing the hardship of those having to raise the money, especially the families of those serving with the army.

The houses of the aristocracy such as Hadham and Gorhambury were pillaged, regardless of their owners' allegiances. Thomas Coningsby, as sheriff, had attempted, possibly with too much enthusiasm, to collect the unpopular and unwarranted taxes levied by the king without Parliament's approval, so it was perhaps inevitable that his house at North Mymms should be plundered. Earl Grey's army's sojourn in Watford, prior to his attack on Royalist Reading, early in 1643 would have involved troops being billeted on householders. The constant demands for recruits, cash and foodstuffs imposed a permanent burden on rich and poor alike. After the Battle of Naseby, large numbers of Royalist prisoners were brought to St Albans to be interned and, more importantly to the townsfolk, to be fed at the expense of the town. Hertfordshire's citizens, however, could be thankful that none was subjected to the horrific siege conditions which afflicted towns across the land, bringing disease, destruction, destitution and death.

The county's trained bands, 4,000-strong, were assembled in Hitchin, when Royalists raiding in neighbouring Bedfordshire looked to be coming a bit close for comfort. Further Royalist incursions around Watford in early 1644 mobilised the defenders once more. Two of the three regiments of Trained Bands under their leader, Colonel Mitchell, were involved in the 1644 siege of Greenlands House in Buckinghamshire. This Royalist garrison had constituted a threat to Parliamentarian communications along the Thames Valley and the house was destroyed by cannon fire.

A notional line of defence along the Chilterns was intended to secure the counties of the Parliamentarians' Eastern Association, and beacons were lit on the heights to alert the county to threats of Royalist raids such as that which struck Bedford and Dunstable in June 1644. The response of the people of Hitchin, rather than rely on help which might or might not arrive, was to root out their weapons and to organise their own defence.

The expectation that the king would attempt a cross-country advance on Cambridge brought a plan to make Hertford the assembly point for the defending forces from London and East Anglia, but when the Royalists swerved away towards Aylesbury, St Albans became the new point of muster, with the army then marching through Great Berkhamsted and Tring. The Hertfordshire men, described as the 'Green Regiment', remained with Major General Browne, the local Parliamentarian commander, into 1645. Hertfordshire also raised a mounted regiment, reputedly numbering into the hundreds, and serving with Colonel Graves during 1645, mainly in the south-west of the country, but diverted to Cheshire, where it may have fought in the Battle of Rowton Heath.

In November 1643, the 15,000-strong army of the Earl of Essex lay in winter quarters in St Albans. Not having been paid, the soldiers were close to mutiny, and several hundred of them were ready to plunder the town. Cash was obtained to take the heat out of the situation, and threats of enemy movements brought a dispersal but did little to address the problems. St Albans remained a forward HQ for the Parliamentarian army throughout the First Civil War, and in 1645 Cromwell had his HQ in Hitchin's Sun Hotel, with large numbers of troops billeted in the town. Berry Close, by the river in Ware, was the location for shooting practice and general military training.

In June 1647, the captive Charles I, though under escort, made what could have passed for a triumphal progress across the county, staying at his Royston Palace, Hatfield House and Theobalds, in Cheshunt, as he made his way to Richmond-upon-Thames. In November large numbers of Parliamentarian troops across the country sought to establish the political aims of the Levellers in the face of official attempts to suppress the movement.

The Army Council designated three official rendezvous, one of which was Corkbush (or Cockbush) Field off Ware Road, in Hertford. Several regiments gathered there, as had been agreed, to put forward the Levellers' radical document, the 'Agreement of the People'. They were then confronted by the army's leadership from their HQ in St Albans, countering what they regarded as mutiny with their own manifesto requiring the troops to pledge allegiance to the Army Council.

The confident and overbearing Fairfax and Cromwell, whose assassination had been a part of the Levellers' plan, outfaced these declared mutineers, many of whom then proved quite amenable to abandoning their officers' ideals and agreeing to take the oath of loyalty, with the consequent collapse of opposition to the army's authority. Eleven ringleaders were arrested and brought from Ware to St Albans Gaol to be court-martialled. In the event only three were condemned to death. Afterwards, they drew lots and one was shot by the other two. As had previously been threatened, other officers were cashiered from the army in a ritual act of public humiliation.

The Second Civil War in 1648 saw skirmishing between the Royalists hoping to free the king and those who remained loyal to Parliament. In one such action in Elstree, the Royalists were repulsed. It had now once more become necessary to raise a Parliamentarian force in the county. Two troops of cavalry and two more of dragoons routed a Royalist force in Barnet and went on to join the Parliamentarian army, which put to flight the main Royalist force at Kingston-upon-Thames. Some of the Royalist cavalry fleeing this defeat passed through St Albans, only pausing in the marketplace briefly in an unsuccessful attempt to solicit the citizens' support.

Another such group of Royalists stopped to rest in St Neots, near Huntingdon, where troops guided by Hertfordshire militia officers from Hitchin took them unawares, conducting them back to Hitchin as prisoners. Having been involved in Charles I's escape to the Isle of Wight, Arthur Capel assumed prominence as a leader during this Second Civil War. Along with Sir Thomas Fanshawe of Ware Park and other local gentry, he raised a company of Hertfordshire men for the Royalist forces and led them to occupy Colchester. His force was soon penned in by blockading siegeworks and he was forced to watch as his hostage son was paraded around by the Parliamentarian besiegers. With no relief in sight, he had no alternative but to surrender.

Those of his colleagues who were fighting in breach of parole were executed out of hand, but Capel was promised quarter by the military and imprisoned in the Tower of London. However, following an unsuccessful escape attempt, he was condemned to death by Parliament and beheaded in March 1649. After the fall of Colchester, hundreds of starving prisoners fetched up in St Albans, many being confined in St Peter's Church prior to their transportation to Barbados via the port of Bristol. Others were moved on to continued confinement in Great Berkhamsted.

A meeting of the Army Council in St Albans Abbey in November 1648 attended by the Parliamentarian leadership, including Fairfax and Ireton, led to an agreement that a 'remonstrance' should be sent to Parliament. The final version was produced by Ireton and Fairfax at The Bull, on Holywell Hill, and sent under military escort to Parliament, demanding that the king be put on trial for treason against his people. This demand, on Parliament's failure to act, led to the army moving in to purge those MPs who refused to countenance such actions against the king, whatever his guilt. Parliament despatched a month's pay to St Albans, but this would only temporarily placate the army. A further mutiny of levellers in the army, affecting troops in St Albans, occurred in the spring of 1649 and was ruthlessly put down by the military authorities.

The execution of Charles I aroused a great deal of sadness in many who had been staunch supporters of Parliament in opposing the royal prerogative. Many throughout the county had suffered physically and materially. While some had lost everything through their loyalty to the crown, some would also bounce back.

Arthur Capel of Hadham Hall and Cassiobury House had been elected MP for Hertfordshire in 1640. Initially, he supported the opposition to Charles I, presenting a petition from the people of Hertfordshire conveying their disapproval of the king's governance. In 1641, he purchased a cut-price barony and morphed into a committed Royalist. He held various offices during the First Civil War, accompanying the queen on her flight to France; his sorry end we have already witnessed.

Other Royalist gentry included Sir William Lytton of Knebworth, MP from 1628, who was one of the commissioners sent to treat with the king in 1644 at Oxford. In opposition to Cromwell, he was a victim of Pride's Purge and was one of forty MPs imprisoned in cellars beneath the House of Commons. Sir John Harrison was the first to be appointed commissioner for customs and an MP. He built Balls Park in 1640 and was knighted the following year. His support for the king cost him his parliamentary seat in 1643 and a fine of over £10,000. After the Restoration he regained his seat and served as a privy councillor until his death in 1669.

The Royalist Ferrers family had been granted extensive lands in Hertfordshire, including Flamstead, Bayford and Markyate Cell. On the death of her father in 1640 and of her brother shortly after, Katherine Ferrers became sole heiress to the Ferrers estates. Her widowed mother remarried Simon Fanshawe and headed for the Royalist capital, Oxford, in 1642.

Fanshawe fought at Marston Moor and was later imprisoned, with the result that many of the family's assets were sequestrated.

Sir Francis Bacon, Baron Verulam, Lord Chancellor to James I, died without heirs in 1626. His Verulam House appears to have passed to Sir Harbottle Grimston, who was an MP and a supporter of Parliament, dying in 1648. His son, also an MP, however, may have hedged his bets during the wars, toeing the parliamentary line but actively working for the king's rehabilitation. The house suffered terminal neglect during the wars and had disappeared by 1665.

William Heveningham, a supporter of Parliament throughout the war, whose father had undergone imprisonment at the king's hands, sat on the court which tried the king but refused to sign the death warrant. Daniel Axtell of Great Berkhamsted was a devout Baptist and an apprentice grocer. He joined the New Model Army in 1643 and fought throughout the campaigns, finally being promoted colonel and commanding the guard at the trial of Charles I at Westminster in 1649. He had no qualms about playing a part in the king's trial and sentencing and went on to commit alleged atrocities during Cromwell's Irish campaign, remaining in the army and opposing the restoration of the monarchy.

On his return to the throne in 1660, Charles II, the merry monarch, took his revenge. Axtell was arrested and, along with other functionaries who had not actually signed the king's death warrant, but were nevertheless held culpable, tried and convicted of regicide. He was taken to the Tyburn scaffold to be hanged, drawn and quartered.

As well as persons, buildings would suffer for their associations. Cecil's old Theobalds Palace was where Charles I was proclaimed king after his father's death there in 1625. It was therefore regarded as an irredeemable and provocative symbol of kingship. By order of Parliament, it was demolished in 1650 and the proceeds from the sale of materials were distributed amongst the army.

It would be from his military HQ in St Albans that General Monk, hitherto a staunch proponent of the Commonwealth, set out on his mission to bring Charles II back as king. At the Restoration in 1660, Arthur Capel's son was created Earl of Essex and Lord Lieutenant of Hertfordshire. He served in Ireland but was recalled in 1677 and became associated with those who opposed the succession of James II, a Catholic. He allied himself with the faction supporting the Duke of Monmouth and, though not involved, was arrested in the aftermath of the Rye House Plot. Imprisoned in the Tower, he would be found dead whilst awaiting execution for treason. The verdict of suicide was not everyone's idea of a satisfactory explanation for his death in custody.

The Rye House Plot of 1683 was a conspiracy to assassinate Charles II and his brother, the future James II, as they returned to London from the Newmarket races. Sir Andrew Ogard's fortified manor of Rye House, near Hoddesdon, had been leased to Richard Rumbold, a former captain in the New Model Army. He was also a prominent local Dissenter; staunch republican and one of the guards at Charles I's execution in Whitehall in 1649. James, Duke of York, had already converted to Catholicism and the king was suspected of contemplating his own conversion. As a result of the presentation of legislation to exclude James from the line of succession on the grounds of his religion failing to pass Parliament, repeatedly being rejected by the House of Lords, what amounted to a Protestant revolution was in the air. The plot developed amid a plethora of unrelated conspiracies, which included a movement to install James, Duke of Monmouth, Charles II's natural son, as heir to the throne.

Only a small number of people needed to be involved in the actual execution of the plot, which hinged on a simple ambush as Charles rode past, but it was thwarted by his premature return to London after a fire in Newmarket. Inevitably, word got out, with the result that informers paved the way for indictments of the accused. As well as the actual intending perpetrators, many other prominent people, who were only vaguely implicated, were arraigned and their assumed guilt proven in evidence-free trials. One woman was burned at the stake; eleven men were hanged, beheaded, or hanged, drawn and quartered; ten men were imprisoned and/or fined; and ten more were exiled or chose to flee to the Dutch Republic. As we have seen, Arthur Capel of Hadham Hall, allegedly, cut his own throat in the Tower of London while awaiting trial.

The plot was seized on by Charles as an opportunity to eliminate much of the opposition, characterised as the embryonic Whig Party. Amongst those tried or threatened with arrest, were fifteen Whig peers, six Whig MPs and the influential philosopher, John Locke, who fled abroad. The Duke of Monmouth, creator of Charles II's new professional army, was obliged to go into exile, and was later beheaded for being encouraged to lead his own disastrous rebellion in 1685, after being abandoned by his erstwhile influential but inactive promoters.

The regular army, the militia and the volunteers

Under the leadership of Monmouth, the Restoration saw the creation, alongside the militia, of a permanent standing army, an entity previously held as anathema. Over the next decades this took greater shape as the expanding colonies required garrisons and as military action proliferated.

By combining eight local companies, a regular regiment of infantry of the line, nominally linked to Hertfordshire, was formed in Jamaica in 1743 as Edward Trelawney's Regiment of Foot. As the 49th Regiment of Foot, this unit fought in the American War of Independence and in 1782, quite unusually as local association was not yet a commonplace, was designated the 49th (the Hertfordshire) Regiment of Foot. It fought in Europe as marines in the earlier part of the Anglo-French Wars, and then back to the Americas for the War of 1812. In 1816 it became the 49th (Princess Charlotte of Wales's) (Hertfordshire) Regiment of Foot.

The Hertfordshire Militia turned out in 1666 to help clear up after the Great Fire of London and to ensure that the fire was not rekindled. The Militia Returns of 1697 recorded that the Hertfordshire Militia, under the leadership of the Earl of Essex, as lord lieutenant, consisted of 1,025 infantry in ten companies, and three troops of horse, each sixty-strong, led by Captains Gore, Charlton and Hookate. After this time, the militia went into abeyance until the Seven Years War broke out in 1756 and a new Militia Act (1757) brought a general resurrection of the militia. This legislation was far from popular and there were violent resistance and the intimidation of the magistrates drawing up lists of those eligible for service.

Opposition to the act had caused riots in Royston, and a request was made to move troops from their station in Baldock to St Albans, as there were parallel disturbances in Great Berkhamsted. Hertfordshire nevertheless managed to raise its required quota of 560 men, who drew their arms from the Tower of London in March 1759. The Duke of St Albans commanded the neighbouring Berkshire Militia. Actual embodiments took place in 1759–62, during the latter stages of the Seven Years' War, and in 1778–83, for the American War of Independence, when the regiment was sent to Kent for training alongside the regulars. These duties were carried out to release regular troops for foreign service while maintaining garrisons at home. In 1780, the militia camped out in London's Hyde Park as part of the force suppressing the anti-Catholic Gordon Riots.

During the Anglo-French Wars, the Hertfordshire Militia assembled in St Albans under the command of the Marquess of Salisbury. They spent time on anti-invasion duties on the south coast, returned to St Albans to take part in the royal review in Hatfield Park in 1800, and then undertook the first of two spells guarding French POWs at Norman Cross on the Great North Road near Peterborough.

In 1811, the regiment volunteered for service in Ireland and, after two years there, returned to Norman Cross, prior to disembodiment in 1814. It was normal for militia regiments to be stationed outside their home areas to avoid conflicts of interest if called out in aid of the Civil Power. Hence, in the winter of 1794/95, it was nine companies of the Derbyshire Militia who were quartered around Hertford and Ware. This, incidentally, provided background material for Jane Austen's *Pride and Prejudice* which, despite no solid evidence of Austen's ever having visited the county, was set in Hertfordshire, with Meryton standing in for Hertford. During periods when the regiments were not embodied, its members were committed to their twenty-eight days' annual training.

Alongside the 'regular' militia, volunteer companies of infantry, of varying quality, were also raised during the early years of the Anglo-French Wars, primarily for local defence in the event of an invasion. These included the Hitchin Volunteer Infantry, the Hertfordshire Rifles, the Standon Volunteer Infantry, the Loyal Hemel Hempstead, St Albans and Watford Volunteer Infantry, and two regiments of the Hertfordshire Volunteer Infantry, all raised and led by local worthies. In 1809, those that remained in existence were integrated into three battalions of local militia based in Hitchin (Midland), Hertford (Eastern), and St Albans (Western), each under the nominal command of the local MP.

In May 1810, local militia, assembled in St Albans for their annual training, mutinied over their pay. It may be noted that the bounties due to local militiamen would be reduced in the following year, so rumours of this impending cut in numbers and remuneration may have been responsible for the discontent. Their militarily inexperienced colonel, Sir John Sebright, completely mishandled the situation, imprisoning a sergeant, the men's delegate, who was then sprung from the St Albans abbey prison under the gatehouse by his outraged compatriots. Whatever the rights and wrongs of the situation, military authority had to be reasserted and once regular troops had been brought in to quell the mutiny, several soldiers, deemed ringleaders, were flogged, while Sir John escaped censure. The army's use of excessive flogging was questioned in Parliament, and the affair was largely hushed up.

VOLUNTEER FORCES IN HERTFORDSHIRE

Following a meeting called in 1794 by the Marquess of Salisbury in Hatfield, as a response to the perceived threat emanating from revolutionary France, five troops of yeomanry cavalry were raised in the county. These comprised a northern troop based in Kings Walden; a western troop based at its captain's property, The Grove, outside Watford; a southern troop based at its captain's house, Theobalds, in Cheshunt; an eastern troop at Albury; and a centre troop based at Brocket Hall, near Welwyn. The motivation behind the raising of these units was initially concerned more with internal security and maintaining the status quo. It is reported that William Wilshere, banker and lawyer, was so concerned by the perceived implications for British society posed by the French Revolution, that he fortified The Frythe, his grand mansion outside Welwyn.

By 1798, however, the government, in the face of threats from the new regime in France, was looking to consolidate anti-invasion defences and so encouraged the expansion of volunteer forces. Additional troops of cavalry were raised at Sawbridgeworth, Beechwood Park and Ashridge, along with a horse artillery battery at Wormleybury, with Wilshere credited as being instrumental in this process. In 1802, the short-lived Peace of Amiens saw the disbandment of some of these troops and the formation of others. After Nelson's victory at Trafalgar in 1805, the threat of invasion had all but disappeared and over the next ten years all bar the Northern Troop had disbanded—the Ashbridge Troop disbanding in 1809.

Within a few years, yeomanry units were encouraged to re-form in anticipation of the civil disorders which were expected to accompany the rocky passage of the Reform Acts in Parliament. So, in 1830–31, seven troops of yeomanry cavalry were raised and formed into the North Hertfordshire Regiment of Yeomanry Cavalry at Baldock with four troops, and the South Hertfordshire Regiment of Yeomanry Cavalry, based on Hatfield House, with three troops, to be joined, a year later, by a fourth, Cashio Troop.

Military infrastructure

CANALS

The Grand Union Canal, a combination of several shorter canals, had been completed in 1805, effectively extending from London to Liverpool. Stretches were used in 1798 to transport troops to Liverpool to quell the uprising in Ireland. The first all-through transit of troops in 1806 took seven days. Subsequent military emergencies saw the boats sailing through the night and halving the duration.

One of the natural obstacles was the Tring Summit, 393ft (121m) above sea level, reached by fifty-seven locks up from Brentford on the Thames. This problem was solved by a succession of locks; reservoirs and side ponds which fed water into the canal; and later on in the century, a prototype inclined plane alongside the canal at Bulborne.

Although the Board of Ordnance entered into a three-year agreement with Pickfords in 1832, the expansion of the railway network would soon make troop movements both cheaper and quicker. The River Lea, flowing across the county from Luton and in places representing the traditional boundary with Essex and Middlesex, was canalised from 1766. It would be used to transport raw materials into the Royal Small Arms Factory and the Waltham Abbey Royal Gunpowder Mills, and their product for distribution to the armed services.

SIGNALS

During the Anglo-French Wars, the Admiralty constructed chains of signal stations to enable orders to be sent quickly to ports, dockyards and naval bases. One such chain extended from London to Norwich and Great Yarmouth. To ensure that the stations were intervisible, the surveyors avoided London's smog by exploiting the high ground and taking the chain north-west from London to St Albans, where the gear was set up on top of the town belfry at the top of the hill. From there it went to Dunstable Downs in Bedfordshire, where it did a dogleg to the next station at Telegraph Hill, Lilley Hoo, at a height of 596ft (183m), re-entering the county to proceed through Baldock and Royston and on into Cambridgeshire.

Each station was manned by a naval lieutenant on half-pay and two trustworthy matelots, with a small hut for shelter. Many types of semaphore signal had been tried using flags, rotating arms, combinations of black balls and lights. The system selected, which consisted of a vertical framework containing six shutters, could form open or closed combinations capable of producing seventeen different letters, either to make words at a rate of six letters per minute, or to be part of a pre-arranged code. These would be read from a distance using Mr Dolland's Admiralty-issue, two-guinea telescope, and copied for onward transmission to the next station in the chain. The process may have been slow, but it was still infinitely quicker than relays of horses.

4

Victorian and Edwardian Hertfordshire 1840–1914

The second half of the nineteenth century would see far-reaching changes in the make-up of the Nation's military, including a reorganisation of the regulars and the development of the Volunteer Force. The necessary preparations for the First World War, however, would leave land-locked Hertfordshire, largely untroubled, secure in the knowledge that the government's 'Blue-Water' Policy would see the Royal Navy remaining the dominant force in Europe and the world. An historic first balloon flight over England was briefly interrupted with a touchdown in North Mymms in September 1784, but it would be another century or more before flight might become commonplace.

The army in Hertfordshire

As a single battalion regiment, following service in China and the Crimea in 1881, the 49th (the Hertfordshire) Regiment of Foot left the county to be merged with the 66th Regiment, becoming Princess Charlotte of Wales's Royal Berkshire Regiment, with a depot in Reading. Ironically, one of the few regiments to be given a local attribution so early on disappeared overnight in this War Office consolidation exercise. This was a result of the Cardwell reforms, which systematically linked regiments to specific counties, which would then become their recruiting grounds. From this time on, Hertfordshire would not again be solely associated with a unit of the regular infantry. The north and south Hertfordshire regiments of yeomanry cavalry amalgamated as the Hertfordshire Yeomanry in 1871, with its HQ initially at Hertford and then at St Albans.

Following service in South Africa in the Imperial Yeomanry (see below), two squadrons were formed based, in 1902, on St Albans and Hertford, but soon, conforming to the standard four-squadron format, a presence in Watford, Barnet and Hitchin was established. In 1852, the 30th (Hertford)

Regiment of Militia established its HQ at Hatfield, and premises were built in Batterdale by the Marquess of Salisbury. From 1855, Therfield Heath, west of Royston, became a training ground for the militia with a small valley scarped to form a rifle range.

When the Cardwell reforms of 1881 brought the militia into the local regimental depot system, with no regular Hertfordshire regiment with which to belong, the militia became the 4th (Extra Reserve) Battalion, Bedfordshire Regiment but were accommodated in new permanent barracks, built in London Road, Hertford, in 1883–84. The militia was still using Therfield Heath for training in 1904 when thefts from its camp were reported in the local press. Militia barracks had been built off Barnet High Street, in 1855, to provide a base for the 2nd or Edmonton Royal Rifle Regiment of Middlesex Militia. In 1881, they became the 7th (Royal 2nd Middlesex Militia) Battalion, King's Royal Rifle Corps (KRRC) and left the area to join their parent regiment's depot in Winchester.

THE RIFLE VOLUNTEER CORPS (RVC)

In the aftermath of the Crimean War and the Indian Mutiny, sometimes referred to as the First Indian War of Independence, there was some dissatisfaction with the army's performance, particularly over a perceived lack of musketry skills. A National Rifle Association was begun in 1859, but many wanted to go further and raise a force of volunteers in those urban areas from which very few were recruited to the yeomanry cavalry.

In 1856, Earl Cowper of Panshanger, had set up the Hertford Rifle Club, which led directly to the first Rifle Volunteer Corps (RVC) being raised in the county. This formed at Hertford in November 1859 and was followed by a further thirteen corps across the county. Not all of them would flourish, but those that did were organised into two administrative battalions, so that the War Office might exercise an element of control over what could otherwise be seen as private armies. As the price of this takeover, the War Office undertook to fund RVC on the basis of how many of their members became 'efficient' in drill, marksmanship, turnout and attendance at weekly parades.

Units were required to provide an orderly room for administration, a secure armoury for the storage of weapons and ammunition, and an indoor space for drills and training on winter evenings. This latter requirement led to the acquisition of dedicated buildings known as drill halls, or of local arrangements to use the premises of town councils, church halls or public houses.

Yeomanry House on St Andrew Street, in Hertford, represents a very early example of a drill hall. It is a four-storey, early Georgian house of 1726 which was acquired for military use in 1860. Behind the house are a hall and stabling. Its painted 'Artillery Barracks' sign on the side of the house very likely dates from the start of the TF in 1908.

In the early days, friction between the nascent RVC and the regular army sometimes surfaced over the degree of professionalism to which the volunteers might be expected to aspire. Lord Ranelagh, a staunch supporter of the RVC and a believer in the independence of the movement, attended a volunteer review at Panshanger in 1862 and took exception to the arrant arrogance and condescension of a visiting guards officer sent by the War Office to supervise a sham fight.

By 1880, the several Hertfordshire corps had coalesced into two rifle volunteer corps: the 1st, of eight companies, with its HQ in Hertford; and the 2nd, of five companies, with its HQ in Little Gaddesden and Ashridge. In the reorganisation of the army in 1887, the two corps, somewhat reluctantly, became the 1st and 2nd (Hertfordshire) Volunteer Battalions of the Bedfordshire Regiment, with newly raised companies added in Tring and Watford. A parallel development had taken place in Barnet, which was the HQ of the 6th Administrative Battalion of the Middlesex Rifle Volunteers. By 1880, Barnet was home to 'C' Company of the 3rd Middlesex RVC, soon to become 'F' Company, 1st Volunteer Battalion, Middlesex Regiment, with its HQ at 14 Union Street, near the militia barracks.

Most of the volunteer movement's figurehead top brass were titled landowners. In Watford, the meeting to explore the setting up of a RVC was chaired by the Earl of Verulam, the lord lieutenant, accompanied on the platform by the 4th Earl of Clarendon, Lord Rokeby and Lord Ebury.

Left: Yeomanry House, 28 St Andrew Street, Hertford, was built in 1726 and acquired for military use in 1860 as the HQ of 1st Hertfordshire's Rifle Volunteers. It later became HQ of both the yeomanry cavalry and the volunteer artillery.

Opposite above: The enormous Ashridge House, in Little Gaddesden, of 1808, accommodated the HQ of 2nd Hertfordshire Rifle Volunteers from 1860, and its park provided training space for field days, especially for the yeomanry cavalry.

Opposite below: The building at 14 Union Street, Barnet, close to the militia barracks, was HQ of a volunteer battalion of the Middlesex Regiment.

Elements of the Hertfordshire yeomanry were led, at various times, by the 2nd Marquess of Salisbury, the Earl of Verulam's son Viscount Grimston, Viscount Malden, and the 5th Earl of Salisbury. Viscount Cranborne commanded the militia battalion; Earl Cowper, in 1901, was honorary colonel of the 1st Volunteer Battalion; and Earl Brownlow of Ashridge commanded the 2nd

Volunteer Battalion. Once these top positions were filled, it was often a struggle to find suitable middle-rank officers.

Many RVC tried to obtain the services of professional men and the 1st Volunteer Battalion's CO was Hertford's leading solicitor, Lieutenant Colonel Charles Longmore. However, officers would generally be drawn from the next layer of society. A list of the officers of the 1st (Hertfordshire) Volunteer Battalion in 1901 includes brewers, seed merchants, assistant masters from Haileybury College, a draper, a banker and an insurance agent, with physicians and clergymen filling their appropriate appointments. Only the adjutant was a professional soldier—a captain seconded from the Royal Inniskilling Fusiliers.

Although membership began with the enthusiasm of the professional and middle classes, as the early leaders found they could not afford to make the necessary time commitments, by the 1870s, membership in the ranks was usually drawn from craftsmen, artisans, and factory workers, The average age of recruits also reduced down to twenty, reflecting that age-group's quest for opportunities for adventure, shooting, sports and the band. Urchins' ridicule of the uniform was offset by the girls it attracted. As volunteers got older and acquired families, they became less willing to give up evenings and weekends. By 1904, only a third of the officers were gentlemen or professionals and the largest groups in the rank and file were artisans and factory hands.

THE HERTFORDSHIRE LIGHT HORSE

The yeomanry was widely regarded as a socially superior clique run by the local aristocracy and recruiting exclusively from the local gentry, their estate workers and tenant farmers. The costs of keeping a horse and of the elaborate uniforms, though subsidised by wealthy patrons, remained a burden.

As an alternative for those who wanted to be volunteer cavalry but with a lower level of expense, units of light horse were raised in several counties. Away from the normal catchment area of the yeomanry, the Hertfordshire Light Horse was such a unit, formed in 1862, meeting at the Railway Inn in Bishop's Stortford and quickly increasing its roll to over one hundred officers and men in two troops with a band.

However, like similar short-lived units across the country, the costs soon escalated out of control. Descriptions of the uniform suggested that economy was not a priority, and anyway, a horse was expensive to maintain. Despite participating in royal reviews and gaining satisfactory grades in inspections, the regimental finances were not healthy. After the regiment's commandant, saddled with heavy debt, resigned, and fled abroad in 1879, the unit would collapse by the time the next year's Army List was published, never to be resuscitated. The unit's HQ was at Silver Leys, outside Bishops Stortford,

Above: The barracks in Bishops Stortford, Silver Leys, built in 1862, of the Hertfordshire Light Horse, was a short-lived unit set up as a cheaper and more inclusive alternative to the yeomanry.

Right: Bishops Stortford, the sculpture of the hart which originally stood over the porch of Silver Leys Hertfordshire Light Horse barracks, now adorning a shopfront in North Street.

where the building still stands as a car-audio shop. The life-size hart which stood over its porch now adorns the shopfront of a former bookshop in North Street.

CADETS IN THE NINETEENTH CENTURY

Following a move from Hertford Castle, Haileybury College was established in 1806 to prepare boys for service with the East India Company (EIC). This connection ceased in 1855 when the Company was relieved of its governmental responsibilities in the Indian subcontinent following the Mutiny. The college then reopened in 1862 as an independent public school in the original buildings.

In 1874, a Haileybury master founded the United Services College, in Westward Ho!, Devon, preparing boys for service in the armed forces.

This college moved to Harpenden and then, in 1906, was absorbed into St Mark's School in Windsor (Berkshire), becoming the Imperial Service College. Coming full circle, in 1942, the Imperial Service College would combine with Haileybury College to be known simply as 'Haileybury', but the tradition of supplying officer cadet candidates to the armed forces would continue.

Although the EIC's ostensibly military training took place at Addiscombe in Surrey, Haileybury always maintained military elements in its curriculum, as peripatetic administrators often found themselves in threatening situations. This element was retained when Haileybury formed a cadet corps in 1886 and attended the inaugural Public Schools Camp, joining contingents from Bedford, Eton, Bradfield and Sherborne at Churn, on the Berkshire Downs, in 1889. Berkhamsted School, in 1891, and St Albans School, in 1903, both formed cadet corps affiliated to the 2nd Volunteer Battalion, joined by the United Services College company for the duration of its short stay in Harpenden.

Toynbee Hall, in Stepney, East London, was set up in 1884 as a centre for social research and reform where students from Oxford and Cambridge could experience first-hand life amongst the working people of London's East End. Formed a year later, the East London Cadet Corps introduced boys to discipline and educational activity.

Haileybury was one of those institutions which supported the project, and in 1906 Clement Atlee became a volunteer at Haileybury House in Stepney, a club for working-class boys. Atlee had attended prep school at Northaw, Haileybury College, and was just down from Oxford. He soon took over the running of the club and became secretary of Toynbee Hall. It must be debateable who learned most from the experience of this contact—the lads or privileged young gentlemen such as Atlee.

The Boer War

By the terms of their recruitment, the yeomanry could not be required to fight outside Britain, nor were they permitted to. However, individual members were free to volunteer for overseas service.

Over 150 officers and troopers of the Hertfordshire Yeomanry, with a Maxim Gun detachment, formed the 42nd (Hertfordshire) Company, of the 12th Battalion Imperial Yeomanry, fighting in the Second Boer War, spending just over a year in South Africa in 1900–01. Attempting to beat Boer commandos at their own game, the Imperial Yeomanry fought as mounted infantry, adopting the tactics of the enemy, based on fire and movement. Previously known as the Hertfordshire Militia, the 4th (Extra Reserve) Battalion, Bedfordshire Regiment was posted to Dublin to replace the 2nd Battalion, Bedfordshire Regiment, which had left for South Africa. However, they too sent nearly 500 officers and men to South Africa early in 1900. Much of their time was spent on garrison duties, but they formed a company of mounted infantry which formed part of General Methuen's mobile column.

Following two and a half years' service under the command of Lieutenant Colonel Viscount Cranborne, during which time they lost over thirty men to disease and enemy action, the battalion boasted the award of nine gallantry medals and around twenty mentions in despatches. The Hertfordshire Volunteer Battalions of the Bedfordshire Regiment were not officially mobilised for the Boer War, but nearly 300 men volunteered to serve in three active service companies attached to the 2nd Battalion, Bedfordshire Regiment.

When three volunteers from the Royston company left town to join them in January 1900, the whole town and the Royston Military Band turned out to wish them 'God speed and good luck'. The return of two of them in May 1901 was greeted with similar enthusiasm. Casualties are recorded on war memorials and rolls of honour across the county, and the two volunteer battalions carried 'South Africa 1900–02' battle honours, as did the 1st Volunteer Battalion, Middlesex Regiment, whose Barnet company had also provided volunteers to fight against the Boers.

Lady Meux of Theobalds Park commissioned six 12-pounder BL guns from Armstrong-Whitworth's Elswick works on the Tyne. They were removed from a Japanese battleship then being built and mounted on field carriages. Although these QF naval guns were superior to those then in use by the Royal Artillery, the War Office refused to accept them. However, Field-Marshal Roberts was persuaded by Lady Meux, and they were despatched to South Africa manned by gunners of the 1st Northumberland Volunteer Battery, largely recruited from the Elswick works. After the war, two of the guns were presented to Lady Meux and mounted outside Theobalds.

The Territorial Force (TF)

A radical reorganisation of the volunteer forces was brought about by a recognition that the primary role of Britain's small but professional regular army was to defend the empire. Since at least half of the regulars were overseas at any one time, an additional dedicated force of trained volunteers was seen as being essential for home defence.

The Territorial Force (TF) would reflect the structure of the regulars, consisting of fourteen self-contained infantry divisions, each comprised of three brigades of four battalions. Each division would have a mounted brigade of yeomanry cavalry; field, heavy and horse artillery; engineers, including signallers; army service corps; and medical units.

Each division would be regionally based, with those units from the same county being administered by its County Territorial Association (CTA).

Hertfordshire's units, which all belonged to the East Anglian Division, were the Hertfordshire Yeomanry, attached for training to the East Midland Mounted Brigade; the Hertfordshire Regiment in the East Midland Infantry Brigade; and the 4th East Anglian Royal Field Artillery (RFA) Brigade.

The RFA unit had navigated a tortuous path to its new incarnation. In the reorganisation of 1881, under which the Rifle Volunteers were integrated into the regular army's regimental districts, the two administrative battalions of the Hertfordshire Corps, by now having no county parent regiment, were, as we have seen, adopted by the Bedfordshire Regiment as the 1st and 2nd (Hertfordshire) volunteer battalions.

In 1908, the Haldane reform of the Volunteer Force saw the two volunteer battalions being amalgamated to become the 1st Battalion, Hertfordshire Regiment (TF), with its HQ at the Port Hill drill hall in Hertford, merely affiliated to the Bedfordshire Regiment as, in effect, its second TF battalion. As a landlocked county, Hertfordshire had no tradition of volunteer artillery units, so when the order of battle for the new TF included a Hertfordshire-based 4th East Anglian Brigade Royal Field Artillery (RFA), it was necessary to start from scratch.

The brigade would consist of one battery and the ammunition column based in Hertford; a second battery based in St Albans; and its third battery based in Peterborough, which was then in Northamptonshire and thus referred to as the Northamptonshire Battery. It had been the intention that the personnel would be drawn from the two Hertfordshire volunteer battalions, now amalgamated, but recruitment was slow and the majority of those becoming gunners would be new recruits.

Once a camp had been held on the ranges at Shoeburyness, in Essex, things began to come together. By 1909, the pattern had been stabilised with HQ and ammunition column at 28 St Andrew Street, Hertford; the 1st Battery at the Artillery Buildings, Harpenden Road, St Albans; and the 2nd Battery at

St Albans, 23 Prospect Road, the home of Thomas Howard, the Regimental Sergeant Major of the Hertfordshire Yeomanry and HQ of 'A' Squadron.

the Clarendon Hall, Watford. The 1st Battalion, Hertfordshire Regiment at Port Hill, Hertford, had companies based in seven other towns and a network of two dozen drill stations across the county, with the four Hertfordshire yeomanry squadrons based in Watford, Hertford, St Albans and Barnet.

The yeomanry regiment nominally aligned with Middlesex was based in Chelsea, so the Hertfordshire Yeomanry's thirteen drill stations reached into Middlesex at Harringay and Hendon, and into Mayfair, in Central London. Arrangements were no less complex in Barnet, where 'D' Squadron, Hertfordshire Yeomanry had its HQ at 51 Salisbury Road; 'B' Company, 7th Battalion, Middlesex Regiment in the Middlesex Brigade of the TF's Home Counties Division was based at 14 Union Street; and the adjacent old militia barracks was occupied by the Middlesex Brigade's Army Service Corps (ASC) company of the Divisional Transport and Supply Column.

CADETS IN THE TF

The establishment of the TF permitted a total of 166 Junior Officers' Training Corps (JOTC) contingents across the nation's schools. In Hertfordshire, these included Aldenham School, Merchant Taylors' School, Berkhamsted, Haileybury College, where a new rifle range had been constructed in 1903, Hertford GS and St Alban's School, altogether contributing thirteen infantry companies. Additionally, there were fifteen companies of the Territorial Cadet Force. Some of these were school-based: Bishop's Stortford College; Queen Elizabeth's School, Barnet; St Edmund's College, Ware; St Michael's School; Watford GS; and the Royal Masonic School, Bushey.

Most were affiliated to the 1st Battalion, Hertfordshire Regiment, with one to the 2nd Hertfordshire Battery, RFA, and several, during the First World War, to the three battalions of the Hertfordshire Volunteer Regiment, formerly the Volunteer Training Corps. These TCF companies also included a Boys' Brigade unit in Barnet; five battalions of the Church Lads' Brigade, nominally linked to St Albans; a company of Watford Boy Scouts; and the Waltham Abbey Cadet Corps which transferred its affiliation to the 1st Battalion, Hertfordshire Regiment after the First World War.

DRILL HALLS AND BARRACKS

Batterdale, in Hatfield, in 1852, became the Hertfordshire Militia's HQ. The Marquess of Salisbury provided a colonel's house with an orderly room and store, and an armoury in a cottage behind it on French Horn Lane. These buildings were recorded in Pevsner's *Buildings of England* as still surviving in 1953.

The militia barracks in Barnet was built in 1855 for the 2nd or Edmonton Royal Rifle Regiment of Middlesex Militia, who remained there until 1881, when they joined their parent regiment, the KRRC, at Winchester. This barracks comprised: an armoury, adequate for the regiment's 1,050 muskets or Enfield rifles; a quartermaster's office and two storerooms; guardroom and cells; adjutant's quarters and orderly room; ablutions; and a private room for the officers. All this occupied an area of two acres and included a parade-ground and came at a cost of over £7,000.

A boundary marker (WD No. 9) has been found in the rear garden of No. 18 Salisbury Road. A plot of land on the corner of Salisbury and Stapylton Roads, forming part of the Militia Barracks site, and empty on the 1896 OS map, had galvanised iron huts built on it by the War Office in breach of covenants. The huts were demolished in 1901 after a court case brought by local residents.

The barracks of the Hertfordshire Light Horse at Silver Leys, on the outskirts of Bishops Stortford, survives as a single-storey building now in use by a car-audio company. There would probably have been ancillary buildings surrounding the barracks itself. The Silver Leys barracks was built in 1864 by Captain Fairman, a wealthy Bishops Stortford maltster who underwrote the unit's expenses until 1878, when he was bankrupted and fled the country. From the evidence of the contemporary OS map, the militia barracks built in Hertford appears to have consisted of a single, long block containing an armoury and administrative offices along one side of a large parade-ground with a second, shorter block containing storehouses fronting London Road. A terrace of seven cottages along the third side and a much longer terrace of sixteen cottages running the entire length of the eastern side of the plot both face onto the parade ground and housed, respectively, senior and junior members of the militia's permanent staff.

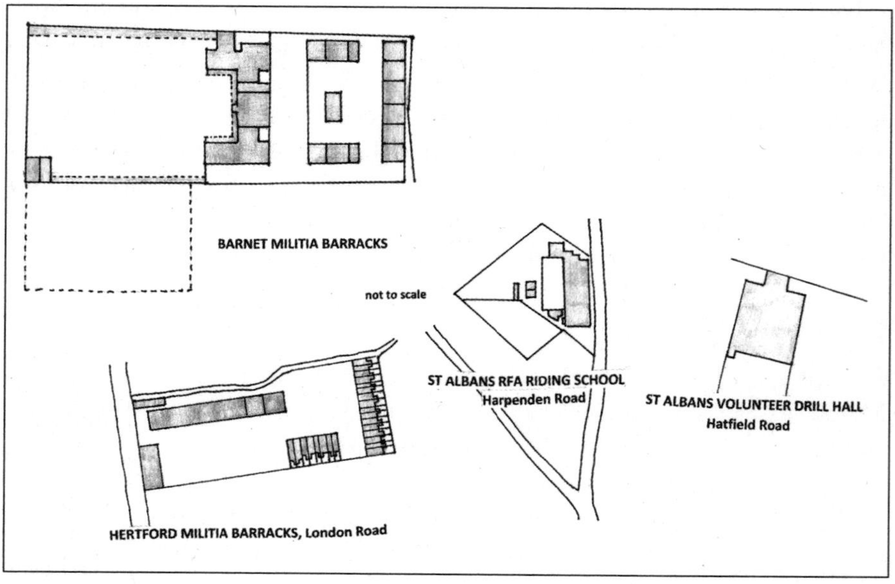

Plans of the militia barracks at Barnet and Hertford, and other premises used by the county's volunteer forces.

A War Department boundary stone (No. 3) remains set in the north-east corner of the present 1960s Fire Station site.

Besides the grand Georgian house on Hertford's St Andrew Street which provided a base for the yeomanry and, later, the artillery, several humbler private houses were used as orderly rooms or HQs for the volunteer units. At 23 Prospect Road in St Albans, the home of Thomas Howard, RSM of 'A' Squadron, Hertfordshire Yeomanry, was listed as their HQ in 1901 and of the re-lettered 'C' Squadron in 1910. Also serving as HQs for volunteer units were private houses in Salisbury Road and Union Street in Barnet, Ramsbury Road in St Albans, and Raynham Road in Hertford.

Some drill halls were intended from the start as community assets. The drill hall in Ware was opened in 1899 as a local initiative to provide a meeting place and leisure facility for the town as well as a home for 'D' Company, 1st (Hertfordshire) Volunteer Battalion, Bedfordshire Regiment, whose commander was a local doctor. It cost £5,250 to build and served as a skating rink in the winter.

The Clarendon Hall in Watford served not only as a drill hall but also as an agricultural hall, roller-skating rink and venue for political and other public meetings. The citizens of Bishops Stortford planned a community project in 1906 to commemorate Cecil Rhodes, combining the drill hall suggested by Lord Kitchener with an assembly room and raising £3,000. While falling short of the required total, enough money had been raised for a perfectly adequate building in the marketplace, meeting the requirements both of the volunteers and of the town's social events.

Existing public buildings were also used by the volunteer forces: Great Berkhamsted Town Hall (1859); the Victoria Hall in Tring (1886); the village halls in Little Berkhamsted (1888); and Widford's dual-use hall (1910). The earlier drill hall in Royston was in Melbourn Street, where an institute had been built in 1855, becoming the town hall in 1900. This building may have served as the drill hall recorded in Melbourn Street prior to the opening, by 1914, of the new building which still stands in Mill Road, which is, as of 2023, in use as the town's Royal British Legion Club.

There was a spate of drill-hall construction around the time of the Boer War when purpose-built halls, often paid for by public subscription, were constructed on Hatfield Road in St Albans (1898), Hemel Hempstead (1898), and Port Hill, Hertford (1898). A second surge came between the establishment of the TF and the First World War, with Hoddesdon opened in 1907, Harpenden's Cowper Road hall in 1908, Widford built by George Paule in 1910, and Royston (Mill Road) completed prior to 1914. It is likely that the Hertfordshire Regiment's drill hall in Station Road, Waltham Cross was built at this time, consisting of a double-fronted house with an adjoining hall behind. Artillery buildings, however, constructed on the Harpenden Road in St Albans, probably prior to 1910, provided very specialist additional facilities: a riding school and a gun park.

Ware Drill Hall, the frontage.

Ware Drill Hall, from the rear.

Bishops Stortford Drill Hall opened in 1906, built at the suggestion of Lord Kitchener and paid for by money collected by the townsfolk.

Above: Great Berkhamsted Town Hall was used as a drill hall before the First World War and as a British Restaurant in the Second World War.

Right: Victoria Hall, Tring, served as a drill hall and later on as a military hospital and a social centre for the troops.

One initiative by a private individual was the Chorleywood drill hall put up in 1913 by Lady Ela Russell, the artist, for her rifle club, and used as a drill station for a volunteer unit based in Watford. The significant feature of all these drill halls was the provision of a large space where up to 100 men could carry out drill. This was usually accompanied by a secure armoury, an orderly room for the unit's administration, equipment stores, and accommodation for the permanent staff instructor.

Hertford, Port Hill Drill Hall, since demolished, was built as the HQ of the Hertfordshire Regiment in 1897.

Widford Village Hall was built as a drill hall in 1910 for a detachment of the Bishops Stortford company of the Hertfordshire Regiment.

Beckett Hall, 28 London Road, Welwyn, was operating as a drill station for a detachment of the Hitchin Company of the Hertfordshire Regiment in 1908.

Right: The drill hall at Waltham Cross, Station Road, was in use in 1914 and has served as an ACF centre.

Below: Chorleywood, the drill hall built by Lady Ela Russell for her rifle club in 1913, was also used as a drill station by the Watford Company of the Hertfordshire Regiment.

Royston, the Mill Road drill hall superseded an earlier armoury in Melbourn Street.

One inducement to volunteer was the social side, with offerings such as a billiards room and regular smoking concerts and dances. The reading room in places where access to a mechanics' institute or public library was not practicable would have appealed to the politically aware or the auto-didact.

TRAINING THE VOLUNTEERS

The RVC were spread out in small units across the country, so opportunities for drilling or exercising in larger formations were relatively infrequent. Shooting could be carried out perfectly efficiently with small numbers, so ranges were built wherever possible to reduce travel. Butts were built in his park at Panshanger, in 1901, by Earl Cowper, in command of the 1st Volunteer Battalion. It had closed in 1894 after neighbours' complaints about stray bullets, to be replaced by a new 600yds (550m) butts for the exclusive use of the Hertford Corps.

Another range was built at Tewin Water in 1877. In response to Lord Kitchener's call for young men to train 'in the use of arms to defend the realm', Cheshunt Rifle and Pistol Club was set up in 1899. The Watford Miniature Rifle Club opened in July 1911 with a guard of honour from the local marksmen. A field day involving 10,000 volunteers from London, Bedfordshire and Hertfordshire was held on Dunstable Downs at Easter 1877, but camps were usually confined to single units which would try to get their members out at least once a year. The Imperial Yeomanry camped at Castle Park, Great Berkhamsted, in 1906 and 1909; at Broxbournebury in 1911 and 1912; and at Luton Hoo, Bedfordshire, in 1914.

The Hertfordshire Territorial Regiment gathered for their annual camp at Broadwater Camp, near Brighton, in 1908, whilst annual camp for the gunners of the 4th East Anglian Brigade RFA the next year took place on the ranges at Lydd, on the Kent coast. Having warned the local fishermen and armed with their 15-pounder breech-loading converted (BLC) field guns, with a range of over 5,000yds (4,600m), and 5in. howitzers with a range of 6,500yds (6,000m), they carried out live firing. They returned in 1911 and continued with a second week in Norfolk.

In 1913, the gunners had the opportunity to practise support work with the infantry at Shorncliffe Camp, in Kent. In November 1908 a pitched battle involving cadets from the Cambridge University OTC, local schools' cadet forces and TF units saw a fighting retreat converging on Royston pursued by the defending home army. Sometimes the amateurs had the chance to battle it out with the professionals. The Annual Army Manoeuvres of 1913 pitted the Brown Force of five regular divisions against the White Force of predominantly TF and yeomanry units. Cavalry were based around Royston.

Hemel Hempstead, where the heavy artillery was off-loaded at the railway station, was the jumping-off point for the 4th Infantry Division, with its HQ on land next to Randall Park and camps on the Highfield Estate and Boxmoor, with a tented camp in Berkhamsted Park. The White Army, threatened on two sides, was forced into a fighting retreat and inevitably succumbed to their opponents' superior numbers, but only after a spirited defence carrying out this very difficult manoeuvre.

Aircraft made an early appearance that year, carrying out unexpectedly effective reconnaissance operations. Few could have imagine that the whole operation of a fighting retreat would be repeated for real one year later at Mons, and even fewer the catastrophic results.

Munitions production

The Smokeless Powder Company (SPC) was founded in 1888 on a new, self-contained factory site near Ware known initially as The Outpost but soon changed to Barwick. High Explosive (HE) powders were manufactured for use in military projectiles: shells, torpedoes, and Small Arms Ammunition (SAA), as well as for sporting guns. By 1892, under the name The Smokeless Powder and Ammunition Company Ltd., filled cartridges were being produced for home consumption and export. In 1912 the company was taken over by Sabulite (GB) Ltd.

The factory was on the banks of the River Rib, whose waters powered the mill, one of whose millstones may still be seen lying in the river. Factory buildings of yellow brick were constructed, now incorporated into the A10 Timber Company. A public house, initially 'The Factory Arms', later renamed as 'The Duke of Wellington' and now a private dwelling named 'Wellington House', was built alongside terraces of workers' housing. Gunpowder Farm contains buildings in the same yellow brick, possibly, including the manager's house. Two small, brick buildings on the east bank of the river, reached by a ford and a footbridge, may be drying houses, and other buildings, as of 2019, were reported as surviving in the adjacent woods.

The extensive factory buildings of the Smokeless Powder Company, Barwick, which manufactured high explosives from 1888 until after the First World War, are, as of 2023, occupied by the A10 Timber Company.

This consciously isolated community in Barwick was provided with a public house: initially 'The Factory Arms'; then the 'Duke of Wellington'; and now a private dwelling known as 'Wellington House'.

5

Hertfordshire in the First World War 1914–18

By the time the First World War had got underway, the whole country had been raised to a state almost of hysteria by predictions of German invasion. These had been stoked by the *Daily Mail* of Lord Northcliffe and the novels of Erskine Childers and William le Queux, among others. Consequently, plans were made to establish a clearly signposted official evacuation route leading from the east coast, where invaders were seen as most likely to arrive, from Essex and Cambridgeshire through Hertfordshire and into Oxfordshire. Arrows were prominently displayed, painted on walls and buildings, along the routes. These would be marshalled by special constables, who would be supported by messengers on bicycles, the Cycle Despatch Corps, and mobile pigeon lofts. Some Essex residents would be channelled along the old Stane Street through Bishops Stortford, but there were twenty-three designated routes with other entry points into Hertfordshire through Buntingford, the Pelhams, Royston and elsewhere, mainly employing minor roads.

All 1.4 million of the weary evacuees, being expected to cover 10 miles (16km) a day, were provided with suggestions for rest stations, including one at Baldock. With minor modifications these plans remained in force until 1916, when the instruction changed to an emphatic 'stay put'. However, as invasion was still felt to be possible as late as the German army's, initially successful, Michael Offensive of spring 1918, emergency regulations stayed in place. One overriding principle, regardless of whether people were to move or stay in their homes, was the absolute necessity to exclude refugees from the roads used by the defending troops.

The military response to the expected invasion, laid down in the November 1914 Plan, would see troops mobilised in the South Midlands, with one entire TF division entraining at Watford, and use also being made of the single-track railway line via Hatfield. As the regular army was despatched to France as the British Expeditionary Force (BEF), many of the TF divisions would mass for training around the concentration areas of Hemel Hempstead, St Albans,

Berkhamsted and Bishops Stortford, both to carry out vital training and to be positioned ready to repulse the invasion.

The deployment of local units

Mobilisation was swift on the outbreak of war. In Hertford, those already committed reported for duty, and recruits were directed to the militia barracks, with the Corn Exchange, the Salvation Army barracks and schools being commandeered as temporary billets. All these men, veterans and innocents alike, would soon be on the move.

THE HERTFORDSHIRE YEOMANRY

The Hertfordshire Yeomanry had completed their 1914 summer camp in June at Luton Hoo, so in August were home when war was declared and were ordered to report to their squadron bases. The regiment then joined the TF Eastern Division at its war station in East Anglia. Enough of the yeomen volunteered for overseas service for the regiment to be reorganised into three squadrons, as per regular cavalry regiments, and promptly deployed to Egypt. Following a brief spell as dismounted troops at Gallipoli the regiment returned to Egypt to be reunited with their horses prior to a campaign against the Senussi. All three squadrons fought in various combinations throughout the Middle East campaigns against the Ottomans in Palestine, modern-day Israel, Mesopotamia (modern-day Iraq), Persia (modern-day Iran) and Syrian coastal ports.

The second-line regiment was raised in September 1914 and lodged in the militia barracks in Hertford. It was then deployed to Essex as part of the mobile reserve and in 1917 was converted to a cyclist unit, remaining on anti-invasion duty. It was then prepared for a Russian expedition, which never materialised, but sent drafts of fit men as infantry to the Western Front to counter the German spring offensive of 1918. The 3/1st Hertfordshire Yeomanry was formed to train men as drafts for the first- and second-line regiments. In 1917, cavalry training was in the process of being reduced and they were absorbed into a reserve cavalry regiment at Tidworth in Hampshire, with the regimental depot joining the combined yeomanry cavalry depot in Canterbury.

THE 4TH EAST ANGLIAN BRIGADE, RFA

The beginning of August 1914 found the 4th East Anglian Brigade RFA assembling at their camp at Bellingham on the Redesdale training area in Northumberland. No sooner had they arrived than they were immediately ordered home. The brigade was then deployed to its counter-invasion stations in East Anglia, based at Euston Hall, near Thetford on the Norfolk-Suffolk border. In May 1915, the East Anglian Division (now renumbered as the 54th Division), given its imminent posting overseas, assembled around St Albans prior to sailing for Gallipoli. However, the artillery would not be going with it and the 4th East Anglian RFA was sent to France but saw no action, shortly rejoining the 54th Division, which by this time was in Egypt as part of the Suez Canal defences.

By the end of 1916, the brigade had been reorganised into three batteries, each with six 18-pounder field guns, and a fourth battery with four 4.5in. howitzers. It was renumbered CCLXX or, more conveniently, '270' Brigade. Action eventually came through 1917 and 1918 with the Battles of Gaza and Jaffa, the latter involving an audacious river crossing, the advance into Palestine and the final leg to Beirut. As well as the first-line TF brigade, second- and third-line brigades were raised.

The 2/4th Brigade (later 348 Brigade) served with the 69th Division, providing drafts to the first-line unit and as Home Defence troops in East Anglia and also as part of the Humber Garrison, having replaced their old 15-pounder guns with modern 18-pounders in 1916. The 3/4th Brigade formed the regimental depot at Hertford and was affiliated to No. 4 Artillery Training School at High Wycombe in Buckinghamshire, training recruits to be sent to the two active brigades.

Those members, usually over-age or medically unfit, who exercised their right to remain in the UK, formed a provisional battery in support of a home-defence Provisional Infantry Brigade. They were based in North Norfolk, with the guns in North Walsham. The Hertfordshire gunners were spared the high casualty rates of the Western Front, but, although only six men are recorded as being killed in action or died of wounds, dozens more died of disease and from accidents.

THE HERTFORDSHIRE REGIMENT

The Hertfordshire Regiment (TF) was holding its summer camp in August 1914 at Ashridge Park and was ordered home to its various drill halls on 3 August, mobilising at Hertford on the outbreak of war. The 1st Battalion soon left the East Anglian Division to join the BEF in France in November 1914. It fought in all the major battles through the entire war on the Western Front, including Ypres, Festubert, the Somme, and the final German Spring Offensive.

In the four years of fighting, the Hertfordshire Regiment lost over 900 officers and men. Three second-line battalions were formed, training replacements for the 1st Battalion and serving in home-defence formations in Yorkshire and East Anglia. A shortage of personnel led, in 1916, to the establishment of a Territorial Force Depot in Hertford which catered to the administrative requirements of the 1/4th, 2/4th, and 3/4th East Anglian Brigades, RFA; the three regiments of the Hertfordshire Yeomanry; and the four battalions of the Hertfordshire Regiment. The 7th Battalion, Middlesex Regiment from Barnet left the Home Counties Division in autumn 1914 for Gibraltar, returning to Barnet early in 1915. It was then sent to France, where it stayed for the duration, fighting in the battles of the Somme, Arras and Cambrai, amongst other actions.

Its second line battalion formed at Barnet in September 1914 and spent time in Gibraltar, Egypt, and France, where it was disbanded in 1916 and superseded by the 3/7th Battalion based in Kent. The Bedfordshire Regiment's 4th (Special Reserve) Battalion, formerly the Hertfordshire Militia, served in the Harwich Garrison before being sent to France in July 1916, its CO winning a posthumous VC in March 1918. As a 'militia' battalion, it did not raise a second-line battalion, but other Bedfordshire Regiment battalions did recruit in Hertfordshire. Its 3/5th Battalion combined with the Hertfordshire Regiment's first reserve battalion in Autumn 1917, and when the 6th (Service) Battalion was reduced to cadre in May 1918, 700 men were transferred to the 1/1st Battalion, Hertfordshire Regiment to make up for some of its heavy losses.

The army in Hertfordshire

Through the early autumn of 1914, Hertfordshire towns became armed camps, with King George V and, ten days later, Lord Kitchener carrying out inspections of troops at Gorhambury as early as September. The region centred on St Albans had been selected as the assembly-and-training area for a succession of divisions as they were mobilised and prepared for action. The first to arrive was the 2nd London Infantry Division (TF) consisting of twelve battalions (13th–24th) of the wholly territorial London Regiment, along with their artillery, engineers, service corps and medics.

The Peahen Hotel in St Albans, first mentioned as standing in London Road in 1480, and rebuilt in 1898, became its HQ until March 1915. Individual battalions of the division were based in Watford, Abbots Langley, Bedmond, Leverstock Green, Hatfield and elsewhere. The divisional artillery of the 5th–8th London RFA Brigades, 2,000 men in all, was centred on Hemel Hempstead, where the Town Hall, Corn Exchange and other halls were requisitioned. along with every school building in the neighbourhood. Boxmoor Hall contained a cookhouse, and horses were picketed on the adjacent meadows. The Army Service Corps and the heavy guns were at Chipperfield, with the RAMC at Piccott's End, and the Divisional Cyclist Battalion at Redbourn. After a period of training around St Albans, the division was redesignated as the 47th Division in March 1915 and sailed for France, its artillery assembling in Cassiobury Park, in Watford. It was followed into the area by the second-line 2/2nd London Division (TF), later the 60th Division, with its HQ in Donnington House, 40 St Peters Street, St Albans, and some of its battalions billeted around Watford, Hertford, and Bishops Stortford.

Between August 1914 and its deployment to France in February of the next year, 4,000 men of the Notts & Derby Brigade, the four battalions of the Sherwood Foresters, of the 46th (North Midland) Division were billeted in Harpenden, whilst the division's Staffordshire Brigade was at Bishops Stortford from November 1914. From May 1915, the 54th (East Anglian) Division (TF) arrived in St Albans with its HQ in Donnington House. This included its Essex Brigade in the St Albans area, and the Norfolk and Suffolk Brigade in Watford. Its troops were probably the first to occupy Gadebridge Camp, but it was still just as necessary to find additional civilian billets.

In July 1915, units of the second line 59th (2nd North Midland) Division (TF) came to the county with its HQ in Donnington House, St Albans and its Notts and Derby Brigade in Watford. One of the St Albans camps was vacated in October 1916 by its Staffordshire Brigade when the division was sent to Ireland. It was replaced by a batch of recruits from a Training Brigade's hutted camp at Crowborough in Sussex. The area around Bishops Stortford, Sawbridgeworth and Much Hadham together formed a key concentration zone for 3rd Army, in 1914 still containing TF divisions earmarked for home defence, but soon to be deployed overseas.

The North Midland Mounted Brigade's HQ was in Stortford's Wheatsheaf Hotel. The old militia camp on Therfield Heath outside Royston saw a succession of units in residence: 1,000 gunners of the RFA in September 1914; 5th Battalion, Royal Welsh Fusiliers from February 1915; followed by the 4th Battalion, Cheshire Regiment; and then a further 3,000 Welsh troops, most likely second-line battalions of the Royal Welsh Fusiliers. Buildings in

The Peahen Hotel, St Albans, served as a divisional HQ in 1914–15 for Territorial Force units undergoing training locally and awaiting deployment to the Western Front.

the town were commandeered, including the British School in Market Hill as a mess, and Church House in Kneesworth Street as a battalion HQ.

Allocated numbers according to the order in which they were despatched overseas, the TF divisions lost their geographical designations. Thus, the 2nd London Division (TF) became the 47th Infantry Division and the 2/2nd London Division (TF) became the 60th Division. Those territorial force

Left: Donnington House, 40 St Peters Street, St Albans, also served as a divisional HQ.

Below: The Wheatsheaf Hotel at Northgate End, Bishops Stortford, served as HQ for a mounted brigade awaiting posting to France. The stabling behind the pub has since been demolished.

personnel who exercised their right to opt for home service, generally on the basis of age or poor health, were organised into provisional battalions for home-defence duties and for training recruits. Along with all these formations came the army's infrastructure.

The London District Signals (RE), with airline, cable and two wireless signal companies, was stationed in St Albans from late 1914. King Edward's Horse was a yeomanry cavalry regiment whose members were expatriate citizens of the dominions. The regiment mobilised at Hunton Bridge, Kings Langley, in autumn 1914 and moved to Bishop's Stortford in April 1915, prior to each of its three squadrons being assigned to separate divisions on the Western Front as reconnaissance troops.

As well as all these TF divisions, elements of Kitchener's New Armies, composed of the tens of thousands of volunteers coming forward from August 1914 onwards, were assembling in the area. By December 1914, there were 3,000 men billeted in Tring in local houses, with the school in the High Street and the Gravelly School in Henry Street taken over as sickbays, the children being distributed around local halls for their schooling. The YMCA gymnasium in the Tabernacle Yard, in Akeman Street, opened as a reading room for soldiers, with bathing in the outbuildings of the museum, the annexe of which was occupied by the RAMC for medical inspections. Purpose-built cinemas opened in Western Road and Akeman Street in 1916.

The 21st Division, inspected by King George V in November 1914, comprising New Army battalions recruited from Durham, Northumberland and Yorkshire, had its HQ in Tring and its men billeted in the surrounding villages. The HQ of the 12th Battalion, Northumberland Fusiliers was in the racquet court of the Rose and Crown PH. Many of these New Army units would ultimately be accommodated in Halton Camp across the Buckinghamshire border. Having said 'goodbye' to the London gunners in 1915, the citizens of Hemel Hempstead became hosts to two batteries of the RFA's 1C Reserve Brigade.

To cope with this vast concentration of troops, it was necessary to construct completely new infrastructure which comprised camps and rifle ranges. Camps, including Britons and Batchwood, whose exact locations remain a mystery, were set up around St Albans. A camp was built by local contractors at Gadebridge near Hemel Hempstead, with a new bridge over the Gade dated 1915. The camp had a substantial guardhouse with the traditional veranda, and thirty-four timber huts on concrete bases, each 120ft (37m) long by 20ft (6m) wide and heated by stoves. There were also stable-blocks, a corrugated-iron cookhouse, ablution blocks, RE workshops and a YMCA hut.

Hertfordshire Prison in Grimston Street, St Albans, became a military detention centre. Ranges were being constructed at Bishops Stortford; Chalk Hill, St Albans; Gorhambury; North Mymms, where whole battalions attended musketry camps; and Warden Hill. However, some divisions had already left for France before they could be readied. All available billets were taken up by battalions of the London Scottish, with the Post Office Rifles being billeted in the Leavesden Asylum. Many schools such as the Parkgate Junior School in Watford were also requisitioned.

Typically, a unit would establish a headquarters in a village school, an officers' mess in a large house, and spread its companies or batteries across farms and cottages in the surrounding area. Despite the appearance of purpose-built army camps, it remained necessary for these makeshift billeting arrangements to continue for the duration. In Hatfield, the organisation of billeting in the town was centred on the workhouse.

TRAINING

A training course for prospective new infantry officers was run in Royston in August 1914, organised by officers from the Cambridge University, Leys School and Eton College OTCs, with most of these officer cadets being assigned to Kitchener's Army. Hertfordshire, as we have seen, however, was soon to receive a procession of established TF divisions making the transition to active service.

Throughout the stay of each unit in the county, intensive training was continuous. This included parades, route marches, shooting on the ranges, gun-drill for the artillery, construction and signalling practice for the engineers. From time to time, ambitious exercises involved several thousand men across wide swathes of countryside, echoing the scale of pre-war manoeuvres.

To meet the urgent need for junior officers, the Inns of Court Senior OTC became an officer training battalion based throughout the war in Berkhamsted. Some 12,000 candidates completed their training there, 2,000 of whom would be killed on active service. At one time, six weeks was the average life expectancy of a subaltern on the Western Front. Training took place in the private parks of Ashridge and Champneys and over the wooded slopes of the Chilterns. Practice trenches were dug on Berkhamsted Common and in Ashridge Park. The camp was centred on the brewery, with the orderly room located in the courthouse and the quartermaster stores and offices in the railway station.

Late in 1915, a school of cookery using improvised field cookers was set up at St Albans. Although No. 309 Company ASC, which spent time in the area on 'local duties', has been linked to this initiative, it is formally listed as No. 35 Horse Transport Reserve Park. It may, therefore, be more likely that one or more of the four ASC companies attached to each TF division would have been responsible for this training to prepare the troops for cooking in the field, prior to their deployment overseas.

In late 1915, the 2/2 London (60th) Division, based around St Albans, had Nos. 517–520 Companies, ASC attached. In the summer of 1916, the Royal Engineers had a tented camp on Bedford Road, Hitchin, with a YMCA hut.

This then became the hutted Bearton/Hitchin RE Signal Depot Camp, with Bearton Lodge as its guardroom. This was a depot for training RE signallers prior to assigning them to RE signals units.

The RE companies attached to the several TF divisions which were temporarily based in Hertfordshire had their HQ in Radlett and carried out their training from a camp in Shenley, with billets in the village. In Much Hadham, an apple store at Home Farm on the Moor Place estate is reported as having served as a munitions store for Wynches Camp, a neighbouring property during the First World War, but there appears to be no material evidence for that. After the success of the Irish Guards' use of a single-shot Holland & Holland deer-stalking gun as a sniper rifle, more of the type were manufactured and went to the front. Just over the county boundary in Northwood, Holland & Holland organised a sniper school.

CADETS

On the outbreak of war, 18-year-old OTC cadets could be commissioned directly into regular or TF units, and by November 1914, Merchant Taylors' School reported that over 500 of their former pupils were serving in the army or the navy, with similar representation from Haileybury.

TF cadets would volunteer through recruiting offices, and many would find themselves immediately promoted as junior NCOs in New Army battalions. In some cases, entire units of TF cadets or Church Lads' Brigaders volunteered en masse in an early foretaste of the Pals' battalions. Although the Boys' Brigade had opted out of the TFC, once war had been declared, the Barnet Boys' Brigade company was re-badged as the 10th Hertfordshire Boys' Brigade Cadets, issued with real carbines to replace their dummy drill rifles, and put into khaki uniforms.

As boys became old enough, they would volunteer or, later in the war, be conscripted. Many joined the Volunteer Training Corps (VTC) while they awaited the call. Youngsters helped with ARP duties, re-settling refugees and gathering salvage and forage. Towards the end of the war, as the newly formed RAF recognised the need for highly skilled technicians, its training regime was reorganised and a boys' training depot set up in Pixmore Avenue, Letchworth, in 1918.

Operations of the RFC and RAF

In March 1914, a twin-seater Bleriot monoplane became lost over Hemel Hempstead whilst returning to its base at Hendon from Paris. Running low on fuel it landed and petrol was found for it.

Despite the local TF unit having seen the same pilot at their summer camp in Kent the previous year, and on the occasion when an aircraft made a landing at the Luton Hoo camp of the Hertfordshire Yeomanry two months later, no one could have imagined the importance that aviation would achieve in the coming war, or how sophisticated aircraft and flying would become. At this stage, cavalry were still regarded as the primary agents of reconnaissance, although this status was in the process of being challenged.

In the early years of the war, the RNAS was responsible for the security of the nation's skies. Unfortunately, despite Churchill, as First Lord of the Admiralty, assuring the public to the contrary, the aircraft of the RNAS, many of them ponderous seaplanes, were incapable of reaching the heights at which the German airships habitually flew. The RFC, a branch of the army, considered itself to be fulfilling a purely offensive role, supporting the ground forces, and primarily on the Western Front. But as the casualties and damage caused by air raids increased, the decision was made to hand all home defence responsibilities to the army.

In order to keep fighter aircraft in the air for as long as possible, a network of landing grounds (LG) was laid down so aircraft could refuel quickly without wasting time returning to a distant base. There were several LGs in Hertfordshire, often operational for only short periods of time in support of the Home Defence (HD) squadrons of the RFC after 1916. The LGs put up flares to help friendly aircraft to land safely at night, but this could easily misfire. On the night of 1 October 1916, the Willian LG, near Hitchin, was bombed by Zeppelin L24. Under attack by fighters, the panicked commander had ordered their bombs to be jettisoned on the first target they saw illuminated. From then on, Willian would be limited to daytime use.

The short-lived night LG at Bishops Hatfield was used by No. 39 (HD) Squadron for only the summer months during 1916 owing to its being prone to fog. Also opening in 1916 for use by No. 39 (HD) Squadron was the night LG at Sawbridgeworth, which was moved to a new site that year, remaining in operation into 1919. A night LG between Hertford and Ware was in use throughout 1917 but was then replaced by a new site at Stanstead Abbots. It was used by No. 39 (HD) Squadron operating F2Bs out of North Weald airfield (Essex) throughout 1918. The LG at Therfield was used by No. 75 (HD) Squadron during 1917. A hangar with bow-string roof, possibly from this site and suggested as of RNAS design, was re-purposed at Tapps Nursery in Baldock from 1920 and can still be seen there. All these LGs had only rudimentary facilities, seldom extending beyond a canvas Bessoneau hangar, refuelling facilities and basic lighting in the form of flares or braziers.

The single exception in the county was at London Colney. In 1916 an LG was developed into a training station and provided with three 1915 pattern flight sheds and a pair of GS 'Belfast truss' sheds and huts. It was used by many squadrons being prepared for service on the Western Front and was designated as, initially, a training squadron station (TSS) and then as the larger No. 41 Training Depot Station (TDS), intended for training American

Tapps Garden Centre, Baldock, occupies a relocated First World War aircraft hangar.

The First World War plane store at London Colney, the last in existence until its recent demolition.

pilots on the big, four-engined Handley Page V/1500 heavy bombers. It remained in use until 1920, retaining the last brick-built First World War plane store in England and other contemporary structures right up until their recent demolition.

Air Defence

Whilst aircraft carrying out later bombing raids on London would generally follow the line of the Thames, earlier raids by Zeppelins had involved crossing the north Norfolk coast and approaching the capital from the north, passing over Hertfordshire.

In October 1915, L13 was engaged by ground fire from Hatfield, and then seen to overfly Watford, St Albans and Hemel Hempstead. For reasons outlined above, however, it was not until September 1916 that Lieutenant William Leefe Robinson, flying a modified BE2c night fighter of No. 39 (Home Defence) Squadron, RFC, from Sutton's Farm airfield, in Essex, successfully downed the Zeppelin L11 over Cuffley. Robinson won a VC for his exploit, but following further operations, he was shot down in April 1917 and captured and imprisoned in the notorious Holzminden POW camp on the Weser river south of Hameln. His unsuccessful attempts to escape brought severe physical maltreatment and long bouts of solitary confinement, from which he never recovered. In his weakened state, he died in the Spanish flu pandemic just weeks after his repatriation, in December 1918.

Within three weeks of Robinson's exploit, another Zeppelin, L31, a new 'super' Zeppelin, was shot down. The loss of L11 must have dented the confidence of the Zeppelin crews, and, although commanded by the most experienced pilot of them all, the decision was taken to abort the raid, jettison the dozens of bombs and incendiaries over Cheshunt, and head for home. The airship was, nevertheless, caught in the searchlights and a BE2c flown by Second Lieutenant Wulstan Tempest closed in for the kill. As had happened to L11 before it, the fighter's incendiary bullets ignited fires, leading to explosions, and L31 crashed into Oakmere Park, Potters Bar. The entire fifteen-man crews of both airships were killed. Tempest survived the war, left the RAF in 1921 and lived into 1966.

Once it was realised that generalised air-raid warnings and the consequent downing of tools was hindering the war effort more than the bombs themselves, it was decided to monitor airship incursions, only issuing local warnings of imminent attack. These warnings were collated in London and the country was divided up into over fifty air raid warning areas. Hitchin lay in Area 43, Hertford in 42, and the southernmost parts of the county in 48, which included Greater London.

After the army assumed responsibility for airship raids through the aircraft of the RFC and the guns of the RGA, the Zeppelins suffered such a high casualty rate that their operations ceased. By June 1917, when heavy bomber aircraft had taken over and were behaving in different ways to airships, a day warning area was designated east of a line drawn through Windsor and St Albans to Norwich, where warnings would extend over a wider area.

In the early years of the war, the Hertfordshire gunners had dug pits to lower their guns' trails, thereby increasing their elevation to fire at incoming

Zeppelins. Given the lack of resulting success, it was necessary to develop specialist AA weapons. Cheshunt and Ware had each been issued with a single 6-pounder Hotchkiss or Nordenfeldt in early 1916, and a QF 3in. 20cwt gun by the next summer. More 3in. guns came to Hoddesdon, Tylers Causeway and Ridgeway in summer 1917, when Watford got a French 75mm auto-cannon. By the end of the war, the London Air Defence Area (LADA) would comprise the peripheral London Gun Barrier, divided into four sectors wrapped around the Central London Sub-Command.

The north-western sector, based on St Albans, was finally equipped with sixteen 3in. 20cwt guns and seven 18-pounders adapted for AA use, all in fixed positions and supported by twenty 24in. searchlights. A narrow strip was left between the Barrier and the central area to allow fighter aircraft to operate from their Essex airfields at Suttons Farm and North Weald.

Keeping the home fires burning

The outbreak of war brought forth a veritable guarding frenzy, mainly generated by the fear of saboteurs, the enemy within. In August 1914, 144 special constables were sworn in at Hemel Hempstead to guard public utilities and, fearing the worst, to quell food riots. On 9 October 1914, fifty special constables were sworn in and paraded at the Royston drill hall to be briefed in their duties by the superintendent. A rota put four of them on duty every night from nine o'clock in the evening until midnight. Hertfordshire's Boy Scouts were mobilised in August 1914, with 1,000 being offered to the chief constable for duty as messengers and for general public assistance. They were allocated in three eight-hour shifts to every police station in the county.

Following Hertfordshire's example, similar arrangements were put into place across the country. Scouts would perform guard duties on vulnerable points such as reservoirs and transport nodes; perform ARP duties such as giving warnings and sounding the 'all clear' with bugle calls; monitor traffic movements while remaining on the lookout for suspicious vehicles; staff first-aid posts; and carry out coast-watching duties.

When most scout leaders joined up, their organisational and leadership roles were largely taken over by 15-year-olds. Comprising old soldiers, the 43rd Protection Company (later to become a unit of the Royal Defence Corps) was based at Berkhamsted to guard Vulnerable Points (VPs) in the neighbourhood.

THE VOLUNTEER TRAINING CORPS (VTC) AND THE HERTFORDSHIRE VOLUNTEER REGIMENT

Very soon, those who were too old to join the armed services or in reserved occupations expressed a wish to do their bit to defend the country. Acting independently, communities set up groups of volunteers, mainly under the label of Volunteer Training Corps (VTC), to undergo military training and to offer their service to the War Office. In November 1914, Tring UDC appointed a sub-committee to consider forming a VTC, based on the rifle club in Western Road, from those ineligible for military service, and to be affiliated to the recently formed Central Association in London.

In Hemel Hempstead, a public meeting in the town hall in January 1915 led to the immediate launch of a local VTC, beginning training with instructors from the London TF units billeted in the town. Men in Shenley enrolled as special constables to guard the Colne Valley waterworks, and then organised themselves, along with their compatriots from Radlett, as citizen volunteers. Loaned rifles by the Metropolitan Police, they shot on the miniature range in the boys' school.

After this initial surge of enthusiasm, recruitment could be slow, as men were unsure of their status as combatants. The War Office was very sceptical, remaining so throughout the war, maintaining the belief that the VTC would rob the army of recruits, and refrained from offering aid. Nevertheless, by the end of 1915, Hertfordshire had raised 2,500 volunteers in four battalions, in Bishops Stortford, Watford, St Albans and New Barnet, with a county HQ in Hatfield. Units raised the funds for uniforms and weapons and gave up time for training and drills.

Despite War Office disapproval, they recruited youngsters who could learn a bit about soldiering prior to call-up. Eventually the War Office faced reality and recognised the existence of this force which would either form a last-ditch defence in case of invasion or else release troops from home defence for service overseas. Each county would be permitted to form a volunteer regiment (VR). The Hertfordshire VR eventually comprised three battalions in Hitchin, Watford and St Albans, with a total of almost 1,400 trained volunteers plus motor and medical sections based in thirteen towns in the county using a variety of premises.

Despite the original idea of training the force as guerrillas that would utilise local knowledge to act as irritants to an invading force, the War Office was determined to treat them as mainstream troops and even raised special service companies to bolster the coast defences. Hertfordshire's three volunteer battalions were fortunately assigned local war stations, either in support of regulars or guarding the lines of communication, particularly the mainline railway routes which traversed the county.

MUNITIONS PRODUCTION

It would take a while for the country to realise the demands made on industry by modern warfare, but few were, ultimately, denied the chance to contribute.

A compact area of North Watford contained a group of munitions factories. The Watford Manufacturing Company opened in 1916 in Greycaine Road, filling aerial bombs and hand grenades; manufacturing fuses for trench mortars; and assembling chemical shells. It had other works on Imperial Way and took over the Victoria Works of Dr Tibbles Vi-Cocoa Factory.

Two of the factories for the Trench Warfare Department of the Ministry of Munitions operated in Watford: NFF No. 24 in Balmoral Road and NFF No. 25 in Callowland and Bushey Mill Lane, next door to which was HM National Ammonal Factory. These factories in Watford were in temporary timber huts and presumably lacked the safety measures normally imposed on such plants.

Part of the Trench Warfare Department works was converted to the filling of gas shells. Apsley Mills and Nash Mills, which suffered an explosion in 1918, were commandeered by the Ministry of Munitions for the manufacture of trench mortar bombs and copper bands for field-gun and howitzer shells. This was alongside the mills' normal output of paper and cardboard to meet War Office demands for the endless military paperwork.

In Hemel Hempstead, Martineau's engineering works manufactured mine-sinkers and the local gas company made toluol, used in the production of high explosives. Featherby's in Bishops Stortford installed fuses into 20lb (9kg) Stokes aerial bombs, which could carry HE, incendiary or chemical payloads. They were then delivered by lorry to Woolwich Arsenal. Sabulite (GB) Ltd. at Barwick produced the explosive material which went into mortar bombs and hand grenades.

The factory covered a site of 126 acres (50ha) and included a tramway network for transporting the unstable product. As well as the magazines, drying houses, rifle butts and factory buildings, the self-contained settlement included residential accommodation for the workers and a public house. The current mobile home park may be occupying the site of the huts which formerly housed the workers. The factory only closed down in 1933.

In Cheshunt, Theobald's Grove railway station had closed in 1908 but was reopened for munitions workers in 1915, before closing once more in 1919. Three days of trials of the new secret weapon—the tank—codenamed Big Willie/Mother, commenced in Hatfield Park in January 1916. The vehicle arrived by train from Lincoln to be put through its preliminary paces. In February, the main demonstration in front of King George V took place successfully, and 150 tanks were ordered from the factories in Lincoln, going into action at Cambrai that autumn—an action which would, with hindsight, be deemed premature.

The demands of the services meant an extreme shortage of labour. Labour Corps companies were raised by the War Office with No. 400 (EMP) Company being based in Hemel Hempstead, but shortages were felt most deeply on the farms. In June 1918, Tring held a recruiting campaign for the Women's Land Army (WLA), with a march starting at the 'Britannia' PH and ending in the marketplace. That same month, a similar march proceeded from Kings Langley to Hemel Hempstead, where a recruitment office had been set up.

The local operation was dependent on organisers who received tip-offs from landowners about farmers who needed land girls and could supply them with a gang of them if necessary. There was a WLA hostel in Hatfield and a central office in Hertford. Out in the countryside, hostels were improvised, as at the kennels in Kinsbourne Green. Rothamsted Experimental Station near Harpenden carried out work on soils, fertilizers, and crops for the Board of Agriculture, which passed their recommendations and advice on to farmers.

Hospitals and medical research

In September 1915, the Middlesex County Asylum at Napsbury became the Napsbury War Hospital, with 1,600 beds for other ranks and a further 350 beds for mental cases, mainly men suffering from what was then diagnosed as 'shellshock' but would now be known as PTSD.

The Federated Malay States (FMS) Hospital at Blackmore End near Kimpton initially had eighty beds, with more beds being added in timber hutting, along with an operating theatre and an X-ray machine, all paid for by colonial subscription in Malaya. Ashridge House Red Cross Auxiliary Hospital functioned as a rehabilitation centre for the St Albans Hospital.

Adjacent to Lady Ela's drill hall, in Chorleywood, is a similarly constructed building. Originally a chapel, it was used during the First World War as a military convalescent facility.

Rothamsted Park's twenty-four-bed military hospital was initially tented but removed to more appropriate accommodation in the golf clubhouse on Harpenden Common. In Aldenham, a twenty-four-bed hospital was set up in a large garage in the grounds of Wall Hall. Initially intended for typhoid cases, it proved unsuitable and became a convalescent facility.

Northcotts Cottage Hospital near the railway station in Hatfield was given by the 4th Marquess of Salisbury as a VAD hospital. In Berkhamsted, The Beeches Red Cross Auxiliary Hospital was one of dozens of such small hospitals run by VADs under the auspices of the Red Cross and the St John Ambulance.

Tring, along with the vast camp over the Buckinghamshire border at Halton, was at the centre of large troop concentrations, so needed enhanced medical facilities. In the early days, as troops flooded into the town, the High Street school and the Gravelly School, in Henry Street, were taken over by the War Office as sickbays. The Victoria Hall was run as an Auxiliary Hospital by the RAMC, aided by male VADs, more of whom needed to be trained by the RAMC sergeant major in charge. The twenty-bed Little Tring Isolation Hospital was provided with extra facilities paid for by the War Office to treat scarlet fever, measles and diphtheria cases, whilst typhoid cases went to the Aldbury hospital. A medical supplies depot was set up in the Market House.

A plan to convert the former Gadebridge RFA training camp at Hemel Hempstead into a 1,000-bed VD hospital was vehemently opposed locally on the grounds that the water and sewage facilities would not cope. Nonetheless, it duly opened in August 1918. However, in June 1919 the patients were moved out, and it was run for a further year as a 350-bed hospital for officers. The camp's huts were auctioned off in December 1920, and one hut was re-erected as the New Mill Community Centre in Tring. Following the development of the site for housing in 2014, the hut was again taken down and moved to the Great War Experience Museum near Bury-St-Edmunds in Suffolk.

Personnel, including some from the Lister Institute were drafted into military hospitals to carry out research into bacteriology. The vaccines produced at Elstree helped finance the research of the institute in its Chelsea laboratories focusing on bacteriological diseases from salmonella to dysentery, meningitis to typhoid. The institute's scientists also found themselves researching chemical warfare, looking at the effects of poison gas, its possible treatments and antidotes. With many of the institute's male staff enlisted in the RAMC, it fell to women to keep the show on the road.

POWs and internment

Libury Hall, which opened in 1902 as a farm colony and refuge for destitute German-speaking men, became an internment camp for older German internees in 1915. Space for 250 internees in brick houses and timber-and-corrugated-iron sheds, increased its capacity to 600. Internees were not forced to work, but opportunities were offered for paid employment. As inmates were civilians, the War Office declined to spare troops so there was no military guard but there was oversight by the police, especially at times of stress, for example, when demonstrations followed the sinking of the *Lusitania*. One sergeant and six or eight armed constables formed the guard when it was needed.

By 1918, there were nearly 600 German POWs working in Hertfordshire. Frith House on Berkhamsted Common housed forty of them working around Tring, and there were 205 in Hatfield. A camp at Hemel Hempstead with a military commandant was based at The Old House and housed eighty more. Marshmoor Camp at North Mymms was a satellite work camp of the centrally organised Patishall Camp, in Northamptonshire. It consisted of a dozen timber huts, which stood in a former woodyard located on the north side of Dixons Hill Road in Welham Green, opposite the sawmill. It accommodated 210 German POWs guarded by old soldiers of the Royal Defence Corps and was served by a siding from the adjacent railway line. The POWs worked in the timber industry, offloading timber from trains, felling trees and processing timber into ammunition boxes and trench-props.

6

Hertfordshire during the Inter-war Years 1919–39

Examples of the 'homes for heroes' promised by Lloyd George were the council houses built in Church Road, Little Berkhamsted, specifically for occupation by returning soldiers. Most communities erected war memorials, and Puttenham, near Tring, celebrated its status as a 'Thankful Village', the only one in the county to which everyone returned safely from the war.

Memorial halls such as those at Bishops Stortford College opened in 1922 or Codicote in 1927 were built as centres of remembrance housing Rolls of Honour. A public subscription for a war memorial also funded the nursing centre in Luton Road, Harpenden, and The Old House in Hemel Hempstead was renovated after its occupation by POWs to provide a social centre for the town. Heath Park, in Hemel Hempstead, and Theobalds Park were graced with tanks, the latter, no doubt thankfully, removed for scrap in the Second World War.

Firms which had expanded into munitions production very quickly found themselves with empty order books. The Watford Manufacturing Company, in Greycaine Road, with other works on Imperial Way and Sandown Road, had overextended its building programme and went bust in 1922. The Building Research Station (now Establishment) moved from Acton, in west London, into Bucknalls, outside Watford, in 1926. Its brief was to 'meet the modern demand for rapid erection and durability combined with economy' in the context of post-war construction, especially of housing.

Until the early-1930s, the military would suffer from the effects of the rolling Ten Year Rule. This official policy was predicated on the misconceived assumption that, since it would take at least ten years for a hostile nation to rearm, it would be unnecessary to maintain even medium levels of military expenditure. The consequent cuts in the armed forces' budgets smothered any ideas of expansion or development, and the RAF's very existence was touch and go at one point in the early 1920s.

Britain, deep in an economic recession, thus failed to maintain any previous military dominance it might have enjoyed in 1918. Not until the mid-1930s would attempts be made to catch up on lost time with a planned programme of rearmament, initially targeted at the RAF.

The Territorial Army in Hertfordshire

At the end of the war, the future of all yeomanry regiments, approaching redundancy as cavalry, was in doubt. Offered the chance, in 1920, of staying as yeomanry cavalry by combining with the Bedfordshire Yeomanry, the Hertfordshire Yeomanry was warned that any such new cavalry unit would necessarily undergo a complete change of role after only two years, becoming either an artillery or an armoured unit in the newly reconstituted Territorial Army. The alternative was to form a completely new field artillery brigade of four batteries, by combining with the county's existing gunner unit.

Thus the 86th (East Anglian) (Hertfordshire Yeomanry) Brigade, RFA came into being in December 1922. Its four batteries, numbered 341–44, were based in St Albans, Hertford, Watford and Hitchin, with regimental HQ at Yeomanry House, St Andrew Street, Hertford. Meanwhile, the Northamptonshire battery in Peterborough had been hived off to join with three Norfolk batteries and form another new field artillery regiment. In 1924, the three distinct elements of artillery—field (RFA), heavy (RGA) and horse (RHA)—coalesced as the Royal Artillery, and in 1938 brigades became regiments, each with four field batteries.

Although there were severe budgetary restrictions, units attempted to maintain a training regime. In 1926, the 86th Field Brigade held its summer camp at Ashridge, but clearly, live firing was not possible there. Two of the brigade's batteries, 343 and 344, in Watford and Hitchin respectively, were partially mechanised in 1927 using hired Morris Commercial six-wheeled lorries.

This modernisation process was only gradual, until in 1933 an annual camp saw the entire regiment fully mechanised using a combination of its own transport and trucks loaned by the RASC. Only in 1937 were pneumatic tyres fitted to the old guns, and it was not until the next year, when there was a little more urgency in the air, that Watford's 343 Battery contrived a summer camp on the Okehampton artillery ranges in Devon. In 1939, land was acquired off Holywell Hill in St Albans for a new drill hall, specifically tailored to the training and operational requirements of the new horseless artillery with their new 18/25-pounder guns.

In 1938, in anticipation of the outbreak of another European war, all TA units were required to duplicate themselves by constructing a new unit around a cadre of existing personnel. Unusually, the 86th Field Regiment found itself eventually contributing to no less than four new units. The core of the original 86th Regiment—RHQ and the St Albans and Hertford batteries—remained as the 86th Field Regiment; the Hitchin battery formed the nucleus of 135th (East Anglian) (Hertfordshire Yeomanry) Field Regiment; and the Watford battery was expanded into the three batteries of the 79th (Hertfordshire Yeomanry) HAA Regiment. Furthermore, in 1942, cadres from the 86th and 147th (Essex Yeomanry) field regiments would form a new 191 (Hertfordshire and Essex Yeomanry) Field Regiment.

In 1919, in recognition of the part Hertfordshire men had played in its fight, the Bedfordshire Regiment became the Bedfordshire and Hertfordshire Regiment. Strangely, when the TA was re-formed in 1921, what had hitherto been the all-TF Hertfordshire Regiment remained an independent, single battalion TA regiment, rather than becoming a TA battalion of the new combined parent regiment. It was reorganised, with its HQ remaining in Port Hill, in Hertford, and four companies distributed across the county in Hertford, Hemel Hempstead, Bishop's Stortford and Hitchin.

Reflecting the experience of the previous few years, a dedicated machine-gun platoon was formed in Bishop's Stortford, and given the expectations of a prolonged peace, a regimental corps of drums was established, based at Ware. Despite the cutbacks to the defence budget occasioned by the Ten Year Rule, the regiment enjoyed summer camps on alternate years in the south-east of England. New drill halls for the infantry built in Letchworth and in Cheshunt opened in 1938.

The TA was tasked with the nation's air defence despite being equipped with only meagre equipment and offered little in the way of training. One of these

Letchworth, Icknield Way, the Hertfordshire Regiment's TA centre, now converted into a dwelling.

Cheshunt, the Hertfordshire Regiment's TA centre, opened in 1938.

newly raised units was 79th (Hertfordshire Yeomanry) HAA Regiment, with RHQ at Clarendon Hall, Watford, two of its three batteries (246 and 247) also in Watford, and the third (248) in Welwyn. The Watford batteries were equipped with old World War One QF 3in. 20 cwt guns, but the third, the Welwyn battery, in the new, up-to-date premises of the Lemsford Lane drill hall, was slated to receive 3.7in. HAA guns, with their attendant predictors

Welwyn, Lemsford Lane, the new TA centre for a battery of a heavy anti-aircraft regiment, which came on stream in 1939, its HQ in Watford. It would be equipped with the latest HAA guns and predictive and sound-location equipment, reflected in the size and layout of the buildings.

Above: Barnet, St Albans Road, the new TA centre built for a searchlight unit, initially badged to the Royal Engineers, but later transferred to the Royal Artillery.

Right: A 3.7-inch, mobile, HAA gun, similar to those issued to the TA gunners in Welwyn, photographed at Tilbury Fort.

and fire-control equipments; and a company of the ATS was affiliated to the regiment as administrative support.

The regiment was embodied in June 1939 to deploy to its wartime station on the Thames Estuary during the rehearsal for war known as the Couverture. In 1937, a new drill hall was built in St Albans Road, Barnet, as the base for 334th AA Company, the searchlight element of 33rd (St Pancras) AA Battalion, RE, later transferred to the RA. For the purposes of the Couverture, the battalion HQ's war station was at RAF Duxford, in Cambridgeshire ,while that of 334th Company was in Baldock.

In May 1939, the government finally passed the Military Training Act, which conscripted all 20-year-olds as militiamen for six months of full-time military training followed by automatic transfer to the Army Reserve. Hutted camps were constructed to house them, controversially, including one on Royston (Therfield) Heath, reported in June 1939 as being occupied by an RE searchlight unit. Another such camp was at Colliers End, Puckeridge.

The assembly of all but the first cohort of 30,000 militiamen was overtaken by the outbreak of war in September, and the legislation superseded by the National Service (Armed Forces) Act, which would introduce a far wider level of conscription. Possibly as a response to growing public anticipation of another European war, the Watford and District Rifle Club had been formed in 1937.

Aviation in Hertfordshire between the wars

During this period, while the RAF was deprived of funds, private flying became so popular that the Automobile Association established a network of very basic landing-grounds where pilots might land and refuel. One of these was just to the north-east of the centre of Hitchin.

Flying was also popular as a public spectacle, as was the 'experience' of being taken for a spin in the clouds. One such showman was Frank Neale, late of the RFC and the RAF. He operated around the Hertfordshire-Essex border and centred much of his commercial activity on Bishop's Stortford. In January 1921, he conveyed over one hundred of the local populace on trips over Stortford in an Avro 504 he had converted to become a three-seater. In 1925, Neale sold up and immigrated to Australia, where he continued to fly and ended the Second World War as a wing commander in the Royal

Letchworth, Icknield Way, the offices of the Irvin parachute company.

Radlett, the experimental hangar and offices of the Handley Page aircraft company.

Australian Air Force Reserve. A flying club opened in 1935 at Elstree, its facilities initially stretching no further than a fuel pump and a shed with a telephone, but soon acquiring two hangars.

Before long, the RAF had designated it a relief landing ground (RLG), and it began to be used by aircraft from Hendon and Northolt. At Broxbourne, a small aerodrome was developed from 1930 as a base for the Hertfordshire and Essex Aero Club. Occupying a clubhouse and a small hangar, these facilities were quickly expanded. At Sawbridgeworth, the relocated LG, known as Mathams Wood, enjoyed a post-war life as a civilian gliding centre.

Irvin Air Chutes was set up in 1919, with a factory in Letchworth in 1926, and GQ Parachutes was established there in 1932. Captain W. E. Johns, creator of Biggles, had been born and educated in Hertford. After distinguished wartime service in the RFC, he remained in the RAF until 1930, when he began writing, inspiring many a young lad to follow in the footsteps of those magnificent men in their flying machines.

The Handley Page factory and airfield in Cricklewood was rapidly being squeezed by the surrounding housing developments, and the decision was made to move to a new site in Colney Street. Flight testing was taking place there by 1929, for which an experimental hangar, 400x200ft (124x62m), had been built, with an accompanying grass airfield. By 1939, the works had produced 124 Heyford bi-plane bombers, equipping eleven squadrons.

Other models for the RAF included troop carriers, a gun-platform for supporting ground forces, one hundred Harrow night bombers, and a torpedo bomber for the Fleet Air arm. The first Hampden bomber, one of the new heavy bombers, flew in 1936.

As Colindale became surrounded by London's northern suburbs in the 1930s, de Havilland found itself in a similar situation to that of Handley Page, being forced to move from Stag Lane to a new site at Hatfield with a clubhouse, swimming pool and sports facilities. In 1934, the de Havilland Technical School moved to a site referred to as Chiswick just off the A1 to the west of Old Hatfield. Despite the site being far from perfect for flying, a flying school and aircraft factory were built there. RAF No. 1 Elementary and

Reserve Flying Training School (E&RFTS) opened in 1935, becoming No. 1 EFTS in the autumn of 1939, flying Gipsy Moths and DH9s. The factory produced DH Dragons and Tiger Moths.

In 1938, a unit of the Civil Air Guard (CAG) was set up at Broxbourne and the club was contracted to run an E&RFTS at Waltham near Grimsby in Lincolnshire. At Broxbourne the CAG numbered over 200 members, with twenty-four aircraft and thirteen instructors. On the outbreak of war, all civil flying ceased, and the Elstree flying field was obstructed with fifty old cars to prevent enemy aircraft from landing. Mathams Wood began operations as an official LG in 1937, hosting army cooperation aircraft, becoming RAF Sawbridgeworth as war broke out.

The Chateau de Madrid, later the Eastbury Park Hotel, a Scottish baronial mansion of 1857, was acquired by the Air Ministry in 1938 as the HQ and

Hatfield, the de Havilland Works offices.

Hatfield, the de Havilland Works canteen.

Hatfield, the de Havilland Works porter's lodge.

officers' mess of RAF Coastal Command. It was necessary to ensure that the operations rooms were protected from aerial attack, something which could only be achieved with difficulty.

The geology of the site consisted of masses of fluid clay, and Ove Arup, an up-and-coming structural engineer, was brought in to construct an underground bunker 195ft (60m) long and 49ft (15m) wide, one of several such constructions he undertook for the armed forces. He sat on the organising committee for ARP and, with others, was an advocate for the underground reinforced concrete mass shelter the government was so reluctant to build.

Air Raid Precautions

Since the First World War and the introduction of the bombing of civilians into the repertoire of war, there had been a concern, especially amongst architects, to explore the protection of civilian populations against the effects of aerial bombardment. This concern was heightened by the experience of the people of Guernica and Barcelona, and architects and engineers connected to the Building Research Station at Garston, including the physicist J. D. Bernal, were involved in the dialogue. The general consensus was for a centralized plan for ARP, but the government shied away from any such undertaking on the grounds of expense, preferring the ad hoc approach of using local authorities, individual employers and households.

Bernal co-authored a book entitled *The Social Function of Science* in 1939 and, after the war had started, would combine with other like-minded scientists to produce *Science in War*, which argued for applied research being used to benefit the populace. Arup, in a similar vein, would later call for a high degree of central control in the building industry to promote consistency and efficiency, but without sacrificing individual incentive and creativity.

Following the government's refusal to provide a centralised ARP system, local authorities, by 1938, were instructed to begin looking ahead to the likelihood of war and were putting precautions in place. Early on Cheshunt and Welwyn Garden City both appointed full-time ARP officers. In April 1938, a public meeting was held in Hertford's Corn Exchange to promote the recruitment of volunteers and opportunities to alert the community to the anticipated danger. Nissen's factory in Hoddesdon was developing a shelter which was easily constructed and therefore widely serviceable. A county-wide ARP exercise was held on the night of 5/6 November. There was a blackout from eleven forty-five at night until two o'clock in the morning, with suitable sound effects from fireworks.

Plans to dig shelters into the hillsides outside Royston were shelved when they were felt to be too far from the populated areas of town. Instead, trenches would be dug at The Warren, with an ARP Control in the town hall replacing the 'glorified chicken house' which had been proposed. In anticipation of civilian casualties from the expected bombing, first-aid posts were set up all over the county, with examples in Hatfield Memorial Hall and in Peartree Lane, Welwyn.

CADETS

By 1921, many of the cadet units which had served to prepare boys for conscription had been disbanded or, in the case of the Boys' Brigade companies, drastically reduced in numbers. In 1926, the Boys' Brigade discarded its militarism and became completely civilian in outlook. So crippling had been the military defeat of Germany and so equally debilitating would the economic depression of the 1920s become that the government had felt justified in applying their Ten Year Rule across the board. However, the War Office gradually became conscious that the cuts forced on them by the recession together with the limitations of the Ten Year Rule contributed to a lack of junior leaders for the armed forces.

Whereas cadet units sponsored by regular line regiments had suffered severe cuts, the public schools had retained their junior OTC units. Royal visits to Merchant Taylors' and Haileybury in 1931–32 were designed to raise their profile and to encourage boys to enrol in the cadet units. Haileybury's cadets formed the Guard of Honour at Hoddesdon for the High Sheriff's reading of the proclamation of Edward VIII's accession. Privileged JOTC units, including Haileybury and Berkhamsted took part in combined exercises on the Duke of Bedford's estate at Woburn with the RAF dropping flour-bombs on them.

Capitalising on the enthusiasm of those such as W. E. Johns, the Air Defence Cadet Corps was set up. Forced to develop independent of an uninterested Air Ministry, it was largely funded by private donations. No. 2 Squadron in Watford was a front-runner in July 1938, anticipating the establishment of the Air Training Corps in 1941.

7

Hertfordshire during the Second World War 1939–45

While the outbreak of war in 1939 made little impression on inland counties, the sudden end of the Phoney War, or 'Sitzkrieg', in May 1940 shocked the whole country into preparing for an imminent German invasion. The three concentric lines of defence defending London constituted a major element in the nation's anti-invasion defences.

The outermost of these lines, Outer London Defence Line 'A', ran along the southern edge of the county but the area to its north was nevertheless seen as safe enough for General de Gaulle, the Free-French leader, and his wife and daughter to have a temporary home at Rodinghead in Little Gaddesden during 1941. For King Peter of Yugoslavia and members of his cabinet was Abdale House, in North Mymms. For the United States' anglophobic ambassador to Britain, Joseph Kennedy, there was Wall Hall. It was also deemed safe enough for some of the myriad secret organisations which flourished in the war, including the SOE and the 'beam benders'.

The county was especially important to the aircraft manufacturing industry and as a training area for the army and the RAF. Many of the county's country houses were requisitioned for a variety of purposes, but, compared with some areas, only minimal damage ensued: Newsells, outside Royston, was burned down; Albury Hall was demolished in 1950; and Brockett Hall suffered superficial damage when the names of Canadian soldiers were incised into the eighteenth-century bridge over the River Lea, which ran through its parkland.

Deployment of local units

Having raised an additional, fourth battery in 1940, 86th Field Regiment remained in the UK, initially in Suffolk and then in Northumberland, on anti-invasion duties before joining 42nd Armoured Division in 1943, equipped with Bishop self-propelled (SP) guns. It trained in Dorset and the

Firth of Clyde for amphibious landings and landed in Normandy on D-Day. Re-equipped with first Priest and then Sexton SP guns it fought its way through North-west Europe, ending up in Bremen.

The force which sailed for the Middle East in October 1941 included 135th Field Regiment, but after being diverted to Singapore, it arrived in time to join in heavy fighting on the retreat down the Malay Peninsula, and then to be taken into captivity. Its CO was the senior Allied officer of the POWs forced to work on the Burma Railway, an event which inspired the film *Bridge on the River Kwai* (which offered an alarmingly misleading picture of the conduct of the colonel, portrayed by Alec Guinness). The regiment suffered heavy casualties both in the fighting, as POWs forced into labour, and also, even more tragically, during the eventual repatriation of the survivors when their aircraft crashed.

Following a spell defending airfields on London's eastern approaches, 79th (Hertfordshire Yeomanry) AA Regiment was deployed to the Harwich gun-defended area (GDA) manning old 3in. HAA guns and LAA Lewis guns and accepting a 100-strong draft of three-month-trained militiamen. In February 1940, the regiment went to France, where it fought to the end, being evacuated from Brittany in the June. Finally, re-equipped with predominantly static 3.7in. guns, the regiment manned six HAA sites in south Wales during the Swansea Blitz.

While 248 Battery transferred to a new regiment, which finished the war in Cyprus, the bulk of the regiment received infantry training at Hitch Wood Battle Camp near Hitchin, and then retrained with mobile equipments prior to landing in North Africa as part of Operation Torch. After crossing to Sicily, the regiment defended air bases and then moved onto the mainland where it supported ground troops and fought its way up to Rimini on the Adriatic coast.

In 1942, formed from cadres contributed by 86th and 147th field regiments, 191 (Hertfordshire and Essex Yeomanry) Field Regiment was one of eleven new field artillery regiments training for the invasion of Normandy. Landing on D-Day+3, it fought its way across France and into the Low Countries where, as a junior regiment, it was disbanded to reinforce other depleted units.

The 1/1st Hertfordshire Regiment (TA) was brigaded with its second line battalion and the duplicate battalion of the Bedfordshire and Hertfordshire Regiment's TA battalion until the end of 1942, employed on anti-invasion duties. The 1/1st Battalion then went to Gibraltar for a year before being posted to Italy, where it was involved in breaking through the Gothic Line. The 2nd Battalion was trained up as part of the all-arms No. 9 Beach Group, tasked with defending the 'King' and 'Love' sectors of Gold Beach in Normandy as the invading troops landed. They then fought their way through the beachheads, protecting the follow-up reinforcement and resupply operations. Having completed its task, the battalion was reported as being broken up for replacements, but it continued to be listed as lines of communication and rear maintenance area troops under Montgomery's 21st Army Group.

The Bedfordshire and Hertfordshire Regiment's 1st Battalion fought in the Middle East and in the jungles of Burma as Columns 16 and 61 of the Chindits, taking part in Operation Javelin as part of the 14th Infantry Brigade. They took off into the jungle on foot, dependent on airdropped supplies. The 2nd Battalion fought with the BEF in France, was evacuated from Dunkirk, and then fought in North Africa and Italy, ending the war in Greece. The 5th Battalion was sent to Malaya in 1942 and went into captivity with the fall of Singapore. The 6th Battalion spent the war on home defence and training activities, a role shared with the regiment's other battalions. For instance, both the 7th and 10th Battalions' were tasked with defending airfields.

Airfields and aviation

Situated conveniently near enough to London but escaping the worst of the bombing, the Watford area was home to several important components of the Allied command and control structure. Bushey Hall (Station 341) was HQ US VIII AAF Fighter Command from 1942 until 1944, when it moved to High Wycombe and became HQ US IX AAF. Nascot Lodge in Watford (Station 549) was HQ Combat Support Wing. Neighbouring Garston Manor was one of three standby RAF Fighter Command operations rooms and the standby administrative HQ of RAF Fighter Command.

Aerodromes of the RAF's 1930s expansion period had been uniformly designed to tight aesthetic criteria and laid out as compact and architecturally distinguished groups of structures fulfilling specific technical, instructional, administrative and domestic roles.

Watford, Nascot Lodge, USAAF Support Command HQ.

In complete contrast, airfields of the Second World War were based on the twin principles of dispersal and concealment. Buildings were either prefabricated or constructed out of easily sourced materials. A wide range of huts such as the ubiquitous Nissen and its American cousin the Quonset might stand alongside temporary brick (tb) buildings with walls a single brick in thickness, cement rendered and buttressed. Such airfields would cover extensive tracts of land and might accommodate large numbers of occupants, with Bovingdon's complement reaching over 3,000 by 1945. Panshanger initially applied the dispersal principle in its early development, but then, when it inherited all the functions of the Hatfield flying school, presumably regarding the threat of aerial bombardment as over, it grouped them together in a compact mass at one end of the airfield.

Hertfordshire was home to only a few operational units. After Dunkirk, No. 2 (Army Co-operation) Squadron flying Westland Lysanders found itself homeless and settled at the Mathams Wood LG, which had earlier become RAF Sawbridgeworth. Most missions were photo-reconnaissance sorties flown at the request of the army, which was seeking up-to-date battlefield information.

However, it had an important secondary role in the selection and training of pilots to service the needs of SOE, dropping agents and supplies into German-occupied Europe. Once re-equipped with Mustangs, No. 2 Squadron was enabled to become more aggressive in its support of ground operations. The squadron belonged to No. 130 (Reconnaissance) Wing within the 2nd Tactical Air Force, formed to provide support for the ground forces, especially around the Normandy Landings, and Sawbridgeworth became the wing's HQ for a few months in 1944.

The airfield was also a temporary home to many of the squadrons equipped with Spitfires, Typhoons and Mustangs which attacked V-1 rocket-launching sites in France, amongst other carefully selected targets, identified by the skilled interpreters of aerial reconnaissance photography. The grass airfield was laid with coir and steel Sommerfield tracking by the Royal Engineers but had concrete perimeter tracks. The station offices were in Shingle Hall,

RAF Sawbridgeworth, Dinghy Store (2901/41); the adjacent pond may have been used for SOE agent survival training in the event of an enforced ditching.

Above: RAF Sawbridgeworth, Shingle Hall served as the station HQ.

Right: RAF Hunsdon, the parachute store (17865/39).

and a T2 hangar, fighter pens and sixteen blister hangars, including the 71ft (22m)-span Dorman Long-type (4630/42), provided.

Remains include the parachute store, general stores, workshop complexes, dinghy shed, fire-engine shed and the station sick quarters. The gymnasium/chapel was removed to become the village's Sawbridgeworth Memorial Hall, which has since, apparently, been rebuilt. Close to the dinghy shed is a pond which has been suggested as a training site for pilots and for SOE agents who, in process of being delivered to the Continent by Sawbridgeworth-based Lysander, might be forced to ditch.

Hunsdon opened in May 1941 as a night-fighter station flying Hurricanes and Havocs equipped with Turbinlites or airborne searchlights and working in pairs. Squadrons flying a wide variety of aircraft were based on the airfield which in 1943 came under the control of the 2nd Tactical Air Force. The three resident squadrons, including ones from Canada and New Zealand, flew Mosquitos against V-1 sites and made spectacular precision bombing raids such as that on Amiens Prison, which freed imprisoned Resistance fighters.

The airfield had two concrete runways, a perimeter track, a general-purpose watch office (343/43), a Bellman hangar, sixteen blister hangars and hardstandings. Elements of the station HQ occupied the old rectory in Acorn Lane and the officers' mess was in Bonningtons, a house in Stanstead Road, one of several other requisitioned buildings used by airfield personnel. The airfield ceased operations abruptly in May 1945.

Bovingdon was constructed by John Laing & Son in 1941–42 as an operational RAF Bomber Command airfield with three concrete runways. There were thirty-six dispersal pans and four T2 hangars, with one of the earliest wartime models of utility watch office (518/40). With the entry into the war of the USA and its close proximity to Bushey Hall (Station No. 341), which served as HQ for US VIII AAF Fighter Command, it was handed over to the Americans as US AAF Station No. 112/341. Bomber aircraft flew in from the USA and raids were mounted on French targets. The station then became a combat crew replacement centre, receiving new crews as they arrived from the USA and providing acclimatisation training for the novel experience of flying in European skies. Additionally, both US VIII AAF bomber and fighter commands established technical sections at Bovingdon to carry out experimental work and flight trials.

The airfield at Nuthampstead was built by US engineer (aviation) battalions in 1942–43, and in September three squadrons of P-38s of the US VIII AAF's 55th Fighter Group flew in as escorts for daylight bombing raids. In April 1944 a bomb group arrived to carry out raids on V-1 launch site targets. The airfield was then returned to the RAF in July 1945.

There was a typical, three-runway layout; a technical site with two T2 hangars and a general-purpose watch office (343/43); an HQ site with an

RAF Bovingdon, the last surviving remnant of the wartime watch office (518/40).

Above: RAF Nuthamstead, hutting once part of the station's hospital.

Right: RAF Nuthamstead, the Norden bombsight vault, installed by the USAAF for extra security.

RAF Nuthamstead, a fusing shed, one of several remaining, in the bomb dump in Scales Park.

London Colney, a Second World War-era Civil Defence garage on this First World War airfield.

operations block and station offices; a complex of instructional buildings, including an Air Ministry (AM) laboratory bombing teacher (1739/41); fifty dispersal pads; and ten dispersed communal sites plus sick quarters.

Several of these structures remain, including the Norden bombsight vault for the safe storage of this jealously guarded instrument, initially denied to the RAF; the operations block and station offices in Nissen huts; the hospital in Bell Farm; and Nissen huts used as fusing sheds or pyrotechnic stores, on the bomb-store site in Scales Park Woods. Although, possibly due to the proximity of the de Havilland experimental facility at nearby Salisbury Hall, the airfield at London Colney was not active during the Second World War, its remaining structures were employed by the Civil Defencer Service which added a motor transport (MT) shed.

FLYING TRAINING

Following the reorganisation of the Air Ministry's training programme, the de Havilland School of Flying became No. 1 (E&R)FTS, flying Gipsy Moths and DH9s. Civilian trainees would undergo an eight-week course prior to induction into the RAF. Once war broke out the Hatfield facility became No. 1 EFTS under RAF control, with forty-eight aircraft and ninety-six pupils; local houses were requisitioned as billets.

In early 1941, Hatfield was operating seventy-two Tiger Moths, with seventy-two pupils at a time taking a six-week course. An RLG had been established at Pound Farm, Sandridge, in flying club days, and it may have been this which was now reactivated. It would appear that use was also now being made of the RLG at Holwell Hyde, but it was not until late 1942 that the transfer of No. 1 EFTS was made to Holwell Hyde / Panshanger when artillery-army-observation-post trainees completed the first course there.

Above: RAF Panshanger, a Bellman hangar, which was transportable and could be erected in just 500 man hours.

Right: RAF Panshanger, a standard Blister hangar (12497/41) with a span of 45ft (14m).

Below: Salisbury Hall, home of the de Havilland research facility, which produced the Mosquito fighter/bomber.

In 1943, the airfield then became RAF Panshanger. Courses were run for pilots from the Fleet Air Arm and from foreign air forces. The airfield was provided with a Uni-Seco administration block-cum-watch office, a Bellman hangar, five blister hangars and instructional buildings. After Hatfield airfield was bombed in 1941 and its premises had been destroyed by fire, the de Havilland technical school moved into Salisbury Hall. In 1940, ten Link Trainers, named for their inventor, were installed in a newly built factory in Warwick Road, Borehamwood, to form the RAF Central Link Trainer School.

RAF DEPOTS

From 1942, Hatfield was the HQ of RAF No. 64 MU, with its main site at Ruislip and three other subsidiary sites. One of them was an advanced ammunition park (AAP) at Woodside Place (TL252069). RAF No. 15 MU was a network of aircraft storage sites spread across a wide area of the country and centred on RAF Wroughton near Swindon, with a purgatory unit at Hatfield, under RAF No. 8 MU, storing incomplete aircraft, and dispersed storage facilities such as the five Robins hangars at RAF Northolt (formerly Middlesex). A single Robins hangar stood in Astwick Avenue, Hatfield, disguised as a garage, with a second Robins, camouflaged as a cowshed, standing nearby.

Sawbridgeworth was an RAF Equipment Park under RAF No. 211 MU, from 1942 to 1945, and has also been associated with RAF No. 247 MU. A total reorganisation of the Airfield Construction Service took place at Christmas 1941, establishing six wings with No. 5351 Wing based in Hatfield, later moving to St Albans. This unit comprised five airfield construction squadrons plus additional specialist flights.

Anticipating the need for airfields to support the invasion of continental Europe, No. 2 School of Airfield Construction, within Technical Training Command, was set up at RAF Mill Green at Welwyn, which then became the central depot of the RAF Airfield Construction Service. This took over the informal arrangements hitherto conducted with Jack Olding & Co. in Hatfield. Opened in late 1942, accommodation remained tented, and buildings were temporary until well into the next year. Practical training began in an exhausted gravel pit beside the LNER railway at Twentieth Mile Bridge, Welwyn Garden City.

The Mill Green site would finally comprise two communal sites, a plant depot and a plant storage site, with the twelve-week training course mainly focused on the operation of heavy plant. The trainees would, for the most part, be employed in the southern English counties constructing Advanced LGs for the 2nd TAF prior to D-Day. They would then be deployed overseas, from Iceland to Malta, Palestine, Egypt and the Portuguese Azores, courtesy of Britain's oldest ally.

Other airfield construction squadrons took part in the advance across North-west Europe. on islands in the Pacific, and in China and Singapore.

However, while they were still around, they were helpful in clearing bomb damage locally. The depot closed in 1948, and the area of the former domestic site, at the top of Ascots Lane, is now occupied by touring caravans and motorhomes.

The army in Hertfordshire

Hertfordshire's role during much of the Second World War was to be a base for reserves and for training. The Barracks, Hertford, was the HQ of the 54th (East Anglian) Infantry Division (TA) in 1939 and was the army's Hertfordshire sub-area HQ within Eastern Command in March 1941. Albury Hall, Bishops Stortford, was HQ XI Corps District in 1940–41 with 15th (Scottish) Infantry Division, 55th (West Lancashire) Infantry Division and 147th (Essex Yeomanry) RHA under command.

The corps had been formed for home defence and was responsible for the defence of the southern half of East Anglia, namely Essex and Suffolk. In addition to those front-line troops who would attempt to delay invading forces, there was a GHQ reserve spread across the south Midlands and Aldershot areas. One component of this force was 136th Infantry Brigade, which in March 1941 (with its HQ at 'Pynders', Grange Court Road, Harpenden) comprised 4th and 5th Battalions, Duke of Cornwall's Light Infantry, 9th Battalion, Devonshire Regiment, 1st Battalion, Royal Irish Fusiliers, and the brigade A/T company.

An army recruitment centre (No. 24) is recorded as occupying St Peter's Institute on Hatfield Road, St Albans. The county's small towns must have resembled armed camps as units were moved around in preparation for home deployments, training and overseas movement. The topographic Edith's Streets website records, 'In the Second World War howitzers were arranged roughly where this road (Falcon Ridge, Great Berkhamsted) lies'. A unit of the Royal Artillery followed by men of the Dorsetshire Regiment occupied three large huts between Beech Drive and Three Close Lane in Great Berkhamsted.

A contingency plan under the codename Rocking Horse Move would see the royal family evacuated to Madresfield, in Worcestershire, if Britain were invaded. The majordomo of this operation was Major James Coats (often rendered as Coates) of the Coldstream Guards, and his force was the eponymous Coats Mission. On permanent standby to see the royal family safely on their way from Windsor Castle or Buckingham Palace was an escort composed of the armoured cars of the 2nd Northamptonshire Yeomanry and the 12th Lancers, with a company of Coldstream Guards. Elements of this force were stationed at Windsor Castle and Wellington Barracks in London, but their main base was the Coldstream Guards' holding battalion's depot at Elstree School, which had been evacuated to Woolhampton House in Berkshire, where it remained after the war.

Although, as household troops, the Coldstream Guards had three regular battalions but no TA element, they raised a 4th (Motorised) and a 5th Infantry Battalion in 1940, and a short-lived 6th Battalion in 1941, with Elstree School hosting both their depot and holding battalion. The Coldstreams' 4th Battalion was part of the 30th (Guards) Brigade within the London District Field Force. According to London Area Operation Instruction No.1, their 'primary role is to deal with air and seaborne invasion'.

Meanwhile, the 6th Battalion, along with the 9th Battalion, Bedfordshire and Hertfordshire Regiment belonged to the 33rd Independent Infantry Brigade (Guards) carrying out anti-invasion exercises with the local Home Guard. The Coldstreams formed a mobile column with a specific responsibility for the defence of the Cheshunt area. Rigorous training was interspersed with ceremonial duties, and in February 1942, two companies of the 6th Battalion attended a drill parade at Merchant Taylors' School. In March, a rehearsal for the St Patrick's Day parade was held there. The line on the eastern side of the county was held by the 2nd Battalion, KRRC which also manned a switch line up the River Lea.

The golf clubhouse at Moor Park, Rickmansworth, was HQ of 1st British Airborne Corps, which was formed in 1944 to coordinate training and planning for all British airborne forces. It was here that the planning for Operation Market Garden, the Arnhem landings, took place. It has also been reported as the tactical HQ of the 1st SAS Brigade in 1944. This, in fact, was a fictional unit, invented for the purposes of deception in projected schemes which drew enemy attention away from real targets. However, the 1st Special Service Brigade, renamed the 1st Commando Brigade in 1944, did come under 1st British Airborne Corps command at Moor Park.

TRAINING

In August 1939, the Royston militia camp was being used for AA training, with 429 S/L Company from RAF Duxford in occupation. A year later, the camp was bombed but there were no casualties. Until 1943, the peak of the bombing, AA units were sent there for initial training, refresher courses or retraining as mobile troops to join the field army overseas, with infantry battalions attending for conversion into AA units.

In 1941, the 70th and 71st Young Soldier Battalions of the Bedfordshire and Hertfordshire Regiment contained over 1,000 recruits, being prepared for joining the regiment's various battalions. The Royal Artillery School of Aircraft Recognition had been at Bishops Stortford but was moved to Deepcut, near Aldershot, in 1944. Over 4,000 instructors were trained there, prior to posting to AA units. As more coast defence batteries and AA functions were turned over to the Home Guard, regular army gunners might be retrained either as infantry or for a different branch of the artillery. The Hitch Wood Battle Camp, between Preston and St Pauls Walden south of Hitchin, was one venue where such training took place.

The 4th A/T Training Regiment (RA) was based at Hitchin. The course lasted eight weeks and 100 gunners graduated every fortnight, joining the 4th Reserve A/T Regiment in Hitchin prior to posting. By 1944, coast artillery gunners were being retrained as A/T gunners for the forces about to take part in the invasion of France. The 3rd Reserve Medium Regiment (RA) was based in Watford. Frogmore Hall was used for Royal Military Police training. Wynches Camp, in Much Hadham, was a tented training camp in 1940, with a mess hut in the village hall carpark. Units of the Suffolk Regiment, the Seaforth Highlanders, Gurkhas and US troops all spent time there in the run up to D-Day. A Reception Centre for repatriated Allied POWs was then used as a German POW camp after the end of the war.

Garston Manor (High Elms Manor since 2010), already accommodating RAF personnel and standing by as an emergency HQ for AA Command, together with Wall Hall, took in another training unit in 1942. This was No. 4 War Office Selection Board (WOSB), which assessed candidates for officer training. Formal interviews were accompanied by intelligence tests and physically demanding problem-solving exercises designed to showcase leadership qualities. No longer would attendance at a public school be in itself sufficient to achieve a commission. Many of the psychological instruments used, such as Raven's Standard Progressive Matrices, had been developed before the war as non-verbal measures of general intelligence.

John Raven worked at the Maudsley Hospital, evacuated to Mill Hill School, and pioneered the treatment of what would later come to be defined as Post-Traumatic Stress Disorder. Coldstream Guards officers went to Merchant Taylors' School to conduct the Certificate 'A' Examinations for the OTC there, where some senior cadets formed a platoon of the local Home Guard company in Rickmansworth. W. E. Johns continued to recruit youngsters to the Air Training Corps, formed in 1941 to prepare youngsters hoping to apply for the RAF.

Hertfordshire Home Guard

The first HQ of the Hertfordshire Home Guard Zone was at 19 North Crescent, Hertford, later moving to the Port Hill drill hall. The zone was initially divided into west and east groups. The HQ of No. 1 Group area (west) was at 'Ferndale', 50 Luton Road, Harpenden with 5th, 7th, 8th, 9th, and 10th battalions under command. After a reorganisation in October 1942, there were three groups: an East Central District, Eastern Sector, comprising 1st, 3rd, 11th and 12th battalions; an East Central District, Central Sector, comprising 2nd, 4th, 5th, 13th, 14th and 15th battalions; and an East Central District, Western Sector, comprising 7th, 8th, 9th, and 10th battalions, with its HQ in Cromwell House, Upper Highway, Hunton Bridge, Kings Langley.

The 'missing' 6th Battalion lay within the Outer London Defence Line 'A', so was attached to London District. Reciprocally, the Cheshunt platoon of the 25th Battalion, Middlesex Home Guard was assigned the Wormley area, where the Outer London Defence Line 'A' crosses the New River, defended by an A/T ditch and sandbagged strongpoints. Additional to the fifteen battalions, there were several other units in the Hertfordshire sub-area.

Three sections of No. 19 Platoon, 'E' (Luton) Company, 6th (34 GPO) Cambridgeshire Battalion were based in Hemel Hempstead, Berkhamsted and Tring. Three sections of a London Passenger Transport Board (LPTB) platoon were based at Boxmoor, Tring bus garage and the Two Waters bus garage at Durrants Hill, Hemel Hempstead, incidentally providing a transport reserve.

Operating under 10th Hertfordshire Battalion, were three railway sections at Boxmoor, Berkhamsted and Tring stations, with their HQ at Watford station and another unit at The Grove, Chandlers Cross, the LMS railway offices. Some vulnerable factories carrying out vital munitions production were allocated LAA weapons.

These were manned by members of the factories' own Home Guard units under command of the local battalion. These were: 'A' and 'C' LAA troops at de Havilland works at Hatfield and 'B' LAA Troop at the de Havilland works at Leavesden (both 13th Battalion); 'A' LAA Troop at the Handley Page works in Radlett (15th Battalion); and Letchworth Home Guard was pictured with Lewis Guns on AA mountings. Employees at Broxbourne CRO formed a platoon of the local Home Guard company to defend the airfield.

Rather than the usual 'A-D' of the regular army, Home Guard companies were initially numbered across each battalion, and platoons were numbered 1–6 within the company. The 7th Battalion, for example, with its HQ at 41 High Street, Tring, had four companies, initially numbered 16–18 and 20 but later re-designated 'A' to 'D'. These were based across its operating area at Hemel Hempstead, Great Berkhamsted, Aldbury and Chipperfield. Two of those platoons in 16 Company, at Dickinson's and Brock's Fireworks, were recruited from employees within those factories.

Alongside the buses of the LPTB platoon, No. 2043 (London) Home Guard Taxi Company was based in Bushey to provide transport as required. A wide range of premises was requisitioned wherever they were needed. In Harpenden, the Victoria Road Schools were used; Cheshunt Great House was occupied; and the lodge at Brookmans Park served as the local Home Guard HQ.

Although the Home Guard was initially formed in the dark days of 1940, when invasion was daily expected and home guardsmen spent time patrolling and guarding VPs, all alongside their day jobs, training was constant and given a high priority. A Home Guard battle school was set up in Tring, before transferring to 'The Limes', Bridge Road, Hunton Bridge, in December 1942.

The GPO, with its own Home Guard units across the country, including three in Hertfordshire, ran its Home Guard training school at Dyrham Park, Barnet.

The Victoria Road schools, in Harpenden, which served as billets for the Notts and Derby Brigade in the First World War has been closed since the 1920s. In the Second World War it served as a Home Guard and Civil Defence base with a first aid centre, a gas decontamination centre, two wards for medical casualties, as well as an evacuee reception centre.

Shooting took place wherever a range could be safely set up, with one operating in the quarry adjacent to South Mimms castle earthworks. The CO of the battalion covering the Stevenage area built a miniature range in his back garden in Hitchin Road. The butts were built of railway sleepers backed by a sandbank 6ft (1.8m) high. Three or four single-shot, BSA 12/15 Martini-action 0.22in. rifles, advertised for sale from 1935, were kept in an unlocked shed outside his back door.

Pistol shooting took place in a factory in Baldock. A full-scale invasion exercise was mounted in Harpenden involving the Home Guard and the ARP on 29 March 1941. As the Home Guard became both more professional and better equipped, their tactics changed. Towards the end of the war, in February 1944, the 7th Battalion established a mobile company, with its HQ in the Baptist Church schoolrooms in Russell Place, Boxmoor. It consisted of three battle platoons plus a support platoon armed with three hand-me-down 2-pounder A/T guns, plus machine guns and A/T rifles. In the 7th Battalion area, women auxiliaries maintained a field telephone line stretching 17.5 miles (28km), linking the HQ in Chipperfield to Bovingdon, Hemel Hempstead and Tring.

In the early days after Dunkirk, the output of the nation's factories largely went to re-equipping the regular army and to supplying our allies, notably the Russians, delivered via Arctic convoys. Despite having to use obsolete and improvised equipment, the Home Guard gradually became an efficient and professional force. However, they had been required to extend their ingenuity in the creation of weaponry, when it was quickly realised that there was an urgent need for effective A/T weapons.

The Blacker Bombard or spigot mortar was invented to fulfil such a need. It could fire a 20lb (9kg) A/T projectile or a 14lb (6.4kg) anti-personnel bomb.

Brookmans Park (TL261052), a spigot mortar emplacement with its central 'thimble' for mounting the weapon and the lockers for storing the bombs.

The spigot mortar was mounted on a steel framework, or 'spider', embedded in a domed, concrete drum, in the centre of a brick-built pit with integral ammunition lockers. Alternatively, it could be mounted as a mobile weapon on a low frame of scaffold poles with spade grips to prevent drift.

Hertfordshire Home Guard battalions were typically allocated thirty equipments each since these weapons were relatively cheap to produce. A photograph on the Hertfordshire Memories website shows Hatfield home guardsmen training with the mobile version. Their pits can still be seen around the county, with one surviving, but now backfilled, in Hertford and three at Brookman's Park, one of which remains in a perfect state of preservation. Another stood outside the Two Diamonds PH in High Street, Stevenage, and one was excavated in Folly Lane, St Albans, in the 1990s. Nowadays, many of the pits will have been filled in and the stainless-steel pintle, showing above ground, may be the only visible evidence for its existence.

Anti-invasion defences

With invasion imminent in the weeks after the Dunkirk evacuation, defences were hurriedly put in place. Having lost most of its armour, transport and artillery in France, the returning BEF, home defence troops and home guardsmen were forced to rely on fixed defences. These consisted of four main elements: a 'coastal crust' of coast artillery batteries and beach defences; the GHQ Line as a continuous barrier of A/T ditches based on natural waterways strengthened by pillboxes and A/T emplacements, stretching across the south and east of the country; towns and nodal points as A/T islands with all-round defences; and supplementary defence lines carving up the country into defensible boxes and killing zones.

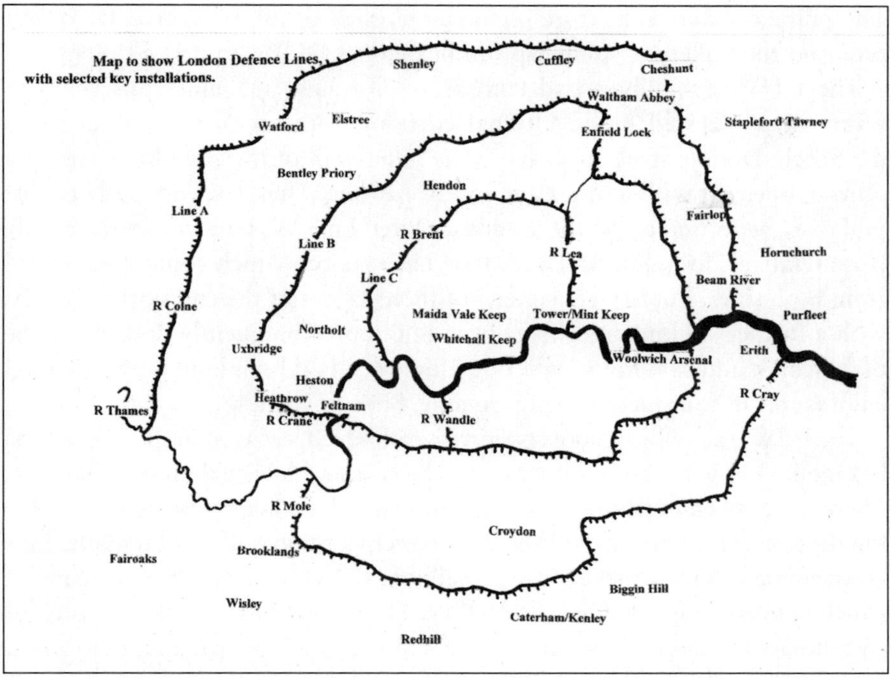

A map of the London defences in early 1941, with Outer London Line 'A' crossing southern Hertfordshire from the Colne to the Lea.

This defensive infrastructure was designed to delay an invading force, allowing time for the Royal Navy to sail from its Scottish bases to disrupt the enemy's reinforcement and resupply operations, while reserves, based in the South Midlands, mopped up any residual invaders. Until the factories were able to replace the lost materiel, especially the armoured vehicles and trucks which would reinstate mobility, the defenders were dependent on these fixed defences. London, in effect one enormous A/T island, was surrounded by three concentric lines of defence, the outer one of which, Line 'A', followed roughly the present line of the M25.

OUTER LONDON LINE 'A'

The line entered the county from the south-west utilising the natural barrier of the River Colne as an A/T ditch. It ran south of Rickmansworth, through Batchworth and past Merchant Taylors' School, and then swung eastwards toward Radlett and Shenley, heading for the Ridgeway. From there it ran to the north of Cuffley and Cheshunt to meet the River Lea at Wormley, exiting the county at King's Weir.

The line followed waterways where possible or made use of high ground, with natural features being supplemented by dozens of concrete pillboxes, long lengths of A/T ditch, and hundreds of A/T blocks and A/T rails.

The pillboxes were a mixture of the large, shell-proof, octagonal DFW3/27 type and the bullet- or splinter-proof hexagonal DFW3/22 and 24 types.

The DFW3/27 pillbox had embrasures for light machine-guns (lmg) in seven faces accessed by an internal corridor, with an eighth embrasure in the porch. Double steel doors set in the inner wall of the corridor accessed a central, open pit with a mounting for an AA lmg. These exceptionally robust pillboxes were unique to the London Outer Line 'A', and unlike their only close relatives, found in Scotland, they had a porch which could be accessed from both sides. There were sixteen of these extant at the end of the century, with a further six known to have been built but subsequently destroyed, one of which, in addition to its eight lmg loopholes, had been built with low-level embrasures in four faces for, presumably, Boys A/T rifles.

The DFW3/24 pillbox, some twenty-five of which survived in the 1990s, was hexagonal but with the side containing the entrance longer than the other five. There were six embrasures for lmgs, with that in the longer base firing over the low-level entrance and its half-height protective blast-wall. Additionally, Line 'A' contained thirty or so DFW3/22 pillboxes of regular hexagonal shape, of which half may survive. One such pillbox (TL311048) has the same protected entrance as the larger Type 24s, with a sixth loophole above and, uniquely, a crenellated roofline, presumably intended to break up its outline.

Unless submerged in undergrowth, pillboxes nowadays present as very visible intrusions in the landscape. However, they would have been afforded appropriate camouflage. One pillbox at Park Lane Paradise, Cheshunt, was remembered by one person interviewed by Fred Nash as having been disguised as a bus shelter, while the heightened pillbox at Bread and Cheese Lane, Cheshunt, was painted as a house with doors and windows.

There were also one-off designs made to fit a particular site like the rectangular pillbox under the railway viaduct at Oxhey; a pentagonal brick

The Ridgeway (TL289035), a version of the DFW3/24 commonly found on Outer London Line 'A'. It incorporates a half-height blast-wall, in this case roofed over, thereby protecting the entrance and allowing for a sixth loophole.

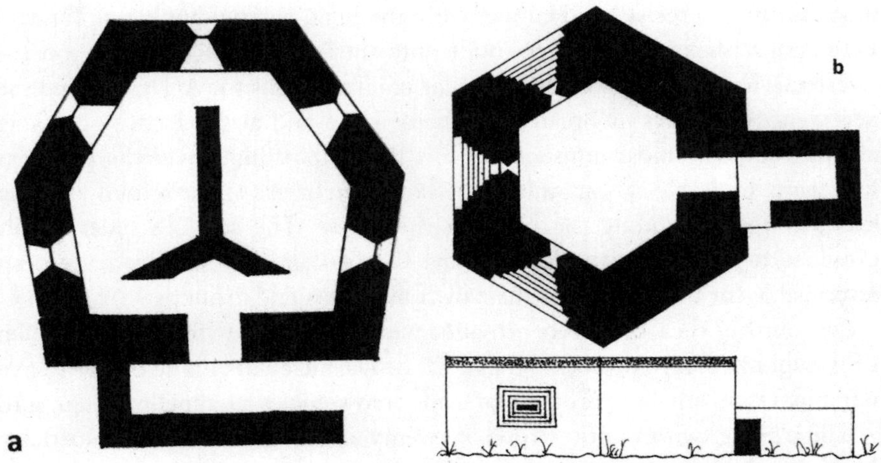

Above left: Plan of a DFW3/24 pillbox found on Outer London Line 'A'.

Above right: Plan based on the DFW3/22 pillbox but with a reduced number of loopholes, greatly thickened walls and a tunnel entrance. This design, which was produced by the Air Ministry, was widely used on airfields. Both Hunsdon and Sawbridgeworth each had up to a dozen of them, many of which survive.

Below left: Top: Section of the standard airfield Battle HQ (11008/41) as built on airfields and surviving at both Hunsdon and Sawbridgeworth. Bottom: Plan and section of the mushroom-shaped F. C. Construction pillbox. It has a cantilevered concrete roof on a central anti-ricochet wall permitting 360-degree fire from the two machine guns mounted on the tubular rail. Some had butterfly-shaped anti-ricochet walls, while others were cruciform. An example survives at Hunsdon, and at least one other there has been destroyed.

Below right: Plan of the DFW3/27 shell-proof pillbox found on the Outer London Line 'A'.

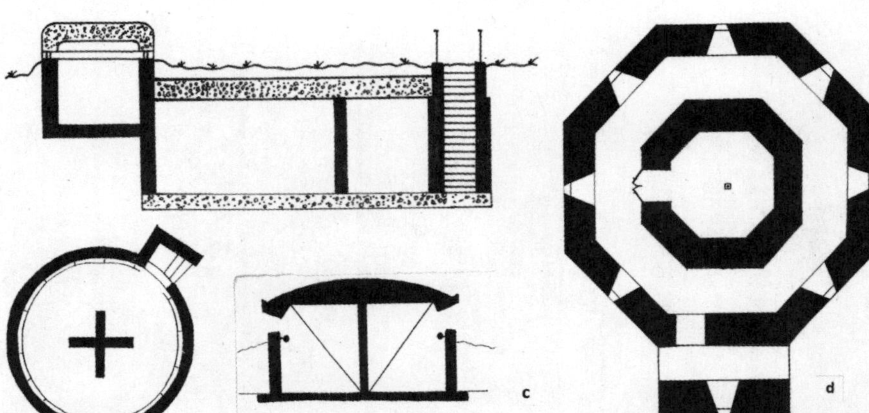

pillbox, open to the sky at Hamper Mill; the long, narrow bunker at Tanfield Farm; a half-hexagonal pillbox built onto the end wall of a factory on the riverbank in Watford; two semi-circular emplacements for A/T guns; and the heightened pillboxes at Bread and Cheese Lane and at the railway crossing in Wormley. The most unusual of all is the pillbox built over the porch at Merchant Taylors' School, built of the same 2in. bricks as the school building itself, and commanding the bank of the Colne. The school's older pupils provided a platoon to the local Home Guard company so may have been responsible for the defence of their own buildings and grounds.

Bridges over the Colne were provided with A/T blocks with slots into which RSJs might be inserted, closing them off. At Darnicle Hill, a line of eighty-five A/T blocks impeded the progress of armoured vehicles, channelling them into a killing zone, with another row of twenty-seven at Woodlands, Northaw. The railway embankment at Potters Bar has fourteen A/T blocks ascending on one side, and a further eleven descending on the other. On the Ridgeway there are double lines of A/T blocks providing strength in depth. Most of these blocks are 3ft 6in. (1.1m) cubes on concrete rafts, but a row of nineteen blocks, 4ft 6in. (1.4m) high, lines the bank of the New River at Wormley.

There are also many smaller conical blocks, and sockets for A/T rails can be seen with odd ones still *in situ*. Fred Nash found evidence for a length of A/T ditch in the Shenley area, possibly connecting two streams and measuring 20ft (6m) wide and 12ft (3.7m) deep. Aerial photographs taken after the war in the areas unprotected

Batchworth (TQ076940), a DFW3/27 octagonal pillbox on Line 'A', with embrasures for seven light machine guns; an eighth loophole in the porch; and a central, open well for mounting an anti-aircraft light machine gun.

Above left: Wormley (TL368052), a non-standard, heightened pillbox with six loopholes and a raised entrance, defending the railway crossing where Line 'A' meets the River Lea.

Above right: Merchant Taylors School (TQ092941), a one-off pillbox built out of the same 2in. (50mm) bricks as the hall porch, commanding the land down to the river.

Otterspool (TQ129991), anti-tank blocks on the riverbank, with one slotted to accommodate an RSJ as part of a roadblock.

by natural obstacles show significant angled lengths of A/T ditch enfiladed in both directions by fire from pillboxes. These ditches ran between the New River in Cheshunt, over Candlestick Lane and Park Lane Paradise, and on to Bread and Cheese Lane, some of them still being discernible as cropmarks.

DEFENCE OF VULNERABLE POINTS

One of the tactics in the summer of 1940 was to create strongpoints out of searchlight sites. Each would receive a concrete pillbox and be surrounded with barbed wire and slit trenches, manned by the S/L personnel and any locally available troops, and under the control of the local field-force commander.

The militia camp at Colliers End was the HQ for all the scattered detachments of 334 Company of 33 S/L Regiment from Barnet, in whose area of operations were seventy-five such sites. This is often the explanation for an otherwise isolated pillbox with little apparent tactical purpose. The pillboxes on the A1081 above Monken Hadley, lying well inside the defences of Line 'A', may represent such examples.

Together with the defence lines criss-crossing the country, towns representing important road, rail or river crossings or junctions were defended as initially, that is, as 'A/T Islands', and later as 'Nodal Points'. These would be surrounded by defences consisting of pillboxes, roadblocks, weapons pits, barbed wire and A/T blocks.

Depending on the size of the town, one or more central buildings would be designated as the 'keep', the final fall-back position. The Spirella factory in Letchworth was identified as the town's keep. Contributors to the national survey of pillboxes carried out by Henry Wills in the 1980s identified at least seven pillboxes which would formerly have ringed Bishop's Stortford, with its important road, rail and river junctions and crossings.

Garston Manor, as it was then called, housing sensitive centres of command and control, lay well outside Line 'A' and dominated the northerly approaches to industrial Watford. It was seen as being particularly vulnerable to an airborne landing by paratroops and was defended by at least eight DFW3/24 pillboxes. These were mainly located to its north-west, but with one, recently restored, on the former access from High Elms Lane. All of them, including

Garston Manor (TL110020), a close-defence hexagonal pillbox, one of several guarding this sensitive site. It has steel shutters protecting five of its loopholes, a low-level entrance flanked by pistol loops and an earth-covered roof for camouflage. The brick formwork is peeling off to reveal the rough-poured concrete.

two at Fortunes Farm, had steel plates over their five main loopholes with a pistol-loop each side of the low entrance. One surviving pillbox, off Fraser Crescent, has an extra loophole inserted into each of its two west-facing angles, an unusual arrangement, showing evidence for local improvisation by its builders, following the advice of RE officers, or not.

Other evidence of elements of these defences of VPs survives: A/T cones at the junction of Bradmore Lane and Station Road, Brookmans Park; A/T cones on the SE side of Woodside Lane, and a ruined Tett Turret at Bell Bar; loopholes in the bridge parapet at Broxbourne on the B194 Broxbourne-Lower Nazeing road as it crosses the River Lea; spigot mortars on the A1000 opposite the end of Bell Lane, close to the entrance to The Cuttings, off the A1000; and a perfectly preserved example of a complete spigot mortar emplacement defending the Brookmans Park BBC transmitting station near to the water tower.

However, many such defences have disappeared over the years. Woodcock Hill Radio Station, incorporating the Sandridge 'Y' Station, was formerly heavily defended; there were armed sentry posts at all the entrances to Radlett village; and at Bovingdon, the water tower, serving as an observation post, was manned every night by home guardsmen who had a telephone link to their CO's bedroom.

AIRFIELD DEFENCES

Airfields were seen as vulnerable from the start of the war and were provided with both AA (see below) and ground defences. Although the construction of hardened defences had been phased out in most contexts by mid-1941, following the successful German airborne descent on Crete, the fear of landings by parachute or glider-borne troops prolonged the active life of airfield defences.

Sawbridgeworth and Hunsdon were both given ample numbers of pillboxes, which ringed the flying area. The level of such allocations was based on a grading, arrived at by General Taylor, the director of fortifications and works at the War Office, in which Britain's 600-odd airfields were given priority rankings based on location, function and vulnerability.

As a fighter station integral to plans for counter-attack in the event of an invasion, Hunsdon was graded IIA status. This entitled it to between fifteen and twenty-four pillboxes, some facing inward and others outwards, manned by 225 troops, topped up by RAF ground staff, with three improvised armoured vehicles and two dozen light machine-guns. Airfields within 5 miles (8km) of important VPs such as Hatfield were graded IIB and afforded a similar level of defence as class IIA.

The remainder of the county's airfields were either omitted from the schedule (Sawbridgeworth and Broxbourne) or arrived on the scene too late to be included (Bovingdon, Nuthampstead and Panshanger). This does not mean that those five airfields remained undefended, as garrisons at Panshanger and Broxbourne were only removed in May 1942. Panshanger had two Allan Williams turrets, and Sawbridgeworth, possibly due to its SOE operations, was heavily defended by pillboxes. Aircraft factories also received defences: three pillboxes defended Leavesden; at Elstree, both an Allan Williams turret on the airfield itself and a pillbox on a minor road at Patchetts Green, defended the airfield; and Hatfield had pillboxes, at least one of which survived into recent times.

In the early months of the war, three gun sites were set up by the Honourable Artillery Company, west of the then A5 road, to defend the Handley Page factory at Radlett. The troops arrived by pantechnicon, were armed with Lewis guns and billeted in local halls and private homes. The airfield was guarded by troops of the Duke of Cornwall's Light Infantry, whose officer flew over the airfield to check that the camouflage was effective.

Later, the defences, which included an Allan Williams turret, were manned by the RAF Regiment and the local Home Guard who built their own armoured vehicle. This was based on a Bentley chassis and engine, with a wooden frame covered in armour plate removed from aircraft to which replacement self-sealing fuel tanks had been fitted.

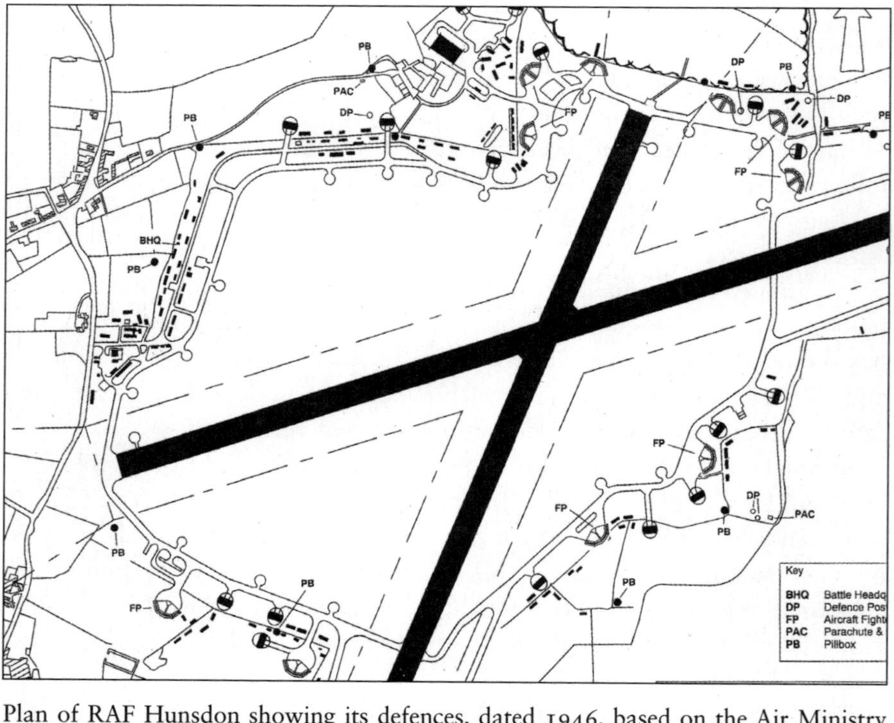

Plan of RAF Hunsdon showing its defences, dated 1946, based on the Air Ministry drawing (1223/46). Note that the surviving BHQ is not as shown on the plan but is nearer the south-east corner of the airfield. (*Paul Francis and AiG by kind permission*)

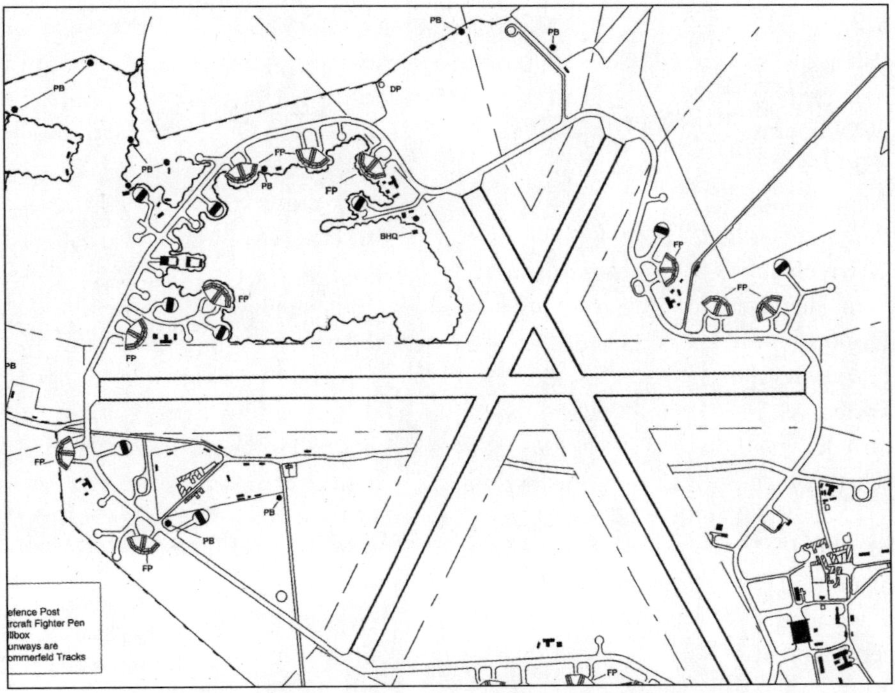

Plan of RAF Sawbridgeworth showing its defences, dated 1952, based on the Air Ministry drawing (1804/52). (*Paul Francis and AiG by kind permission*)

Across the county's airfields a wide range of pillbox types may be seen. Both Hunsdon and Sawbridgeworth were defended by the Air Ministry's shell-proof variation on the standard, hexagonal DFW3/22 pillbox. Greatly thickened sides, a tunnel entrance, a reduced number of loopholes and steel-plated prefabricated embrasures made these formidable obstacles to any ground assault.

At Hunsdon, these robust pillboxes were supplemented by at least two of the mushroom-shaped FC Construction pillboxes as well as smaller Air Ministry types. Two of the three pillboxes at Leavesden were improvised out of concrete blocks, with the third built of poured concrete in brick formwork. All three vary in shape and have different conformations of loops: one is hexagonal, with three armoured loopholes in its long base; one is almost square, with a porch projection and three wide loopholes, for heavy machine guns or A/T weapons; and one is pentagonal, with four loopholes in three of its sides. Defence posts were built at Radlett, a mixture of rectangular DFW3/23 pillboxes with open compartments for mounting LAA machine-guns, and hexagonal, splinter proof DFW3/22 pillboxes.

Defence of an airfield was directed from a battle HQ. At Panshanger this was an adapted blast shelter, but Hunsdon and Sawbridgeworth each received an example of a new design rolled out in 1941 (11008/41). This lay

Above: Hunsdon (TL429144), an Air Ministry-design pillbox.

Left: Hunsdon (TL425143), an FC Construction 'Oakington' or 'mushroom' pillbox.

Radlett (TL157047), an Allan Williams turret defending the airfield. Manned by two men, the turret was armed with two light machine guns, one of them on an anti-aircraft mount, and could be rotated 360 degrees.

Above: Hunsdon (TL425133), the standard battle HQ.

Right: Panshanger (TL274126), a shelter which doubled as the battle HQ.

Sawbridgeworth (TL464183), a thirty-three-man sleeping shelter equipped with bunk beds.

largely underground, was entered through hatches and vertical ladders, and had a raised concrete cupola supplying 360-degree visibility for the defence commander. Interestingly, the surviving standard BHQ at Hunsdon is not in the location indicated on the AM plan dated 1946. In February 1942, the RAF Regiment was established, taking in many existing defence personnel from airfields. This and the developing role of the Home Guard may account for the withdrawal of regular troops from airfield garrisons such as Hatfield, Leavesden and Radlett.

Survival of many of these features is generally good. There are Air Ministry pillboxes, sleeping shelters, BHQs and ammunition stores at Hunsdon and Sawbridgeworth. One Allan Williams Turret at Radlett *in situ*, and another from Panshanger, have been relocated to Sywell Aviation Museum in Northamptonshire. However, one from Elstree was moved to Salisbury Hall Museum and then, disappointingly, disposed of.

Secret Hertfordshire

Perceived as being far enough distant from obvious bombing targets but sufficiently close to London, Hertfordshire hosted a variety of secret organisations and projects. Initially known as the inscrutably labelled Inter-Services Research Bureau, the Special Operations Executive (SOE) expanded into a network of training centres and development workshops.

RAF No. 80 Wing, known as the 'beam-benders', was formed with its administrative and control centres in the county to thwart the Luftwaffe's use of directional radio beams that would guide their bombers onto planned targets. Whilst much of the operation to intercept enemy communications was centred on Bletchley Park, in Buckinghamshire, both listening posts and many of the support structures which developed and produced the relevant technology were located in Hertfordshire.

SPECIAL OPERATIONS EXECUTIVE (SOE) TRAINING AND OPERATIONS

From 1939, SOE and its forerunner organisations set up two types of establishment in Hertfordshire: SOE Stations, which were dedicated to developing infrastructure and the kit for their agents, and Special Training Schools (STS), where agents were trained for their specific tasks and equipped with the necessary equipment to accomplish them. When the Government Code and Cypher School (GC&CS) took over Bletchley Park in Buckinghamshire, the Statistical Research Department of the War Office was removed to Aston House, near Stevenage, since demolished.

Under the unpretentious cover-name of War Office Signals Development Branch Depot No. 4, its focus was primarily wireless research, but this was soon shifted to the development of weapons and, importantly, explosives. It soon became SOE Station XII, focused on the research and development of both weapons and tactics. The adjacent chalk quarry afforded the opportunity to test the viability of the gadgets it came up with such as limpet mines and time pencils. The former used a delaying mechanism based on dissolving aniseed balls, half a million of which would be manufactured in a factory in Welwyn, while the latter employed variable amounts of acid to detonate explosive charges.

By 1945, the site had expanded to include separate men's and women's hutted camps; a dozen large huts for stores; isolated explosive stores and packing sheds; and underground explosives stores in the magazine area. As official enthusiasm grew and SOE's activities expanded, more extensive premises were needed.

Bride Hall, in Ayot St Lawrence, with ample hidden storage facilities in its medieval barns, was SOE's weapons acquisition department as Station VI. In Old Welwyn, The Frythe, a former hotel, commandeered in 1939 by Military Intelligence, became SOE's engineering section, Station IX, for the research and development of specialised weapons and equipment, ultimately occupying 20,000ft^2 of extra workshops and hangars. Its impressive list of products, documented in 1945, included simplified small arms: pistols and sub machine-guns; folding motorcycles which could be delivered by parachute; and submersible canoes and midget submarines. Also in Old Welwyn, the North Road Garage acted as a store for The Frythe and housed the repair depot for SOE's MT section.

Radio training was carried out at the Yeast-Vite factory, in Whippendell Road, Watford, Station VIIb, with the wireless research section, Station VIIc, housed in Allensor's joinery factory, in King George's Avenue, Watford. Located on the Barnet bypass, The Thatched Barn, in Borehamwood, was a roadhouse owned by Billy Butlin, whose holiday camps had already been commandeered as training camps by the Royal Navy. It was requisitioned as Station XV to develop camouflage techniques relevant to SOE's activities, including producing authentic clothing, disguises and aids to concealment. It employed film technicians, artists, and magicians, or illusionists, such as Jasper Maskelyne. Old Gorhambury House, outside St Albans, provided accommodation for SOE staff as Station XI. RAF Sawbridgeworth operated flying training courses for pilots flying Westland Lysander aircraft on clandestine SOE operations, delivering agents and supplies into German-occupied Europe.

Brickendonbury Hall, outside Hertford, was initially requisitioned by Section 'D' of SIS for weapons development, explosives trials, and sabotage planning and training. It began by teaching basic espionage tradecraft and subsequently developed into SOE Station XVII. As its training role expanded, it would become Station 17, training SOE members to utilise the output of

The Frythe, Welwyn, was Station IX, the research and development arm of SOE, specialising in their less conventional weaponry and gadgetry.

Brickendonbury was originally SOE's Station XVII but moved across to a training role as STS17. Its graduates took part in some of the better known of SOE's attempts to set Europe ablaze.

Wall Hall served as STS39, training personnel of the Political Warfare Executive. It was also home to a War Office selection board, putting army officer candidates through their paces.

Aston House. Amongst the students' practice targets were the railway sheds at Hitchin and RAF Radlett.

Some of the 1,200 graduates of Brickendonbury were those involved in the assassination of Heydrich, the assault on the Norsk-Hydro heavy water plant in Norway, and the sabotage by blackmail of the Renault, Peugeot, and Dunlop plants in France. Briggens, in Stanstead Abbots, was set up as STS 38, a Polish Training Section for the Chicociemni, the 'silent and unseen' elite of the Polish army, preparing to be parachuted back into Poland. Frogmore Farm and Frogmore Hall, at Watton-at-Stone, near Stevenage, acted as holding stations for them as STS 18. Brockett Hall, sometimes described as STS 20, complete with its 'von Ribbentrop Room', which trumpeted its interned owner's Nazi sympathies, was primarily sequestrated by the War Office as a maternity hospital, but it is also reported to have hosted a training centre for Polish agents involving total immersion in a simulated Polish environment, with the language, food, clothing and traditions all designed to ensure that agents, immediately and seamlessly on arrival, would resume their place in Polish society.

Other Polish trainees initially shared premises at Briggens with SOE's false document section, but as forgery operation expanded under Station XIV, the Poles removed to Audley End, in Essex, in 1941. Gardeners End, at Ardeley, near Stevenage, was STS XIX, training first Polish and then Czech agents. Towards the end of the war, it trained German POWs, known as 'bonzos', to be parachuted into Germany in Operation Periwig. They would either hand themselves in, revealing themselves to have been blackmailed or otherwise pressured into working for the British, or allow themselves to be captured so they could 'betray' the existence of an extensive, but fake, German underground resistance organisation, adding an extra layer of confusion to the last days of the chaotic Third Reich. Austrian POWs, tasked with preventing the destruction of artworks at the end of the war, constituted a further group, also referred to as 'bonzos'.

In 1943–44, Wall Hall at Aldenham, as STS 39, was a training centre for the Political Warfare Executive (PWE), concocting and peddling black propaganda, much to the consternation of the Reithian BBC, which, jealously guarding its impeccable reputation for transmitting only the truth and nothing but the truth, saw the PWE as a threat to its integrity and refused to transmit its fake news. Albury Hall, in 1940, already requisitioned by the army, is reported as being used by SOE for training agents. There were tunnels and underground rooms which may have been connected to this activity, but the house was demolished in 1950.

RADIO COUNTER MEASURES (RCM), THE 'BEAM-BENDERS'

As the Luftwaffe's bombers homed in, apparently unerringly, on British targets in 1940, it was discovered that they were following radio beams. These were transmitted from Kleves and Lorrach on the German/Dutch and the German/French/Swiss borders respectively and designed to intersect over the designated target. The RAF, having discovered the existence of this beam, named *Knickebein*, was tasked with countering it, setting up No. 80 (Signals) Wing for this purpose. No. 80 Wing's first HQ for their RCM operation was established at Garston Manor, formerly the Road Research Laboratory, in Autumn 1940, with a standby operations room in a local garage.

In October 1940, the HQ was moved to the Aldenham Lodge Hotel in Radlett, demolished in 1964, closer to the London/Birmingham GPO trunk cable. With the operations room's expansion into 'Newberries', on Radlett golf course, from late 1941, the Aldenham Lodge Hotel continued as the administration centre for 80 Wing, which by now consisted of 2,000 personnel and over one hundred outstations such as that at Potters Bar. The operations room and HQ staff were lodged in two nearby houses: 'Lamorna' and 'Tintern', with 'Heathwood' as a WAAF hostel. Sick quarters were in 2 Beech Avenue, with Shenley military hospital as backup. Howards Garage, on Watling Street, was the MT section, and Radlett Hall on Watling Street the service's NAAFI canteen.

Once the problem—code-named Headache—had been identified, the solution—Aspirin— could be applied. A network of paired jammer stations, known as 'meacons' (a portmanteau of 'masking' and 'beacon') was set up. In Harpenden, a meacon jammer was installed at Kennels Farm, Kinsbourne Green, off the old A6 road near the entrance to Luton Hoo. Paired with a meacon at Elstree, it was one of fifteen such combinations countrywide. The RCM HQ, which controlled jamming devices, received information from watchers and from 'Y' stations and ordered the jammers into action.

A fire control officer, a member of Colonel Turner's department, was also based in the operations room to activate decoy 'Starfish' fires (see below). In the centre of the operations room was a large plotting table on which was recorded information about incoming enemy aircraft, particularly any hostile pathfinder unit preceding raids, and guiding the bomber force to its targets. This information was sent direct to Fighter Command HQ at Bentley Priory.

Once it had been realised that the enemy had the capability of jamming the coastal radar, three monitoring stations were set up early in 1942, becoming 'J' Watch, with lodgers at radar sites as necessary. A former night-club/roadhouse on Watling Street called 'The Houseboat' had only opened for a few months in 1935. It was now commandeered as the base for the jamming unit from March 1943.

The Wireless Intelligence Development Unit (WIDU), based at RAF Radlett, flew its Avro Ansons carrying airborne listeners to identify the German beam settings and relay the details back to base for action by ground stations. In late 1943, needing to expand out of their workshops at The Houseboat, the radio section of RAF No. 100 (Bomber Support) Group's development unit moved from Radlett to Norfolk as the RAF's radio engineering section.

THE INTERCEPTION OF ENEMY COMMUNICATIONS

The three existing intercept stations operated in 1938 by the army, the Royal Navy and the RAF were supplemented by three more, including Woodcock Hill, in Sandridge, near St Albans. This was run by the GPO on behalf of the Foreign Office and MI6 for the Radio Security Service (RSS), dedicated to intercepting diplomatic radio traffic. A large H-shaped building with two tall aerials was built to expand the existing facilities on site, with a farm of rhombic aerials on telegraph poles pointing in the direction of interest.

In 1940, after its base with MI5 in Wormwood Scrubs prison was bombed, the RSS in the guise of the Radio Analysis Bureau, known as V(w), was moved to a new home in Arkley View, Barnet, under the rather prosaic *nom de guerre* of PO Box 25 Barnet. It acted as a clearing house for intercepts from amateur radio 'hams' for onward transmission to GC&CS at Bletchley Park. The big house, already in use by the GPO as an intercept station, housed all the analysis, intelligence, direction-finding control and administrative functions. The extension of intercept work, teleprinter terminals, and the expanding activities of classifying and collating the product of enemy wireless networks necessitated the addition of huts in the grounds.

An orderly room and a base for the Bletchley-bound motorcycle despatch riders stood nearby, with messes opposite. Other large houses, including The

Lawns, Scotswood, Rowley Lodge and Meadowbank, were taken over for training, transmitting, intercept work, messes and billets. Ravenscroft Park, in High Barnet, also housed an intercept training centre. Many illustrious dons were recruited to the site for traffic analysis and work on radar and VHF communication, adding to the wide spread of listeners contributing their gleanings to the system. In Harpenden, Rothampstead Manor housed No. 1 Special Wireless Group of the Army 'Y' Service, with listening posts at Shenley and Markyate. Boxmoor House has been suggested locally as the likely location of the SOE radio listening post reported in the village.

The resources of local industry were also enlisted into the wireless intelligence effort. In 1920, the British Tabulating Machine Company moved out of London to Letchworth and set up a new factory. Working to a brief from Alan Turing, company design engineers, under the codename 'CANTAB', produced the prototype *bombe* which enabled the cracking of the Enigma codes at Bletchley Park. Some 210 machines were built and delivered there by army truck in a deliberately low-key operation. The production of parts was contracted out to other local firms such as Spirella, in Icknield Way, which produced wiring, while the drums were engineered at the Ascot government training centre in Pixmore Lane.

Letchworth, the Spirella Company manufactured parts for the computers used at Bletchley Park. The building also formed the 'keep', the fall-back position at the centre of the town's Home Guard defence plan.

INTELLIGENCE AND COMMUNICATIONS

Brookmans Park Transmitting Station had opened in 1929 as part of the BBC's scheme to improve services across Britain, serving London and the Home Counties. Marconi transmitters were installed along with generators, as there was no electricity supply to the site until 1939. In 1940, a powerful new 140kw transmitter was installed to increase the range to include Occupied Europe, necessitating a significant extension of the original building.

The building was camouflaged with paint, and the windows were bricked up with metal shutters, while a military guard camped in the driveway. Air Ministry regulations initially restricted the height of the two aerials to 200ft (61m), but they were later raised to 500ft (154m). A repeater station at Elstree linked GPO research department transmitters and receivers. Aldenham House Country Club was requisitioned for the BBC's use as an overseas broadcasting station. RAF Barkway radio station opened in 1942 for the GEE navigation system, which enabled Allied bombers to follow intersecting radio beams onto their targets.

As part of the decentralisation of government departments from London, Glenalmond in St Albans housed the Central Registry, Section V, V(d), MI6/SIS, until 1943; Hexton was home to Section 'D', of the Political Intelligence Department of the Political Warfare Executive; and MI5 maintained a safe house in Radlett.

An enigmatic and intriguing snippet in the news section of Airfield Review No. 151 in June 2016 reported that 'the once secret Post Office

Brookmans Park opened in 1929 for the BBC. More powerful transmitting equipment was installed in 1940, enabling broadcasts to German-occupied Europe.

telecommunications unit on the site (Hatfield airfield) has now been demolished'. The source of this information was *The Moth* of March 2016. In Hemel Hempstead, a house called 'The Arches', at Felden, was used by the Polish Radio Intelligence Company from May 1943. There has been much discussion on the internet as to the identity of this house, which is thought to have reverted to its pre-war name of 'Widgeons'.

Air defence

Garston Manor was earmarked as an emergency reserve HQ for Anti-Aircraft Command, and Cupid Green in Hemel Hempstead was 1st AA Division's ordnance workshop. Mobilised in Watford, 79 HAA Regiment was assigned to RAF establishments, including Bentley Priory, and the airfields at Duxford, North Weald, Martlesham Heath and Debden, deploying a mix of old 3in. 20cwt guns and Lewis guns. The regiment was then moved to the Felixstowe and Harwich GDA prior to joining the BEF in France.

London's Inner Artillery Zone (IAZ) took in the south-east corner of the county, with Theobalds Park, Cheshunt, accommodating an AA Operations Room and training camp, some of whose huts near to the New River appear to have survived. Close to Theobalds, stands Gunsite Stud, a possible former practice battery. Two of the IAZ batteries also stood close by: Albury Farm (ZE11) was unarmed, but manned by 302 Battery, 99 HAA Regiment in August 1940; and Burnt Farm, Goffs Oak (ZW3), was armed in 1940 with four First World War-vintage 3in. mobile guns. Reported unarmed in 1942, it was manned by 469 Battery, 132 (M) HAA Regiment in 1943, one of the very first regiments to integrate ATS women into a combatant unit, where they operated height-finding, predictive and gun-laying radar devices. It is then recorded as subsequently being armed with four 3.7in. and four 4.5in. HAA guns. By June 1942, Battery HM1, from Lemsford Lane TAC, armed with four static 3.7in. HAA guns, was defending Hatfield's airfield and factory.

RAF airfields, munitions factories and utilities were given LAA protection where it was available. The Handley Page works at Radlett (VP548) was provided with four of the nation's meagre supply of 40mm Bofors guns in May 1940, as well as a pair of Lewis guns. Similarly, Hatfield airfield and de Havilland factory (VP547) had four 40mm Bofors guns in May 1940, both stations being manned by Troops of 36 AA Regiment's 145 Battery. Watford had LAA cover for the Hawker / de Havilland shadow factory at Leavesden (VP131), and one of the Waltham explosives works' numerous LAA positions lay over the river in Cheshunt in January 1940. Near the start of the war, 117 Battery of 30 LAA Regiment with its HQ in The Manor House, in Melbourn Street, Royston, defended four airfields in Cambridgeshire and Bedfordshire.

Theobalds, Cheshunt, housed a gun operations room controlling anti-aircraft defences.

By early 1941, targets in the Royston area were defended by 346 Battery, 36 S/L Regiment, based in the militia camp, with its HQ still in Royston Manor House. RAF Hunsdon (VP611) was first allocated four Lewis guns but by 1942 was equipped with four 40mm Bofors guns mounted on static platforms. In the early days it had been additionally defended by parachute and cable (PAC) equipments which involved the launching of rockets. From these there unfurled parachutes with suspended steel cables intended to slice the wings off low-flying aircraft attacking ground targets.

Eventually, Home Guard LAA units would take a major responsibility for many of these targets, with LAA Troops at Hatfield, Radlett and Leavesden armed with a variety of weapons, including Hispano-Suiza and Oerlikon 20mm cannon, and even twin Browning 0.5in. heavy machine guns removed from disabled bomber aircraft.

On the declaration of war, 33 AA Battalion RE drew its equipment from its mobilisation stores in Buntingford, and its Barnet-based 334 Company was deployed to Colliers End militia camp, Puckeridge. Like all the other RE searchlight battalions, it transferred to the RA as a searchlight regiment in 1940.

Early in the war, single searchlights had been first installed on permanent sites, that reported at the John Warner School, Hoddesdon (TL380103) being a possible example. Subsequently, they were clustered in threes, before being finally reorganised as more closely spaced single lights, to reflect the evolving solutions to night-time bombing raids. By the time of this deployment in March 1941, the AA strategy had largely been worked out with belts of lights illuminating 'indicator' and 'killer' zones, maintaining demarcation lines between the night-fighters and the guns. Hertfordshire lay in the killer zone, where searchlights were consequently spaced at intervals of 6,000yds (5,540m).

Consequently, in October 1941, 33rd Regiment was ordered to de-cluster and to establish forty-eight, single-light S/L sites across the Hertfordshire-Essex-Cambridgeshire-Suffolk borders, with 334 Battery generating an extra 'E' Troop of six lights to defend RAF Hunsdon. Sites in Hertfordshire included Amwell, Rye House, Willian, Wyddial, Reed, Bishops Stortford, Walkern and Brent Pelham. This deployment lasted until April 1943, when 33 Regiment was transferred to Kent. It was replaced by 93 (Mixed) Searchlight Regiment, with its RHQ in Moor Park, Rickmansworth. This was responsible, in March 1943, for three S/L Batteries, each with four troops of six lights. With HQs at Hatfield and Watford, two of 93 Regiment's batteries operated across Hertfordshire, with troops based in Knebworth, Offley, South Mimms, Holtsmere End, Stanborough, Hunton Bridge, Sopwell and Dagnall.

The HQ of Watford's 342(Mixed) S/L Battery was 'The Russells', a house of 1718, now Russell House apartments on Hempstead Road. Roe Hill House, Hatfield, was HQ, 301(M) S/L Battery. As a mixed battery, training was held there for the women of the ATS who served in the battery. The house, built in 1905, has since been demolished and flats built on the site. Although occupying some of 33 Regiment's former sites, its expanded territory extended further west into Buckinghamshire and Middlesex.

From early on in the war the 1st HAA Tractor Battery (RA) occupied Pendley Manor's stables in Tring, with Nissen huts and workshops alongside Station Road. The unit was equipped with heavy transport, mainly AEC Matador 6-wheeled trucks and specialist gun-transporters. Its function was to service HAA batteries in London but also further afield, by transporting guns and servicing all the HAA batteries' many trucks. While detachments of the unit's complement of sixty were out on the road, those spending time in camp were billeted in the Manor's stable-block.

THE ROYAL OBSERVER CORPS (ROC)

In Watford the original ROC control centre was in the GPO building in Market Street. In 1943 it moved to a purpose-built two-storey brick control room surrounded by single-storey sections in Cassiobury Drive. Designed in 1941, this became the prototype for many of the others built across the country.

The network of ROC posts established before the war, was manned and maintained by volunteer observers. Some posts, such as that at Elstree, occupied the roofs of high buildings and others sat on exposed hilltops and it was down to individual local initiative to provide appropriate protection against the elements. An official shed known affectionately, or not, as the 'rabbit hutch' might be provided on some sites, whilst others gained more substantial structures, raised on platforms with partial overhead cover allowing use of the post instruments.

Observations were reported by telephone or radio to the central control in Watford and thence relayed to the local fighter command filter room at Bentley Priory. In order to achieve enhanced warning of raids, the development of a new long-range plotting board (LRB) was proposed. Faced with Air Ministry scepticism, 17 Group Centre at Watford, along with post office engineers, improvised its own prototype and demonstrated its successful operation. Occasional exercises were held to test the whole system. Observers were usually men in reserved occupations, but some youngsters were recruited on the basis of their success in aircraft-spotting and identification competitions. Many of them also had better hearing and eyesight than some of the older observers.

In September 1942, the Cuffley ROC post (G1) was the first to spot the JU86H flying at a hitherto unimaginable height of 38,000ft (11,000m). As priorities changed, several hundred WAAFs were redeployed from Fighter Command to the ROC in 1943. Also working alongside the ROC, on occasion, and utilising supposed ROC membership as their cover were the members of the highly secret RSS in their base in Barnet. The Watford-based 17 Group was one of those ROC units cooperating with RAF 80 Wing. On one occasion the Watford controller tracked a brand new, but thoroughly lost German Dornier 217 and fooled it into landing in Kent with its brand new Knickebein receiver equipment intact.

Watford, Cassiobury Drive, the double-height control room for the wartime Royal Observer Corps posts of Group 17.

BOMBING DECOYS

Initially airfields, but later urban areas were provided with decoy sites designed to draw bombers away from their intended targets. The first decoys were constructed to protect airfields early in the war. Dummy airfields with mock-ups of aircraft, often designed and built by technicians from film studios, were known as 'K' sites. At Holwell Hyde, dummy buildings representing the footprint of de Havilland's Hatfield factory were built alongside the dummy aircraft and scrap cars parked outside on painted roads. The contractor was Sound City (Films) Ltd. of Shepperton.

By 1942, those more ambitious sites such as Holwell Hyde were shut down because of the high expense of maintenance, whilst the direct threat of attack was diminishing. On 'K' sites, the aircraft were moved around regularly by the resident ground crew to suggest an active airfield worthy of the Luftwaffe's attention. Expensive to construct and maintain, this programme was ended in June 1942 as large-scale attacks had largely ceased by then.

Night-operating 'Q' sites simulated the lights of taxiing aircraft and runways, the procedure being to illuminate on the reported approach of enemy aircraft and to extinguish just as they came into hearing range, affording the intruders a fleeting glimpse of the lights being hurriedly extinguished. Very soon, as bombing switched to civilian and industrial targets, more appropriate types of decoy were developed.

'SF' (special fires) or Starfish sites replicated the fires and explosions occurring in built-up areas, whilst other decoys specifically simulated the lights of factories (FL), railway marshalling yards (MY) and locomotive fireboxes, using combinations of lights, sparks and fires. While it is obviously impossible to gauge the overall effectiveness of decoys, it can be said that most decoy sites were bombed during the war, diverting those bombs from their genuine targets and bringing new experiences into the lives of the bewildered inhabitants of isolated areas.

Examples of decoys in the county include Barley, for RAF Bassingbourn, and Barnet, for RAF Northolt; Holwell Hyde, as part of the 'M' (Industrial) Series, for de Havilland's Hatfield aircraft factory; and two 'C' (Civil) Series decoys for Luton at Bendish and Flamstead. As the war progressed, decoys were adapted to meet new needs. Hatfield was provided with two 'C' Series decoys in 1942–43 at a modified Holwell Hyde and a new site at Essendon. Luton's two decoys, located in Hertfordshire, became permanent Starfish sites in August 1941, operating into summer 1943 and sporting specialist effects to mimic the Vauxhall factory and the town's marshalling yards. Essendon adopted techniques to simulate the last-minute shutting of doors in a blacked-out factory: often merely light boxes with hinged lids; while not very sophisticated, perhaps, they were perfectly effective when observed from 15,000ft up in an approaching bomber.

A further way of avoiding becoming too inviting a target for bombing was the application of different camouflage techniques.

The de Havilland Hatfield complex, with its factory and flight school, was vulnerable to aerial attack. A report of a camouflage survey carried out in 1940 described the aerodrome as conspicuous: the hedge painting across the flying field was in good condition but of bad design; and the camouflage of the factory itself was good but was emphasised by contrasting light-coloured aprons. The recommendation was for the LG's camouflage to be redesigned and the plant's aprons to be textured.

The 1940 camouflage survey of the Colney Street, Radlett, works of Handley Page noted a serious deterioration, in that the building works for the factory's recent extension had created a highly conspicuous scar in the landscape, not previously present. While the hedge pattern was good, the painting had faded. The conclusion was that the situation needed close monitoring.

A very different sort of deception was carried out at Hatfield in 1943. Eddie Chapman was a safe-cracker and burglar who fell into German hands while imprisoned for crimes committed in Jersey. He volunteered his services as a German spy and saboteur and was parachuted into England, charged with blowing up the de Havilland factory in Hatfield, which was known to be building the revolutionary Mosquito aircraft. He was immediately arrested on landing but was helped to set about planning how to blow up the factory's powerhouse, ostensibly putting the whole plant out of action.

The magician Jasper Maskelyne was then recruited to construct a realistic scenario for this non-explosion. He used papier-mâché, painted tarpaulins, timber and other visual effects to create a scene of apparent devastation, which German aerial reconnaissance aircraft were enabled to photograph unhindered. The early edition of the *Daily Express*, which was flown to neutral Lisbon, recorded the bombing, and due, obviously, to the alertness of the censor, the story immediately disappeared from domestic editions, thereby satisfying any qualms the editor might have held about publishing fake news.

Chapman (aka Agent Zig-Zag, in British intelligence's XX (Double-Cross) System) reported his success back in Germany and was allegedly awarded the Iron Cross. Chapman's exploits as a double agent would continue throughout the war and included mis-reporting V-1 and V-2 strikes, so that the German despatchers failed to correct their aim when the missiles consistently missed their intended targets in central London, either overshooting or falling short. In amongst continued criminal behaviour, one of Chapman's legal post-war projects was a health farm in Shenley, and he died in St Albans in 1997, aged 83.

Munitions production

AIRCRAFT FACTORIES

The de Havilland Hatfield factory complex produced both the Rapide and its military version, the Dominie, used for airborne wireless instruction or as a light transport aircraft for, amongst other tasks, collecting ATA pilots from their delivery points. Dominie production moved to the Brush Works at Loughborough (Leicestershire) in 1943 to allow greater concentration on the Mosquito, which had been developed by Geoffrey de Havilland and his design team at Salisbury Hall, in Shenley. This was despite opposition from MAP, which, somewhat grudgingly, ordered just fifty of them in March 1940 as bomber and reconnaissance aircraft. However, by the end of the war, getting on for 4,500 had been built at Hatfield, Leavesden and at other shadow factories.

Salisbury Hall was not an airfield but had two runways laid nearby with the intention of being able to fly aircraft off to Hatfield for testing. This was to solve the problem of the long delays to the prototype Mosquito's maiden flight when the aircraft had to be dismantled and taken to Hatfield by road. In the event, however, just three aircraft were flown off from Shenley, as the runways were not successful and had soon been ploughed up by disgruntled local farmers. A team was assembled by Airspeed, at Hatfield, to develop the Horsa glider for airborne operations, and a dedicated hangar was built at Salisbury Hall. This hangar was later relocated to Astwick Manor when the de Havilland technical school moved there. The Vampire jet fighter made its first flight in September 1943 but did not enter RAF service until the end of the war.

Salisbury Hall, a hangar/workshop.

Handley Page at Radlett continued to build over 500 Hampden bombers, with greater numbers built by Shorts, in Belfast, and English Electric, in Preston, and Samlesbury, in Lancashire. The second prototype Halifax heavy bomber flew from Radlett in August 1940. with the first production model two months later. Almost 6,200 were built altogether, equipping seventy-six RAF squadrons, with a third of those coming out of Radlett and a further 700 from Leavesden. The original flight sheds at Colney Street, Radlett, were extended to spread northwards along Park Street. The experimental hangar, the two-storey block alongside and the Ministry of Aircraft Production B1 hangar survived into the 1990s.

Leavesden was bought by the Air Ministry in 1940 in order to establish a shadow aircraft factory administered by de Havillands. Extensive hangars, offices, control tower and workshops were built and a 3,000-yard runway laid. Production began on the Handley Page Halifax, over 700 of which were constructed there. From late 1941, No. 2 Factory built the Mosquito, completing almost 1,400 of them. Finished aircraft were delivered to their destination airfields by mainly female ATA pilots of No. 5 Ferry Pilot Pool based at Hatfield.

Fairfield Aviation at Elstree/Aldenham was contracted throughout the Second World War as a civilian repair organisation (CRO) by MAP. Redwing Aircraft Company's premises in Croydon (Surrey) were bombed and the whole operation, initially repairing damaged Blenheims, was moved into

Radlett, Handley Page's B1 hangar, designed by the Ministry of Aircraft Production for use on airfields and aircraft factories.

Elstree, Type 'R' hangar supplied by the Ministry of Aircraft Production for the Civilian Repair Organisation, operating on this club airfield. It measured 240×120ft (74×37m) and may have been erected by a Watford firm.

Odhams print works in Watford with a workforce of 1,100. Repaired aircraft were then delivered to Elstree by road on RAF Queen Mary transporters to be checked over and test flown.

As working under camouflage netting proved impracticable, MAP provided a large R-type hangar, a pair of joined Super Robins, and a blister hangar, also laying a 3,150ft (970m) concrete runway, so that larger aircraft might be flown in for repair. Many RAF aircraft, including nearly 500 Wellingtons and over 1,200 Lysanders, were tested, repaired and modified in these new hangars provided by MAP for the purpose. The military aspects of the airfield were closed down at the end of 1945, when club flying resumed.

Surviving buildings include the MAP 'R' hangar and the now radically modernised Robins hangars. The first watch office was attached to a hangar and accessed by ladder; it has subsequently been succeeded by three further ATC towers. Also part of the CRO network was Broxbourne, where the Hertfordshire and Essex Aero Club was awarded contracts to repair and service light aircraft, mainly Miles Magisters, from Reading, and Percival Proctors, from Luton. Canadian-built Harvard trainers were also modified to meet RAF requirements and spare parts were manufactured for Percival marques and Bristol Beaufighters, aircraft being delivered and collected by the ubiquitous ATA pilots, flying without benefit of armament, radio or crew.

OTHER WARTIME PRODUCTION AND DEPOTS

Irvin and GQ of Letchworth collaborated in 1940 to develop a safe and efficient static line for dropping airborne troops. Parachutes and associated equipment were produced for aircrew and airborne forces alike, with production expanding into the neighbouring Spirella building, with the

Bondor factory in Baldock being requisitioned by MAP for the production of parachutes. Brocks, the firework manufacturers of Hemel Hempstead, produced signal rockets, parachute flares and Verey lights. HMS *Aeolus*, named for the god of the winds, was an RN depot located behind 51 Tring High Street that supplied kites and balloons to the navy for shipboard AA defence and for meteorological recording.

As well as MI9, the official escape and evasion organisation, and SOE-sponsored workshops, private companies were involved in supplying specialist items to order. One such company was Platignum, in Stevenage, which, as well as producing aircraft parts and cap badges, also produced pens containing maps and compasses for escaping POWs, and a pen containing a poisoned dart for secret agents. Much like Platignum, other factories continued to manufacture their normal products, despite much of their capacity being devoted to meeting contracts for munitions.

Based in former mills specially adapted for papermaking, Dickinson's, of Hemel Hempstead, continued to manufacture paper and cardboard products but also produced 20mm cannon shells for aircraft and other essential accessories for aircraft such as fuel pumps and spark plugs. They also made 'Window', the aluminium foil strips dropped by RAF bombers to blind enemy radar. Creasey's, of Knebworth, built army lorries, and Corby, Palmer & Stewart, in Great Berkhamsted, made army uniforms and parts for Mosquito aircraft.

Jack Olding of Caterpillar Island, Hatfield, became the sole agent for the US Caterpillar Tractor Company in 1939, initiating a school for the instruction of RE and RAF personnel in the use of heavy plant, which later evolved into the RAF Airfield Construction Service at Mill Green, using local disused gravel pits for training. US-built Grant and Sherman tanks and Canadian Ram tanks were imported and prepared prior to issue to armoured units. British-built Churchill tanks, bulldozers and earth movers were adapted to the requirements of General Hobart's 'funnies': flail tanks and 'Crabs' for clearing minefields; armoured bulldozers; flamethrower-equipped Crocodile tanks; and AVREs armed with Petards, mortars firing 40lb (18kg) HE charges. All these and others comprised the RE's range of assault vehicles, with which the 79th Armoured Division was equipped for clearing the beaches for the Normandy landings.

Featherby's (later Millars), in Bishops Stortford, hydraulic engineers with an on-site foundry, carried out repairs to tanks, and Dyrham Park, north of Barnet, was home to the workshops of No. 21 Army Tank Brigade prior to its departure for North Africa and Italy in 1942. A central ordnance depot was located in the film studios at Elstree, and the East Central District's REME Command workshop was in Buntingford.

The Building Research Station at Garston found itself providing wartime building bulletins, which served to provide ideas and develop building materials to meet the requirements for instant factories, army camps and airfields using new materials and techniques, with the repair of bomb-damaged housing as another area of focus. Their output was prodigious: in one eight-week period over 800 factory designs were produced.

These designs, including those for small huts for military use, were all subjected to rigorous testing before their acceptance by the War Office, the Ministry of Supply, the Air Ministry and the other supply agencies putting out contracts. The eternal balance to be sought was the use of minimal materials for maximal weather resilience at a time when all building materials were in short supply and at a maximum level of demand, and labour was scarce. Additionally, the construction of scale models of the Mohne Dam enabled Barnes Wallis to develop a strategy for its destruction by the 'bouncing bomb', more properly, a mine.

Professor J. D. Bernal—previously voicing the Building Research Station's anxiety regarding the lack of ARP planning—had joined the Ministry of Home Security, becoming one of Earl Mountbatten's scientific advisers. He supplied the concept of the Mulberry Harbours, thereby ensuring the success of the D-Day invasion, and even landed on the beaches on D-Day+1 to analyse the conditions for himself. At war's end, he also evaluated the various commercial proposals for the prefabricated houses which would replace the many dwellings destroyed or severely damaged by bombing.

Hertfordshire was home to many of the principal designers and builders of the huts which so many organisations, both military and civil, would require during the war. In 1939, Messrs. Nissen Buildings Ltd. of Rye House, Hoddesdon, in production there from 1922–60, had redesigned the 1917 model of their prefabricated Bow Hut to create a more spacious building which admitted more light. Waiving royalties for the duration, the Nissen company saw thousands of their curved steel huts, and their derivatives, being produced for every conceivable use. More specifically, they were used on airfields and in barracks, camps, hospitals, stores depots, hostels (for industrial workers and land girls) and munitions factories.

The Air Ministry alone erected over 103,000 Nissen huts during the war. Nissen also developed a version of their hut with the curved roof to serve as an air-raid shelter, offering protection against both incendiaries and gas. Whilst Nissen huts were basically curved corrugated iron roofs mounted on brick dwarf walls with end walls of either half-brick or timber and felt, many other designs of huts were constructed from prefabricated panels mounted on timber frameworks. The TF Nash Construction Company, housebuilders of St Albans, produced a hut constructed from easily sawn panels made of cement and sawdust, and marketed as 'Nashcrete'.

The Handcraft Hut was designed and produced by the Universal Asbestos Manufacturing Company of Tolpits Lane, Watford. It was constructed from reinforced asbestos-cement panels with a seven-sided profile. Laing huts were prefabricated in a purpose-built factory in Elstree. The pitched roof was covered in corrugated asbestos sheeting lined with plasterboard, and the timber walls were covered inside and out with plasterboard and weatherproofed with felt sheeting. The interior layout allowed for a dormitory with twenty-four beds, or twelve single cubicles either side of a central corridor. All of these huts were capable of being configured into larger complexes.

A Maycrete hut at Letchworth Nursery School, with sawdust and cement panels laid horizontally between concrete uprights, up to window height, was linked in an H-shape, with air raid shelters on the ends. Many of these huts were quite distinctive but others less so, only identifiable by the detailing of their roof-trusses. Many of these huts were repurposed as housing after the war, both officially and by squatters, and some survive to this day, while modern adaptations of some of them are still being manufactured.

HERTFORDSHIRE'S RAILWAYS

LMS central staff were evacuated from their HQ in Euston House to The Grove, a sixty-room country house outside Watford, now a hotel and conference centre. Three dozen timber huts were erected there, and distinctive air raid shelters were excavated alongside the house, one of which housed the control staff.

A comprehensive telephone system connected the railway operators to the armed services, the emergency services and ARP. At the same time, LNER staff were evacuated to The Hoo, in Hitchin, a seventeenth-century house with landscaped gardens, which was demolished in 1958. Emergency railway control centres, hardened structures built of brick and concrete and resistant to bombs of up to 500lb were built at Watford for the LMS and at Knebworth for the LNER. By 1943, fixed radio transmitters had been installed at Watford and Knebworth, two out of a couple of dozen such locations nationally.

Additionally, mobile sets mounted in 30cwt (1,527kg) Karrier Bantam road van, were stationed at Watford and at New Barnet. The protected control room at Knebworth, extending over two floors, was intended to house the Kings Cross staff of the LNER but was inadequate and had to be extended, with some staff accommodated in adjacent shops and a stabled railway coach.

To make the running and staffing of the railways more efficient, some wartime changes were made. Passenger services were withdrawn from Watton-at-Stone and Stapleford for the duration, and Attimore Hall Halt, on the Welwyn-Hertford branch line, was open only to freight, serving its adjacent factories. There was also expansion of the system when Lemsford Road Halt opened for workers in 1942 and new sidings were extended to serve military facilities, listed in an official document in the same year. These included the War Department records and pay office, in the old militia barracks in Barnet;

189 Field Ambulance RAMC, in the Thatched Barn on the Barnet Bypass; the War Office depot and mobilisation store, at Buntingford; 54th Divisional Signals, at Bishops College, Cheshunt; the Colliers End militia camp; the Ministry of Food PLA Buffer Depot No. 29, at Hemel Hempstead; and the RAF airfields at Hatfield Hyde, Hunsdon and Nuthampstead.

Watford, The Grove, base for a troop of volunteer cavalry in 1794 and taken over as offices by the London, Midland and Scottish Railway Company (LMS) in 1940.

Knebworth, the protected railway control room of the London North-Eastern Railway Company (LNER). It has been used as a church and currently, with an added floor, serves as apartments.

Hospitals and welfare

The RAMC, assisted by Queen Alexandra's Imperial Military Nursing Service, deployed over 120 British general hospitals during the war using a number of stopping-off locations between, mainly, overseas deployments. Those RAMC hospitals which had been evacuated from France in the summer of 1940 were accommodated temporarily at home. The former London Orphan Asylum (latterly known as Reed's School) in Watford became a military hospital for the duration. The 10th, 11th, 14th and 20th British General Hospitals (RAMC) spent time in Watford before new deployments to Gibraltar in November 1940, to Madagascar in June 1942, to India in January 1942 and to Bayeux in June 1944 respectively. Others of these hospitals in transit spent short periods of time in Hoddesdon and Hitchin.

Hatfield House was loaned by Lord Salisbury from 2 September 1939 right up to the end of the war. According to the official records, a succession of British general hospitals occupied Hatfield House for stays of between two and twenty months. The 17th British General Hospital came from France to Watford via Leeds before ending up at Hatfield House for fifteen months between November 1940 and February 1942, when it left for India. Several of these hospitals were formed at Hatfield before embarking on their travels. In all, sixteen RAMC hospital units passed through Hatfield, nine of which originated there. (See Appendix 10 for the full schedule.)

In anticipation of high civilian casualties and recognising the shortcomings of existing hospital arrangements, in 1939 the Ministry of Health was charged with establishing a national network of free hospitals. Existing hospitals were commandeered, new hutted hospitals constructed, a blood transfusion service set up and medical supplies stockpiled, all as parts of the Emergency Medical Service (EMS).

Prior to America's entry into the war, US army medics arrived in Britain to discuss the integration of medical services, with the subsequent allocation of some of the EMS facilities to the US army. Watford would become the HQ of the (chief) surgeon's office of the Eastern Base Section, Communications Zone, ETOUSA, administering the US army's medical provision. His staff comprised twelve officers and twelve enlisted men. Its region extended from the Scottish border to the Thames, taking in the eastern half of the country, which included major elements of the VIIIth and IXth USAAF.

North Mymms Park had become an auxiliary hospital in 1940 under the auspices of the British Red Cross but with the lady of the house, Mrs Burns, as commandant. Initially there were fifty-five beds, but this was later increased to sixty-six. The hospital treated almost 4,500 patients, both members of the armed services and civilian victims of air raids. After 1942, the Park was also the location of a large, hutted US general hospital.

Following a four-month stay by the 1st Surgical Auxiliary Group, the 1st US General Hospital arrived in January 1944, staying there until September, and sending a detachment to set up a new hospital in Herefordshire prior to D-Day. It was followed in January 1945 by the 7th US General Hospital for only a brief stay on its way to France. The hospital buildings consisted entirely of large numbers of Nissen and timber huts. At the end of the war, the hospital became a demobilisation camp for the ATS and other women's services. A US 750-bed general hospital is also recorded in Panshanger Park, built by the Ministry of War Production.

Shenley Psychiatric Hospital, the medical superintendent of which was the CO of a local TA unit, was built by Middlesex County Council during the 1930s. In 1939 many of its patients were discharged. Throughout the war, the hospital admitted both military and civilian casualties.

Watford General Hospital, with its Peace Memorial Wing, was taken into the EMS under the control of University College Hospital and staffed by nurses of QAIMNS. Its original 206 beds were increased to 310 to receive war casualties. Its patients included POWs from camps in the neighbourhood. Ashridge House was offered as an EMS hospital in 1939. Over thirty huts, each holding forty patients, were constructed as wards, along with an operating theatre, dispensary and laboratories. The hospital closed in 1946 and had been completely cleared away by 1980. Abbot's Langley Hospital had been an industrial school but was taken over as an annexe to Leavesden Hospital and requisitioned as an EMS facility in 1939, with brick-built huts in the grounds. The Bishop's Stortford Workhouse was also absorbed into the EMS, with two complexes of huts and a new nurses' home added.

St Bartholomew's Hospital, one of a only a handful of centres investigating the use of penicillin, was evacuated to Hill End Hospital, a mental health facility near St Albans. In Elstree, the Lister Institute, dedicated to promoting research into preventive medicine, contributed to the production of antisera and vaccines as well as, from 1940, research into biological warfare. This had been outlawed internationally in the Geneva Protocol of 1925, but research continued to ensure that defensive measures might be implemented, were they to become necessary. Its research into nutrition produced the National Loaf on behalf of the Federation of Bakers, set up in 1942, specifically to develop a replacement for white bread and to avoid bread rationing, which was only imposed after the war.

WELFARE

Most small towns, particularly those within easy reach of airfields or army camps, provided dedicated social facilities. Elstree Studios incorporated a 550-seat auditorium for hosting shows for the troops. In Bishops Stortford, 13 Apton Road became an officers' club run by the American Red Cross, and cinemas were permitted to open on Sundays to provide entertainment for the many US army engineers building the nearby airfield at Stansted.

A 300-bed hostel was opened by the American Red Cross on The Causeway in early 1944 to allow USAAF personnel, even thousands of miles from home, to enjoy leave. Royston's Congregational Church Sunday School was commandeered as an American Red Cross GI Club. On Akeman Street in Tring, the Victoria Hall was a venue for dances, and there was a YMCA Club in Tabernacle Yard, and Watford's YMCA in Clarendon Road.

Provision was also made for civilians to benefit from centrally planned feeding arrangements. Berkhamsted Town Hall served as a British Restaurant, cooking and serving communal meals, and in Bishops Stortford the British Restaurant was combined with the communal feeding station in South Street. One of the NAAFI's five main warehouses was in Watford.

Under the auspices of the Directorate of Army Psychiatry, civil resettlement units (CRU) were set up from 1943 for repatriated Allied POWs. When the trickle became a flood in 1945, it was agreed that the use of hutted camps, which were too closely associated with their previous accommodation, would be avoided. It was therefore decided that returning POWs should be housed in more luxurious settings graced with table service.

Twenty country houses were chosen, with Hatfield House being selected as the organisation's first unit and HQ. The units were managed by RAMC psychiatric and medical officers and staffed by members of the ATS. The POWs attended the week-long course in groups of sixty. In July 1945, publicity for the voluntary scheme was boosted when Hatfield House received a visit from the king and queen. The experience created by the overlap of personnel who had worked in both WOSBs and CRUs led to the establishment of the Tavistock Institute of Human Relations in 1947.

Air Raid Precautions (ARP)

Over 300 bombs fell fairly evenly across the whole of Hertfordshire during the war, the worst incident being a V-1 hit in Watford which caused many deaths and destroyed over fifty properties. In October 1940, a lone Junkers 88 bomber was distracted from its planned target by AA gunfire and dropped its bombs on the de Havilland factory in Hatfield, killing twenty-one workers and damaging parts being made for the new Mosquito fighter-bomber, then in the development stage. Crippled by anti-aircraft fire, the aircraft crashed nearby.

The previous month, five people had been killed when a pair of houses in Ware were bombed, and a parachute mine killed seventeen people in Bells Hill, Barnet, in November 1940, with at least a further dozen bombing victims in the Barnet area. A parachute mine landed on Tamworth Road in Hertford in September 1940, killing eleven people. Another such bomb on Cheshunt swimming baths destroyed the changing rooms but caused no casualties.

Between June 1944 and March 1945, eighty-two V-1 'doodlebugs' fell on Hertfordshire. The first of them hit Mill End, Watford, damaging over

300 houses but causing no fatalities. However, thirty-seven people were killed by the V-1 which fell on Sandringham Road, Watford, in July 1944. The Royal Masonic School in Bushey had a narrow escape when a V-1 careered across the roof of the school, at a height below the level of the clock tower, and exploded 400yds away. St Audrey's Senior School in Endymion Road, Hatfield, was less lucky when in October 1944 a V-1 destroyed the school along with houses in adjacent streets, killing nine residents. A V-1 fell on shops in Hertford but there were no casualties.

Thirty-four V-2 rockets would land between September 1944 and March 1945, making the county the local authority with the fourth highest number of such incidents after London. This was possibly the consequence of misleading information being fed back to German controllers through the XX System, sometimes resulting in rockets overshooting the capital and landing to its north. A V-2 landed on Calton Road, Barnet, killing twelve people, injuring a further 135 and demolishing eleven houses. Another V-2 landed near Little Gaddesden, fortunately causing no casualties. V-2s landed on Waltham Cross High Street on 2 January 1945, on College Road the next week, on Highbridge Street, and on allotments at Bishops Stortford the same month. On 29 March 1945, the very last enemy bomb to land on British soil was a V-1 which landed in a field near Datchworth without causing any casualties.

Despite the Building Research Station's plea for a centralised approach and Bernal's limited efforts to carry out proper scientific research into the effects of different types of bombing, provision remained ad hoc. Towns were responsible for merely following Home Office advice regarding ARP, resulting in varied levels of provision. In Harpenden, the Victoria Road schools, which had been closed since the 1920s, became the focus of local ARP, with a first-aid centre, a gas decontamination centre, two wards for medical casualties, as well as an evacuee reception centre. The town's ARP control was underground behind

Watford, The Grove, one of four entrances to air-raid shelters provided for LMS staff.

the fire station in Leyton Road, and an emergency fire station and air raid siren were located by the water tower in Shakespeare Road.

Concrete trenches were dug on the Heath Road common, with space for 400. In Bishops Stortford, one of several public shelters was built with a concrete roof, electric lights and seating for 700, while schools, business premises and private houses used existing cellars. In New Barnet, the town hall served as the ARP registration centre and the CD control was in the basement of East Barnet Town Hall, with an ARP reporting centre incorporated into the Dissenters' Chapel in Totteridge Lane. On the corner of Lytton and Leicester Roads in East Barnet was the fire station, built in 1905, with a sub-station at the Clockhouse Garage in Hampden Square.

As we have seen, The Grove, a country house outside Watford, (TQ081988) became the HQ of the LMS Railway Company, evacuated from Euston in September 1939. Four air-raid shelters (ARS) with pre-cast barrel-vaulted concrete panels for roofs were excavated, each containing square blocks of passages linked by corridors. Their entrances may still be found in the hotel grounds.

Agriculture: the Women's Land Army and harvest camps

Following on from the experience of the First World War, the Women's Land Army was reformed, and eventually, there would be over 2,100 land girls working in Hertfordshire. Training, for those fortunate to be enrolled on the two- to-three-week course, was carried out at Oaklands Agricultural College, in St Albans. However, some land girls, as they were officially known, were directed straight onto farms or nurseries, where they learned by either the tried and tested 'standing next to Nellie method' or being thrown in at the deep end.

Girls could be based in twos and threes on farms, or they could be assigned to work gangs based either in purpose-built hostels or billeted in large houses. Pendley Manor at Little Gaddesden accommodated thirty-four land girls in 1942. Other hostels were located in the St Albans golf clubhouse; Barnes Lodge, at Kings Langley; Watton, at Stone; Hollybush Lane, Hatfield Hyde, on what is now the ICI playing fields in Welwyn; in a prefabricated building in Rushden; in Berry Green House and Berry Green, Cheshunt Park; and Beaney, at Ringshall, on the Ashridge Estate.

There was a WLA depot for heavy agricultural equipment at Nettleden, and specialist courses for such skills as tractor driving were offered at Oaklands. Here, girls were taught to maintain, service and drive tractors using various attachments for ploughing. They also learned to diagnose faults and, where possible, repair their machines. All this, plus a bit of general animal husbandry, took a week, with both written and practical tests on Friday afternoon and

Potters Bar, Ganwick Farm, the Robins hangar provided by the Ministry of Supply for this farm with its complement of POWs.

Saturday morning. Oldings of Hatfield imported John Deere tractors from the USA and also developed their own models as mechanisation gradually advanced. As well as the land girls there were the lumberjills of the Timber Corps, some of whom were based near Berkhamsted. The timber might be shipped out on the Grand Union Canal on barges crewed by women.

There were never sufficient agricultural workers to meet the ever-increasing targets of the war agricultural committees, so POWs and schoolchildren were drafted into farm work. As well as long summer evenings spent harvesting or fruit picking, schools held protracted harvest camps. Merchant Taylors School, through its cadet corps, ran a couple of such camps in 1944, which generated 7,000 hours of voluntary work. Ganwick Farm, on Waggon Road, Potters Bar, became a camp for POW farmworkers, operating into the late 1940s, where the Ministry of Agriculture erected a Robins hangar and two Nissen huts, all still extant.

Warehouses in Beggars Lane, alongside the Grand Union Canal, in Berkhamsted, stored food stocks for emergency distribution, part of a network of buffer depots, an essential element in a strategic initiative by the Ministry of Food. Another Robins hangar was erected at the buffer depot in Bell Lane, Shenley, and ended up at the Salisbury Hall de Havilland Museum.

POW Camps

Batford, Camp No. 95, on Common Lane, in Harpenden, opened in May 1943 for 600 Italian POWs. They were initially accommodated in tents, which were gradually replaced by rows of huts with the standard water tower. By July 1944, the camp had been designated an Italian labour battalion camp, with the inmates, no longer enemy combatants, employed on local farms. In November the Italians moved out into hostels or lodged on farms and 750 German POWs moved in, mainly to be employed in agriculture. The camp had satellites at Hatfield Hyde, Lemsford and Stanborough.

The Wynches Camp at Much Hadham, Camp 411, covering forty acres (16ha) had been a training camp for the army, before holding a reported 10,000 POWs, first Italians and then Germans, as well as repatriated Allied POWs. Royston Heath, Camp 29, opened in 1941 with 300 Italian POWs in eight huts. Photographs show POWs working on the harvest, guarded by soldiers with fixed bayonets. By 1944, the site comprised twenty large huts, surrounded by a 12ft (3.7m)-high barbed-wire fence, accommodating the Italian former prisoners who were employed in agricultural work and general labouring.

In 1944, they were moved on and their places taken by German POWs. In 1948, the huts went to the local council as public housing. The precise sites of neither Gorhambury Park Camp nor The Arches, Felden, Hemel Hempstead, have ever been identified. Both shared the designation as Camp 235 so were probably linked. The Arches may only have operated after 1945, having been in use until then by the Polish radio intelligence company.

Rushden WLA hostel became an Italian POW camp, and Meesden, Camp 128, was a German work camp. Dancers Hill, at South Mimms, Camp 33, consisted of two tented compounds. The guards were accommodated in huts, an unusual, if understandable reversal of the usual arrangement in those circumstances, as the Geneva Convention stipulated the opposite situation should obtain. One of the prisoners' compounds was surrounded by a double wire fence. The second, containing only five tents, was guarded by two watchtowers.

8

Hertfordshire in the Cold War and Beyond 1945–2024

It should be remembered that the Women's Land Army continued in being up until 1949 and that POW camps were only gradually being relinquished up to that date. POWs began to be repatriated by late 1946 but more were still arriving from their stay in Canada. Batford Camp was not closed until July 1948, after which it served as public housing until 1958.

The US general hospital in the grounds of North Mymms Park was finally handed over to Hatfield RDC for adaptation as public housing, over 150 Nissens and timber huts being partitioned and supplied with a water supply and a low level of electric power. Fifty of the Nissens were auctioned off in 1955.

The Mill Green airfield construction camp housed displaced persons for a while after the war and was only relinquished by the RAF in 1948. It then housed construction workers for the Welwyn Garden City and Hatfield Development Corporation. The domestic area is now a caravan park.

Not until 1963 was the old Royston Militia Camp adopted as the site for a new school. The equestrian facilities at Theobalds have been used by the Metropolitan Police for Mounted Branch training.

The armed forces in Hertfordshire

Whilst hosting few active defence facilities in post-war Britain, Hertfordshire nevertheless is home to important defence assets of command and control and munitions development and production.

THE REGULAR ARMY, TA AND ARMY RESERVE

The TA was reconstituted in 1947 with the Hertfordshire Regiment and the 5th Battalion, Bedfordshire and Hertfordshire Regiment in 162 Infantry Brigade. The Hertfordshires and brigade signals were based in Hertford barracks. Retaining its HQ in Barnet, 479 HAA Regiment was reconstituted, only to be disbanded in 1954 ahead of the total closing down of AA Command. It was absorbed into 286 Regiment in St Albans in 1955 as a field artillery regiment armed with 5.5in. medium guns towed by Matador tractors attached to 54th (East Anglian) Division.

Two batteries from Hitchin and Hertford moved into the Lemsford Lane drill hall in Welwyn, with the third battery at Croxley Green. By 1961, the Hertfordshire element of 286 (Hertfordshire and Bedfordshire Yeomanry) Field Regiment had been reduced to a single 'R' Battery at St Albans, with one section at Croxley Green and the Light Aid Detachment (REME) at Welwyn. An army recruiting office was located in St Peter's Institute in Hatfield Road, St Albans.

As the Cold War became progressively colder, an attempt was made by the new Conservative government to resurrect the Home Guard. Groups of former home guardsmen, like those who had shot in their CO's back garden in Stevenage and gone on to form the Stevenage Home Guard Rifle Club after the war, sometimes stayed together for mainly social purposes. However, shooting for fun and camaraderie was one thing, but going back to compulsory drills was something else, so recruitment was slow as the country was reluctant to go back into uniform.

Hertfordshire's Home Guard gained national notoriety for naming a weekend exercise in September 1952 as Operation Lumbago. It was felt by Churchill and the War Office that portraying the new force as a collection of

St Albans, Camp Road, the converted bakery which became a TAC for the artillery. It has since been demolished for housing.

Hemel Hempstead, the TAC now redeveloped.

'old crocks', as the *Daily Graphic and Sketch* so sensitively put it, might not be conducive to raising the profile of the force. Only Churchill's enthusiasm kept the idea alive, but out of a projected strength of 900,000, recruitment never exceeded 80,000, with many of those enrolled being retired officers and older veterans rather than the healthy young technicians the task demanded.

Hitchin Army Reserve Centre, currently still in use.

Following Churchill's resignation in 1955, the force, robbed of its most ardent supporter, dwindled away, until finally being disbanded in 1957.

New drill halls were built in Tolpits Lane, Croxley Green (1951) and Hemel Hempstead (1955). In 1987, the Holywell Hill drill hall in St Albans was demolished to be replaced by a leisure centre, and a redundant bakery in Camp Road was acquired and converted as a TAC for the 201 Hertfordshire and Bedfordshire Yeomanry Medium Battery, 100th (Yeomanry) Field Regiment RA (TA). This unit would later be equipped with the FH70 155mm howitzer but not the space or the personnel required, realistically, to sustain this hefty weapon. It closed in 2000 to be re-developed for housing. The Bedford Road ARC in Hitchin was refurbished for re-opening in 2023, and as of 2024, it houses a company of the 3rd Battalion, Royal Anglian Regiment, and 'D' Squadron of 254 (East of England) Medical Regiment.

CADETS

As of 2023, uniformed cadet organisations are growing in popularity, offering opportunities for training in life-skills and character-building activities in a disciplined environment. Bedfordshire and Hertfordshire ACF is organised into five companies, each with eight detachments across the counties, including Hertford, Hitchin, Royston, Watford and St Albans.

There are eight ATC flights in the county, including those at Letchworth, Harpenden, Hatfield and Stevenage. The county's six sea cadet detachments include Welwyn, St Albans and Stevenage. The CCF thrives in a number of

Haileybury College, the rifle range of 1903, upgraded in more recent times. (*Mike Bardell*)

schools. At John Warner School in Hoddesdon, the detachment has grown from thirty members to 120 and gained independence from its partner detachment at St Edmund's, Ware, which shares its training with Goff's Academy in Cheshunt. The CCF at St Albans School is combined with Marlborough Science Academy and includes army and RAF sections, whilst that at Queen Elizabeth's, Barnet. is affiliated to the Royal Engineers.

Other CCF contingents operate at Aldenham's and Haberdashers' Aske's Schools in Elstree; Haileybury College, its cadet unit dating back to 1886; Merchant Taylor's, in Northwood; Berkhamsted School, affiliated to the Welsh Guards, and possessed of an RAF section; and Queens' School, Bushey. The Rickmansworth ACF trains alongside the Royal Masonic School for Girls.

HMS *WARRIOR*, PERMANENT JOINT HQ, NORTHWOOD

In 1953, NATO's eastern-Atlantic military-command structure was set up at Northwood. In 1960 the C-in-C home fleet moved to Northwood, and three years later the RN element was commissioned as HMS *Warrior*, soon to be joined by NATO's Channel Command. Cold War planning located the NATO Wartime Civil Agency for Ocean Shipping, the body responsible for coordinating trans-Atlantic merchant shipping, at Northwood. An assessment by the Joint Intelligence Committee in 1967 helpfully anticipated that the Northwood HQ would attract two airburst 1–3 megaton bombs in any Soviet assault. Eastbury Park, acquired by the RAF in 1938, burnt down in 1969, and the RAF then vacated the site.

In 1971, the post of C-in-C fleet was established, joined by flag officer submarines in 1978. By 1980, Northwood was the primary control centre for the Royal Navy's nuclear submarines carrying Polaris ICBMs as the nation's nuclear deterrent. The expeditionary force to the Falkland Islands in 1982 was directed from Northwood, and in 1996, the Permanent Joint HQ was established. In 2019, Joint Forces Command was renamed Strategic Command. The buildings, radically rebuilt in 2010, host four permanent joint tri-service HQs, including NATO Allied Maritime Command, all staffed by 2,000 personnel. The Royal Navy Reserve (RNR) unit HMS *Wildfire* resumed its place on the Northwood campus in 2011.

RAF AIRFIELDS

At the end of the war, there had been a gradual run-down of aviation sites. Nuthampstead served as a sub-site of RAF Nos. 94 and 95 MUs between 1945 and 1954, but after a period in care and maintenance, the airfield was finally shut down in 1959. RAF No. 2 Squadron at Sawbridgeworth was one of the last units to belong to No. 123 (Rocket Projectile) Wing in 1947 before its transfer to Germany where the wing was disbanded.

Bovingdon was assigned to the 3rd USAF Air Division in 1949 and supported contractors flying civilian aircraft during the Berlin Airlift of 1948–49. With the effective return of the USAF to Britain, Bovingdon housed its transport aircraft and also hosted flights by the US navy's Privateer and Mercator spy planes, normally based at Blackbushe, in Hampshire. American use had tailed off by 1962, but the RAF used Bovingdon for its communications flights up until 1969. Much of the site is now occupied by a prison but a fragment of the watch office may still stand.

Hunsdon was placed in care and maintenance in May 1945 and finally closed in July 1947. Very little remains beyond the parachute store (17865/39), some sleeping shelters, the BHQ (11008/41) and some Air Ministry-designed pillboxes. After the end of the war, Panshanger's involvement in training pilots continued when it became No. 1 Reserve Flying School in 1947, flying Tiger Moths. Re-equipped with Chipmunks it operated until March 1953, when it closed and reverted to use by private aircraft. Broxbourne had resumed private flying after the war but never recovered from a disastrous fire, and the club moved to Stapleford Tawney, in Essex.

Prior to the acquisition of the US missile systems which would constitute the nuclear deterrent carried in the Royal Navy's submarines, a number of homegrown projects were initiated. One of de Havilland's projects was the intermediate-range ballistic missile (IRBM) Blue Streak. This missile was designed to be 'hot-launched' from underground silos. In 1959, when the system was expected to go into deployment as a weapon of retaliation after a Soviet first strike, owing to its proximity to their place of manufacture in Hatfield, RAF Duxford. in Cambridgeshire, was added to the list of possible Blue Streak silos. The redundant ROTOR site at Chenies (see below) was also considered as a possible location for a silo, but in the event, the missile never reached the production stage.

Defence against nuclear attack

AIR DEFENCE

After the descent of the Iron Curtain, a complete reorganisation of Britain's AA defences, known as ROTOR, was carried out. This relied on electrically operated HAA guns receiving their instructions from a network of radar stations housed in a mixture of temporary surface buildings and underground bunkers.

Chenies, between Bovingdon and Chorleywood (TQ015999), was a ground control interception (GCI) radar station planned for 1953 and linked to the sector operations centre at Kelvedon Hatch, in Essex. Considered to be in a 'safe' inland area, its R8 surface, double-height control building was housed in unprotected, prefabricated SECO huts of wood-fibre and asbestos panels.

It had originally been located at Heathrow but, instead, was transferred to this greenfield site, the only such station to be accommodated in anything other than a pre-existing structure.

The Fighter Command control unit from Heathrow removed to Chenies in 1954, when its existing staff was replaced by No. 163 Signals Unit. There being no domestic accommodation onsite, personnel were brought in by bus every day from RAF Bovingdon, 2 miles away. The only radars installed at Chenies were six Type 13 and 14 radars mounted on plinths in the surrounding fields, with an American FPS3 radar scheduled to arrive in mid-1953, but there were never plans to install the latest Type 80 radar, which had begun to appear in some of the south-coast stations. However, this lack would soon become academic, as rapid developments in aeronautical technology rendered AA Command redundant, and it was disbanded in 1956.

The ROTOR stations, including Chenies, had closed by 1958, when a new plan based on fewer, more powerful radars, coupled with surface-to-air missiles (SAM) came into operation. With new equipment housed in a brick building, the Chenies site then became an RAF Strike Command communications centre, connected into the NATO network, and manned round the clock on a four-shift rotation. Aerials, one of which was 100ft (31m) high, were mounted on wooden lattice masts.

Then, in the mid-1980s, it became the location for a Meteorological Office radar. According to Subterranean Britannica's reports and a more recent site visit, most of the ROTOR-era buildings have been demolished, and it is unlikely that any radar plinths have survived, with nothing being readily visible.

THE ROYAL OBSERVER CORPS IN THE COLD WAR

At the same time that ROTOR was being developed, the ROC, having been stood down in 1945, was resurrected to continue its role as an aircraft-spotting body. In 1948 it was proposed to equip ROC posts with radar as and when the appropriate low-level sets might become available. This plan would be overtaken by events, but it was a team consisting of two men and a woman from No. 17 Group, Watford, which was selected as the first team to operate the system.

A wholesale reorganisation of the existing posts saw several hundred being relocated and additional posts installed. As opposed to the haphazard improvisation of many of the wartime posts, a purpose-built structure was commissioned from ORLIT of Colnbrook in West London. The new post was a cuboid measuring roughly 10×7×7ft (3×2×2m), constructed from prefabricated concrete panels, half of which would be roofed over to protect the instruments. Type 'A' stood on a concrete raft at ground level, and Type 'B' was raised around 6ft (2m) off the ground by concrete legs and accessed by an integral stair. The tracking instruments were mounted on a wooden pedestal in the open section. The Watford HQ of No. 17 Group until 1953, and of No. 5 Group until 1968, remained in Cassiobury Drive in the wartime sectional surface building.

The same factors which signalled the end for HAA artillery, namely speed and height of flight, also saw the end of visual aircraft spotting as a viable early-warning technique. As it happened, however, far from becoming redundant, the volunteers of the ROC were quickly assigned a new role within the UK Warning and Monitoring Organisation.

Coping with the threat of nuclear attack implied a need to locate strikes and to assess the level of radioactive fallout. This was a job the ROC could carry out, its network of 1,500 posts, spread across the whole of Britain, being ideally situated for the task. ORLIT was again commissioned, this time to produce an underground post. This consisted of another concrete box measuring 20×8×7ft (6×2.5×2.3m), buried around 6ft (1.8m) underground and accessed down a vertical, steel rung ladder, in a 15ft (4.5m)-deep shaft entered through a hatch. Inside were two bunks, a chemical toilet, a desk, and a radio or telephone, all lit by a strip light powered by a car battery. On the surface were instruments which recorded the size and location of a strike and measured ambient radioactivity. These very basic instruments were gradually improved over the years.

The existing group HQ in Cassiobury Drive was upgraded in 1961 to a 'semi-sunken protected' bunker, retaining its double-height control room,

Brent Pelham, a fine example of an Orlit 'B' elevated ROC aircraft spotting post.

with galleries overlooking the plotting table, but all under a more robust roof and equipped with better ventilation equipment. However, following another reorganisation of ROC Groups, Watford was declared surplus to requirement in 1968, with its functions transferred to the Metropolitan Sector HQ at Uxbridge, in the London Borough of Hillingdon. It was retained until 1973 as the metropolitan area training centre but released for public sale in 1974, whereafter it would accommodate a veterinary practice.

Of the county's sixteen posts, ten changed their location at some stage in their lives, often having been originally sited in poorly drained locations unconducive to their new subterranean existence. The scheme which saw the closure of the Watford HQ also saw the closure of six posts, leaving the remaining ten spread across three groups, only being closed in 1990 when the ROC was stood down as part of the 'peace dividend'.

Of these ten, six appear to have survived, including Ashwell, Hertford and Brent Pelham, which retains a fine example of a Type 'B' ORLIT post, adjacent to the later underground post.

Left: Hertford (Bramfield), the underground ROC post with the instrumentation for locating nuclear strikes.

Below: Watford, Cassiobury Drive, the protected ROC Group 5 control centre, built in 1961 and operational until 1968, being used only for training until 1973.

COMMUNICATIONS NETWORKS

National defence during the Cold War was predicated on the ability to retaliate swiftly to any nuclear attack by activating the nuclear deterrent. The 'mutually assured destruction' doctrine was entirely dependent on early warning systems and effective communications.

The network of intervisible microwave towers for the transmission of information in the event of a nuclear attack, whose best-known example is the GPO/BT Tower in London's Tottenham Court Road, was named 'Backbone'. The GPO Tower was intended to be the model for all of other towers, designed to be built as concrete cylinders. However, the Backbone tower at Pimlico (TL088045), linked to Stokenchurch (Buckinghamshire)

Below left: Pimlico, the microwave tower which was part of the 'Backbone' early-warning system.

Below right: Barkway, the radio tower used as part of the GEE bomber guidance system and then by the USAF in the same system as the Bovingdon tower.

to its west and Kelvedon Hatch (Essex) to its east, is a guyed steel lattice construction, originally designed as merely a link to another tower at Tring, which never materialised.

The towers, which carry parabolic dish aerials, are generally located in open country to avoid damage from the bombardment of urban areas. Pimlico also had further microwave links to towers at Dunstable to the north, and to Harrow Weald to its south, linking with Birmingham and London respectively. This connectivity became more important than its projected role in the mainline Backbone network. Pimlico is also co-located with the Bedmond tower, part of the Home Office 'Hilltop' network, which was used for the co-ordination of the police and TA in internal security operations.

Another Hilltop radio station (TL355364) at Reed, near Royston, also linked to the ROC control at Bedford. The Sandridge wartime intercept station was rehabilitated as a further Hilltop station, today signposted 'HOSDB' (Home Office Scientific Development Branch). The USAF also operated its own parallel network of microwave communications relay stations linking its bases in the eastern counties. Aerials at Barkway (TL372365 and 381364) and Bovingdon (TL013047) were all used by USAF(E) 10th Communications Squadron, based in the United Kingdom 1959–62, and remained in military use until 2011. Pimlico continues in use with British Telecom and Belmond is a TV repeater transmitter.

EMERGENCY MEASURES

Provision was made for the continuance of national government after a nuclear attack using a mix of underground bunkers and the decentralisation of governmental functions. Region 4 would cover the eastern counties, and a Sub-Regional Control (4.2) occupied the basement of the five-storey Sovereign House, the recently demolished government offices in Hertford. This protected bunker would, in the event of a nuclear attack, have accommodated a local commissioner, representatives of key government ministries, armed forces, police, a BBC studio, and members of medical, health and welfare organisations, in all a staff of 180 personnel. The two-level bunker had walls 20–30in. (50–75cm) thick; its own borehole for water, with 150,000gal. (675,000L) stored in permanent tanks; a generator with reserve fuel capable of powering the whole operation for one month; a filtration system which would rinse fallout dust; and an aerial to enable communication with other bunkers; and the BBC's transmitters. The bunker was given a protection rating of 400—a meaningless figure until compared with the rating of the average domestic building: 5–10.

Local authorities were similarly required to parallel such provision for a complement of around eighty. The basement of Hertfordshire County Hall would act as the main wartime HQ, with parallel accommodation in the Hemel Hempstead District Council offices as a standby wartime HQ. Both locations, however, were described as inadequate. Three Civil Defence (CD) control centres had been planned for the county: the North Control in

Hertford, Sovereign House, whose basement contained Sub-Regional HQ 4.2, a subsidiary of the regional seat of government in Cambridge. It has recently been demolished. (*Subterranea Britannica and Howard Martin*)

Hitchin, which was never completed; the Western Control, at Carpender's Park in Watford, possibly in the old house which had been a girls' school and was demolished in 1960 for USAF married quarters; and the South-west Control built in the former Reed's School, Watford, between 1953 and 1956, where government departments continued to occupy buildings into the 1980s.

Dacorum Borough's Emergency Centre was built in 1966 in the basement of the civic centre in Hemel Hempstead. In the 1950s, London was divided into four sectors with the wartime HQ for the North London Group of boroughs (sub-region control 5.1A), established in a single-storey bunker at the Barnet Council site in Partingdale Lane, on the boundary of the old Borough of Barnet. Despite grave misgivings over the efficacy of all these measures, characterised by the declaration of 'nuclear-free zones' by some authorities, the Thatcher government continued to urge local authorities to maintain the pretence of offering dubious security against nuclear attack.

Just one year before the collapse of the Soviet Union, the St Albans and District Emergency Centre, located in the basement of the Council Offices, was built in 1989 to replace an earlier bunker in the basement of the Magistrates' Court. Bunkers such as that in Partingdale Lane might continue as a local control, in this case, Barnet Borough Emergency Control, but many simply lapsed. Since 1990, most national and local bunkers have been disposed of or have been adapted for document storage, as at Dacorum, where the heavy blast doors have now been removed.

Another measure taken by the government to ensure any survivors of a nuclear attack might be fed was the establishment of buffer depots stockpiling staple foods such as flour, sugar, tinned fish, meat, vegetables, margarine, and milk powder. The Ministry of Agriculture, Fisheries and Food (MAFF) administered depots across the country, equipped to deliver relief to stricken areas.

Depots in Hertfordshire included The Drift, Royston; two in Hoddesdon: (No. 19) and 4 Hertford Road (No. 4F); Marshmoor Sidings, Hatfield; New Ground, Tring (No. 4M); Goodwyns Halt, Hemel Hempstead (No. 36); and 90 Manor Way, Borehamwood. A very small proportion of these depots stored mobile bakeries. Fuel depots and the pipelines which supplied them, vital components of NATO infrastructure, would be closely guarded, and one task for the police would be to shut petrol stations down to deny mobility to civilians, who, in any case, would have been ordered to stay put but might have been tempted to escape densely populated potential target areas.

To ensure that roads remained completely open for use by the armed forces and the delivery of emergency supplies, many major roads were designated as 'essential service routes' (ESR). These would be controlled by armed soldiers of the TA. In Hertfordshire, they included the M1, A1, A41 and A10 (ESRs 3, 4, and 5) as well as the cross-country A110 (ESR 4a). Troops would prevent these roads from being clogged by motorists attempting to escape from London, even were they able to obtain any fuel.

Additionally, a Military Road Route System was designed to link military ports, strategic airfields, and centres of production with minimal interference from civilian traffic. The A1 (STAG) and M1 (BAT) were the key north-south routes in this system, while the A41 and A414 (ELK) allowed traffic to or from Colchester Garrison or the US military port of Felixstowe to access the west of England whilst avoiding London. At the same time that efforts were under way to keep refugees off the roads, rural county councils, especially those bordering conurbations, were devising plans for barring urban refugees. Martial law in region 4 would be administered by the officer commanding Colchester Garrison, and in 1982 the regional police commander was the chief constable of Suffolk.

Had Hertfordshire residents been able to see the Soviet Union's target list, they might have felt reassured that only three local sites were listed: Hatfield and Hitchin, listed as major defence contractors in government documents, and the Northwood command centre. On the other hand, had these sites been targeted, the whole county would have been obliterated as collateral damage.

Munitions production

De Havilland and its licensees built over 3,000 Vampire jet fighters which remained in service with the RAF until 1966. The improved Venom entered service with the RAF and the Royal Navy in 1952, its naval version being deployed on aircraft carriers until 1962. The Sea Vixen served with the RN into the 1970s under the Hawker Siddeley label. Coming into service in 1947, a new 6,000yds (5,540m) long runway with half-width extensions at each end was laid at Hatfield.

De Havilland built several large hangars at Hatfield, including a flight-test hangar for the Comet programme in 1952–54. When it was built, it was the largest aluminium building in the world, designed to accommodate the four Comet aircraft which would later provide the basis for the Nimrod airborne early-warning aircraft. The Comet hangar has a clear height of 45ft (13.8m), a clear floor area span of 200ft (61m) and a length of 330ft (101m). There is an integral block of offices, a fire station and a six-storey air traffic control tower, added in 1954. Fifty years later it would be converted into a sports-and-leisure centre. A new assembly hall opened at Hatfield in September 1986 for the BAC 146, but the de Havilland offices fronting the A1 were facing demolition in 1988.

The Hatfield site provides an overview of the post-war aeronautics industry. The de Havilland Propeller company, on Hatfield's Manor Road site, had switched production to turbo-alternators for guided missiles, operating through the 1960s and developing and testing Firestreak, Sea Dart and Blue Streak, among others. The same site accommodated engine test facilities for such as the Olympus engine for the aborted TSR2, considered the ancestor of the Tornado; test beds for Rolls Royce and Saunders Roe; and for the Merlin, Gnome, Ghost and Gem aircraft and rocket engines.

The majority of this extensive complex with all its history was demolished in the early 1990s, leaving little as a reminder. The de Havilland administration and canteen building now houses Hatfield Police Station, with adjacent gatehouse buildings in commercial use. Astwick Manor, in Coopers Green Lane, became the former British Aerospace (previously de Havilland) Technical School, which had moved from Salisbury Hall 1947–48 into the manor house, with residential student accommodation added in the 1950s, along with the re-erection of the Airspeed aircraft hangar from Salisbury Hall.

The manor has since been converted to apartments and the hangar demolished. Now standing at Duxford and housing storage facilities for the Moth Club members who keep the old DH models flying is a hut from de Havilland's original site in Stag Lane. Formerly housing the company's offices, it had been taken to Hatfield as the de Havilland Museum and, after de Havilland's demise, to Farnborough, where it was refurbished before final relocation to the domestic site at Duxford.

Leavesden became de Havilland's main aero-engine production facility after the war, continuing this work under Bristol Siddeley, and then Rolls Royce until 1994. Factory 1 then became a film studio, since completely rebuilt, and Factory 2 was demolished.

Hatfield, the de Havilland Comet hangar.

In Colney Street, Handley Page developed the Hastings as a passenger-and-freight aircraft for the RAF, the largest such aircraft to date, and given priority over the civil Hermes. It arrived in service in time to contribute significantly to the Berlin Airlift. It could carry thirty-two paratroopers; thirty-two stretcher cases or twenty-eight seated casualties; fifty troops with

Hatfield, Astwick Manor, once the de Havilland Technical School, removed from Salisbury Hall.

their equipment; or jeeps and light artillery pieces, remaining in service until 1977. In 1952 it was necessary to expand and modernise the factory buildings in order to accommodate the new V-bomber project.

The Handley Page Victor, together with the Avro Vulcan and the Vickers Valiant, comprised Britain's bomber force for delivering nuclear weapons. The Victor first flew in February 1956 at Radlett, and eighty-six of them were subsequently built. When the RAF relinquished responsibility for the nuclear deterrent to the Royal Navy's Polaris nuclear-powered submarines in 1969, some Victors were converted into aerial-refuelling tankers and others to fulfil airborne-radar and long-range reconnaissance roles. Victors refuelled the Vulcans which bombed Stanley airport during the Falklands Conflict of 1981, only being finally retired in 1993.

In the 1960s, the company designed an air portable hangar for the RAF capable of being erected by six men in little over four hours that would house a pair of fighter aircraft. The final aircraft supplied to the RAF was the Jetstream, a twelve-to-twenty-seat passenger aircraft. By this time the company was in financial trouble, and although sixty-odd Jetstream airframes were constructed at Radlett, they were completed elsewhere after the company went into administration in 1970.

Since the war, several defence companies have been based in Stevenage. In the 1960s the government, in reaction to the overcapacity resulting from the existence of too many aircraft manufacturers, insisted on mergers. The Stevenage New Town Development Corporation encouraged high-tech firms to the town and built them bespoke factories, mainly on the Gunnels Wood Road industrial area. English Electric Aviation Ltd., having established a factory in 1955, became the British Aircraft Corporation (BAC) in 1960 and produced the Swingfire and Vigilant A/T missiles and the Thunderbird and Rapier SAMs.

De Havilland, by now Hawker Siddeley Dynamics, established a new factory in 1956 in Stevenage. As weapons development gained in complexity (it *was* rocket science, after all) research and development facilities at Hatfield, for de Havillands, and at Stevenage, for the BAC, required extensive estates. De Havillands won the contract to develop the Blue Streak, an IRBM. This project, not expected to be completed before 1969, was cancelled in 1960.

English Electric, meanwhile, had won the contract for Blue Water, a surface-to-surface ship-borne missile. When this, too, was cancelled in 1963, 1,500 jobs were lost and the company was forced to consolidate all its work in its remaining Stevenage factory, then continued as BAC. Matra Marconi was an Anglo-French collaboration launched in 1990. Its Stevenage factory was taken over from GEC in 1999 by British Aerospace.

From 2001, MBDA, a joint venture between Airbus, BAE Systems and Leonardo, based on the Stevenage site opened in 1954, has been developing a range of missile systems. Weapons systems previously developed by BAC have continued in production, along with the Storm Shadow cruise missile and the air-launched ground-attack Brimstone, both for use by the RAF. Other companies engaged in servicing the aviation industry were W. H. Sanders Electronics, manufacturing aircraft radar components in its 1954 Stevenage factory.

Virtually all the premises on the Gunnels Wood Road and its environs have been demolished and replaced by new factories such as the massive Airbus plant. IrvinGQ in Letchworth worked in conjunction with Martin-Baker's ejector-seat manufactory to provide essential safety systems for jet combat aircraft such as the Hawk, Jaguar and Typhoon, along with parachute braking for the aircraft themselves. The development of aerial drop equipment, including parachutes and pallets for aerial delivery, has continued to 'enhance the capabilities of airborne forces'.

RAILWAYS

In 1953, plans were put into place to establish emergency railway control centres in British Rail's Eastern region for the evacuation of Kings Cross to Knebworth, of St Pancras to St Albans and of Euston to Bricket Wood. By 1956, protected centres had been completed at Knebworth and Bricket Wood. Further plans were in place for the evacuation of the 2,400 HQ staff to Frogmore Hall, Watton-at-Stone; district engineers to a private house in Stevenage; some of the King's Cross staff to the Knebworth control centre, which would require supplementary hutting; and the seventy-five-strong staff from the district engineer's office in Stratford, east London, to Hertford East Station.

The wartime emergency control centre at Knebworth (TL249202) dating from 1939, but brought up to scratch in the 1950s, stands immediately to the south of Knebworth Station. Used until recently as a church, it now serves as housing. The post-war Bricket Wood (TL135021) Type 'L' building of 1954 survives, along with unprotected office buildings, initially as a store for Travis Perkins and currently as the depot for a scaffolding company, at the north-east end of the station carpark. These were two of only three such bunkers completed in the region, since at St Albans only the concrete floor slab was ever laid. An Eastern region mobile emergency control based at Hitchin was sold off in 1979.

Fortunately, it has never proved necessary to mobilise any of these precautionary facilities.

Appendix I

Prehistoric Forts and Defended Settlements

Arbury Banks, Ashwell (TL262387), hillfort
Gatesbury (TL395240), late Iron Age ditched enclosure
Gorhambury (TL118079), Iron Age dwellings within enclosure
Hexton, Ravensburgh Castle (TL099295), hillfort
Letchworth, Wilbury Hill (TL202325), hillfort
Redbourn, The Aubreys (TL095113), hillfort
St Albans, Prae Wood, Verlamion, supposed successor *oppidum* to Wheathampstead
Welwyn, Iron Age settlements
Wheathampstead, the Devils Dyke and The Slad, may represent a Belgic *oppidum*

Appendix II

Castles, Moated Sites and Strong Houses

Earthwork castles

Anstey (TL404330) large motte and wet moat

Barkway, Periwinkle Hill (TL373360), possible ploughed-out earthwork castle

Great Berkhamsted (SP995082), motte and bailey, later developed in stone

Great Wymondley (TL215285), motte and bailey within a larger enclosure

Hertford (TL325125), motte and bailey, later developed in stone

Pirton (TL147316), oval motte, bailey and possible village enclosure

Sandon, The Mount (TL329346), a possible ringwork, later adapted as a mill mound

South Mimms (TL230026), motte and bailey with a timber keep embedded in its motte

Therfield (TL331371), motte, bailey and possible village enclosure

Walkern Bury (TL305260), oval ringwork with an outer bank and ditch

Widford, Barrow Hill (TL417168), possible motte with a water-filled ditch

Stone castles

Benington (TL297236), earthworks and a square Norman keep

Great Berkhamsted (SP995082) motte with keep, bailey walls and square tower

Hertford (TL325125), motte, remains of masonry tower and walls, and C15 brick gatehouse

Hoddesdon, Rye House (TL386099), imposing C15 brick gatehouse and three sides of a square moat contained within a larger five-sided ditched enclosure

Strong houses

Barkway, Newsells Park, demolished following a fire in 1943
Bygrave (TL266361), traces of two fortified manor houses licensed in 1386
Hadham Hall, Little Hadham (TL452228), its west range contains an altered C15 gatehouse
Hatfield (TL236085), Bishop Morton's palace of 1480–90, includes a hall and gatehouse range, with a further gatehouse fronting onto the high street
Hunsdon (TL419128), house of Sir John Oldhall incorporating a-C15 gatehouse
Knebworth House (TL230207), quadrangular brick house with C15 gatehouse, built by Sir John Hotoft and added to by the Lytton family
Much Hadham, The Palace (TL431196), former residence of bishops of London now encased in later re-building
Rickmansworth, the Manor of the More (TQ081940), double moat of grand courtyard house
St Albans Abbey Great Gatehouse of 1357 (TL144071)
Shenley, Salisbury Hall (TL195028), moated house built by Henry VIII's Treasurer
Standon, The Lordship (TL393214), four-centred archway and reconstructed corner turret of the courtyard house of 1546

Moated sites

Albury, Cockhamstead (TL419252), moat
Aldenham, Penn's Place (TQ166969), moated site consisting of two rectangular islands
Ardeley Bury (TL301271), square moat
Ashridge, Great Coldharbour Farm (SP988112), possible moat
Ashwell (TL263395), moat; and Mobbs Hole (TL263437), moat.
Ashwell End (TL252402), moat
Aston Bury (TL276217), possibly once moated
Astwick Manor (TL204100), irregularly shaped moated site
Bengeo Temple Farm (TL340178), moated grange of templars turned over to hospitallers
Brent Pelham Hall (TL434309); Down Hall Farm (TL436306); and Chamberlains Moat (TL434316), with a large rectangular platform
Brickendonbury (TL329104), moat
Broxbourne, Hell Wood (TL356047), moat, and Factory Farm (TL350051), moat
Buckland (TL339339), moat, and Bull Moat (TL356340), moat

Caldecote (TL236384), moat

Cheshunt Great House (TL346027), foundations; Half Moat Manor (TL345025), the site of Cheshunt Manor, moat (TL348003); and Theobalds Palace, Cedars Park (TL355011), moated manor

Clothall, The Gables (TL272315), moat; and Kingswoodbury Lodge (TL291314), moat

Colliers End, Roughground Wood (TL37.20), rectangular moat 360x86ft (110x26m)

Cottered, Lordship House (TL319292), C15 moat; and further moats at TL323292, and TL330282

Eastwick, Home Wood (TL432124), moated site; similar moat (TL430125) across the valley

Epping Green, Woodcock Lodge (TL290068), moat; and Birchwood (TL284058), moat

Furneux Pelham Hall (TL428280), one arm of a moat to west of the house; and another moat at TL425291

Gilston, Overhall Farm (TL440135), moat; further moats at TL440112 and TL445123

Great Munden, Baxters Spring (TL340240), moat; and Mill Farm (TL344250), moat

Hexton, Pegsdon (TL117303), moat

High Down House (TL144305), moat

High Wych, Blounts Farm (TL457179), almost circular moat; and Mathams Wood (TL463180), moat

Holwell, Lordship Farm (TL161329), moat

Hormead Hall (TL405304), circular moat

Hunsdonbury, Olives Farm (TL409126), moat

Jenningsbury Farm (formerly Juvenellesburg) (TL341119), moat enclosing 4 acres (1.75ha)

Kings Langley, Little London (TL077018), expanded moated site for royal hunting lodge

Layston, Owles Hall (TL376287), traces of a circular moat

Letchworth, Norton Bury (TL236349), moat

Little Hadham, Old Green Street (TL455220), two arms of a former moat

Long Marston (SP894156), moat

Monken Hadley, (TQ245976), moat

Much Hadham, Brands Farm (TL415190), moat; Green Tye (TL440183), moat; Kettle Green (TL417182), wet moat surrounding later house; Camwell Hall (TL417176), vestiges of moats; The Lordship (TL429199), dry moat with causeway; and South End (438166 and 441169), moats

Newnham (TL242376), rectangular moat perpetually fed by springs, house demolished

Northchurch, Marlin Chapel Farm (SP964071), large, moated enclosure in the north-west quadrant of which is a smaller square enclosure measuring 310×275ft (95×85m), with a partly water-filled moat

Nuthampstead, The Warren (TL420343), unfinished moated site

Pirton Grange (TL123329), moat with timber-framed gatehouse with portcullis; Burge End, Hammonds Farm (TL144324), moat; and Rectory Manor Farm (TL141320), moat

Reed Hall (TL360356), moat with parts of a manor house dated to 1430; Bush Wood (TL371357), moat; Gannock Grove (TL368355), moat; Queenbury (TL362359), moat; and Reed End, Mardleybury (TL350365), moat

Roxford (TL304104), moat adjoining River Lea

Sandon (TL324342), moat; Five House Farm (TL338338); Friars Grange (TL319329), moats; Roe Green (TL314335); and Wood Farm (TL324325), moats

South Mimms, Fold Farm (TQ225975), moat

Stanstead Abbots (TL402139), Moat Wood, moat

Stevenage, Whomerley Wood (TL246236), moat

Stocking Pelham Hall (TL448294), two arms of a moat; and (TL454293), moat

Thorley, Moor Hall (TL467189), manor site with one arm of a moat on the north

Throcking Hall (TL338300), moated platform with brick revetment and foundations; (TL336302), and (TL337300), moats; and Broadfield Hall (TL324310), water features, probably former moat

Thundridgebury (TL368174), D-shaped moat

Wareside, New Hall Farm (TL389162), two opposite arms of the moat remain; and Bakers End, Castlebury Farm (TL393171), large pond may be evidence of a moat (TQ104944),

Watford, Oxhey Hall (TQ103944), moat surrounding later house

Watton-at-Stone, Well Wood (TL283190); and Chapel Wood (TL283188), earthworks of a possible ecclesiastical, defended site

Welham Green, North Mymms, Dixon's Hill Close, Pancake Hall (TL227051), moat

Wyddial Hall (TL374319), pond may represent the corner of a former moat; and Beauchamps (TL382314), three sides of a moat

Wymondley Priory (TL219279), moat

Appendix III

Licences to Crenellate

1346 Waytemore Castle, Bishop's Stortford, to Bishop of London
1357 St Albans Abbey, to Abbot and Convent
1386 Bygrave House, to John of Thornbury, knight of Totnes (Devon)
1426 Manor of the More, Rickmansworth, to Henry Beaufort, Bishop of Winchester, Bishop Winton of Durham, at al
1443 Rye House, Hoddesdon, to Andrew Ogard, William Oldhall, Robert Whytingham, et al.
1447 Hunsdon House, to Richard, Duke of York
1458 Manor of the More, Rickmansworth, to Ralph Boteler of Sudeley (Gloucestershire)

Appendix IV

Airfields and Other Aviation-related Sites

ASTWICK MANOR (TL205100) in Coopers Green Lane, Hatfield, the de Havilland technical school, moved from Salisbury Hall in 1947–48, with residential student accommodation added in the 1950s, and the re-erection of the Airspeed aircraft hangar from Salisbury Hall.

BALDOCK (TL253337) Tapps Garden Centre occupies a First World War hangar of unknown origin, but sometimes described as RNAS design, and possibly from Therfield LG.

BARKWAY (TL372365 and 381364) two aerials used by the RAF from 1942 for the GEE navigation system then, 1959–62, by 10th Communication Squadron USAF(E) as a signals link for bases in the eastern counties. The facility closed in 2011.

BISHOPS HATFIELD (TL216112) Short-lived Night LG used by 39 (HD) Squadron for only a few months during 1916 owing to its propensity for being fog-bound.

BOREHAMWOOD (TQ206968) an industrial unit in Warwick Avenue housed the RAF Central Link Trainer School from 1940, with ten Link Trainers.

BOVINGDON (USAAF Station 112/341) (TL005045) was built as a bomber airfield before being handed over to the USAAF, using it, initially, as an operational bomber station, then as a combat crew replacement centre training newly arrived aircrew. After the war it operated for both the RAF and the USAF as a communications hub housing transport aircraft. The USAF pulled out in 1962 and the RAF in 1969. Much of the site is now occupied by a prison.

BROXBOURNE (TL378065) began as the base of the Herts and Essex Flying Club in 1930. A Civil Air Guard unit trained until 1939, then a CRO repairing light aircraft throughout the Second World War.

BUSHEY HALL (TQ140950) (USAAF Station 341) SE of Watford, from 1942–44, this neo-Jacobean house of *c.* 1880, formerly a hydrotherapeutic establishment, was HQ US VIIIth AAF Fighter Command, until its removal to High Wycombe. It was demolished after the war.

EASTBURY PARK, Northwood, Watford (*c.*TQ100926) the Chateau de Madrid, later Eastbury Park Hotel, a Scottish baronial mansion of 1857, was acquired by the Air Ministry in 1938 and served as HQ and officers' mess for RAF Coastal Command from 1939; centre for administration of RAF Photo Reconnaissance operations; and an Operational Research Station in 1941. A buried Nissen hut, covered in concrete, was set up as an operations centre, only replaced by a permanent construction in 1944. The house burnt down in 1969.

ELSTREE (Aldenham) (TL162965) Opened as a flying club in 1935, with two hangars and a clubhouse; within two years it was being used by Hendon, and a year later by Northolt as an LG. It was used throughout the Second World War by Fairfield Aviation to test, repair and modify RAF aircraft in new hangars provided by MAP for this purpose. Proctors and Lysanders were some of the aircraft using the airfield. Surviving buildings include a MAP R-type hangar, a pair of recently rebuilt joined Super Robins, and a Blister.

GARSTON MANOR (TL114014), now reverted to its original name of High Elms Manor. An adjacent house named Bucknalls was built in 1855 and became the centrepiece of the Building Research Establishment campus. It was set up as a standby RAF Fighter Command operations room, possibly codenamed 'Magic'. A second standby facility codenamed 'Radium', which may have initially been located in Garston Manor itself, moved to Aldenham Country Club, now part of Haberdashers' Aske's School. Both were fully manned and operational by June 1940. Garston Manor is also recorded as housing at different times: RAF Fighter Command's administrative department and the HQ of RAF No. 80 (Radio Countermeasures) Wing.

HATFIELD (Chiswick) (TL206090) developed by de Havillands in the 1930s to replace Stag Lane in North London's expanding suburbia. A flying school and aircraft factory were built despite the site being far from perfect for flying. No. 1 (E&R) FTS became No.1 EFTS in autumn 1939, flying Gipsy Moths and DH9s. The factory produced both the Rapide and its military version, the Dominie, used for airborne wireless instruction or as a light transport aircraft for, amongst other tasks, collecting ATA pilots from their delivery points. Dominie production moved to the Brush Works at Loughborough in 1943 to allow a greater concentration on the Mosquito. The surviving administration/canteen building is now Hatfield Police Station.

HERTFORD (Ware) (TL347132) site astride the present A10 possibly used as a night LG during 1917, but abandoned the following year for a site at Stanstead Abbots.

HILLEND FARM (TL165115) RLG established by the RAF during the Second World War and used by No. 1 EFTS Hatfield.

HITCHIN (Willian) (*c.*TL223296) This daytime LG was bombed by Zeppelins in October 1916, presumably by panicked flyers jettisoning their bombs on either the first target they recognised or a lucky strike on a landing ground.

HITCHIN (TL185303) Automobile Association landing ground in the 1930s, with a maximum landing run of 700yds (650m).

HUNSDON (TL426138) operated fighters and fighter-bombers from May 1941 to May 1945. It was equipped with two concrete runways, a Bellman hangar and sixteen Blister hangars. It came under the 2nd Tactical Air Force in 1943 and carried out raids against V-1 launch sites and other specified targets.

LEAVESDEN (TL095003) Bought by the Air Ministry in 1940 as a shadow aircraft factory administered by de Havillands of Hatfield. Extensive hangars, offices, control tower and workshops were built, and a 3,000yds runway laid. After the Second World War the site stayed in MoD hands but was leased to Rolls Royce to build aero engines. Flying ceased in 1994, and the site now operates as film studios.

LONDON COLNEY (TL178021) A landing ground was developed in 1916 into a training station and provided with three 1915-pattern flight sheds and a pair of GS 'Belfast truss' sheds and huts. It retained the last plane store in England until its recent demolition. It was used by a number of squadrons being prepared for service on the Western Front and was designated as, initially, a training squadron station (TSS) and then a training depot station (TDS). It closed in 1920, and was not used by the RAF in the Second World War, possibly owing to the close proximity of Salisbury Hall and Radlett. The remaining structures were, however, employed by the Civil Defence organisation which added a MT shed. The brick-built First World War plane store and workshop and the Second World War MT shed built by CD survived until very recently.

MATHAMS WOOD (TL460180) in use as an LG from 1937 and by Lysanders in 1940; the precursor of RAF Sawbridgeworth (qv)

MILL GREEN (TL248103) RAF Airfield Construction Service (see Welwyn below)

NUTHAMPSTEAD (TL435345) (USAAF Station 131) opened in 1943 for a USAAF fighter group escorting bombers on raids. The last year of the war saw a bomb group carry out 195 missions. The airfield was a storage site until 1954 and closed in 1959. Several buildings and elements of the bomb dump survive.

PANSHANGER (Holwell Hyde) (TL266126) began as a bombing decoy for de Havillands, at Hatfield, with a mock factory and airfield. It then developed as an LG for No. 1 EFTS, gradually taking over altogether from Hatfield. In 1947, de Havilland Aeronautical Technical School, once again, became No. 1 Reserve Flying School until 1953. The airfield site may now be developed for housing.

POUND FARM (maybe TL170106) has been recorded as being an RLG for de Havillands, Hatfield, in its flying club days. Pound Farmhouse is located on Sandridge High Street.

RADLETT (TL155036) The aerodrome opened in 1930 with test-flight hangars soon to be expanded on the Park Street site to accommodate the large Handley Page aircraft being built throughout the Second World War. In 1952 the main runway was extended for the Victor programme. With the demise of Handley Page in 1969, the airfield closed, and the main site was demolished. The Park Street flight-test sheds and offices survived at least into the 1990s.

SALISBURY HALL (Shenley) (TL195028) The Tudor house within its moat was the secret workshop where de Havilland developed the Mosquito. It is now an aircraft museum housed in hangars mainly imported from other airfields.

SANDRIDGE (Hillend Farm) (TL165115) LG for No. 1 EFTS, 1939–45

SAWBRIDGEWORTH (TL480154, re-sited to TL459177) a night LG used by No. 39 (HD) Squadron opened in 1916 and in operation until 1919. The site was then used for civilian gliding and flying, becoming an advanced LG from 1937. Army cooperation flights began using the ALG, known as Mathams Wood, and in 1940 it opened officially as RAF Sawbridgeworth. Fighter squadrons of the 2nd TAF flying Mustangs and Spitfires operated during 1943–44, carrying out sorties against German defences during the D-Day campaign.

STANSTEAD ABBOTS (TL393112) was used as a night LG by No. 39 (HD) Squadron, operating F.2Bs out of North Weald (Essex) throughout 1918.

STEVENAGE (TL225250) aircraft factory opened in 1954 by English Electric to replace their cramped facilities at Luton and continued in use by the British Aircraft Corporation, its successor company, and the predecessor of British Aerospace (later BAe).

STEVENAGE (TL238234) De Havilland factory built in 1956 and continued in use by Hawker Siddeley.

THERFIELD (Heath Farm) (TL304371) LG used by No. 75 (HD) Squadron during 1917

WATFORD, Nascot Lodge (USAAF Station 549), 87 Langley Road, was HQ combat support wing and base for 1584 Quartermaster Battalion, Mobile Aviation, 1942–45.

WELWYN (TL272132), RAF Mill Green, No.2 School of Airfield Construction, and the depot of the RAF Airfield Construction Service.

WOODSIDE PLACE (TL252069) Advanced ammunition park (AAP) under No. 64 MU, supplying RAF No. 11 Group with mainly small arms ammunition (SAA), 1941–46

Appendix V

Barracks, Drill Halls, TA Centres and Army Reserve Centres

Ashridge, drill station for 'F' Company, 1st Battalion, Hertfordshire Regiment (TF), in 1908; no dedicated building identified but likely to have been Ashridge

Ashwell, drill station for 'E' Company, 1st Battalion, Hertfordshire Regiment (TF), in 1908; no dedicated building identified

Baldock, drill station for 'E' Company, Hertfordshire Regiment (TF), in 1908; no dedicated building identified, but old town hall opened c. 1880.

Barnet, #14 Union Street, HQ 'F' Company, 1st Volunteer Battalion Middlesex Regiment (ex 12 Corps; ex 3 Corps, Middlesex RVC), in 1902, then 'B' Company from 1907. #51 Salisbury Road: HQ 'D' Squadron, Hertfordshire Yeomanry, in 1908. #High Street, militia barracks (1855) base for 2nd or Edmonton Royal Rifle Regiment of Middlesex Militia; 7th (Royal 2nd Middlesex Militia) Battalion, KRRC in 1881; in 1908: 'F' Company, 1st Volunteer Battalion Middlesex Regiment; in 1911: 'B' Company, 7th Battalion Middlesex Regiment; 'D' Squadron, Hertfordshire Yeomanry; Army Service Corps: Middlesex Brigade Company, Divisional Transport & Supply Company; in 1914: No. 2 Company, 3rd Volunteer Battalion, Hertfordshire VR; in 1935: records and pay office, RCT; demolished 1980 for Spires Shopping Centre. #St Albans Road, drill hall built in 1937 for 334 Company, RE (TA); in 1947: 470 HAA Regiment; in 1955: 1557 Transport Company RASC; in 1961: 56 Squadron (City of London) Signal Regiment; in 1965: 240 (Hertfordshire) Tank Transport Squadron, RCT; in 2014: 240 (Barnet) Transport Squadron, Royal Logistic Corps. In current use as ARC

Bishops Stortford, #Silver Leys, barracks of the Hertfordshire Light Horse, 1862–79

#White Horse Yard, North Street, 'C' Company, 1st (Hertfordshire) Volunteer Battalion, Bedfordshire Regiment, in 1902. #Market Square, drill hall, 1906; 'C' Company, Hertfordshire Regiment, 1908–50

Braughing, drill station for 'C' Company, 1st Battalion, Hertfordshire Regiment (TF), in 1908; no dedicated building identified

Cheshunt, #Crossbrook Street, drill hall, 1938; in 1914, drill station for 'H' Company, Hertfordshire Regiment (TF)

Chorleywood, #drill hall, built 1913 by Lady Ela Russell, for her rifle club; drill station for 'D' Company (Watford), 1st Battalion, Hertfordshire Regiment (TF), 1914

Croxley Green, #Dickinson Institute, opened 1895, Rifle Club and Church Lads' Brigade drill hall. For TAC, see Watford.

Great Berkhamsted, #Town Hall (1859) HQ, 'F' Company (half), 1st Battalion, Hertfordshire Regiment (TF), in 1908

Harpenden, #Cowper Road, drill hall for 'C' Squadron Hertfordshire Yeomanry, in 1904–08; drill station for 'B' Company, 1st Battalion, Hertfordshire Regiment (TF), in 1908

Hatfield, #Batterdale, Hertfordshire Militia HQ, 1852; demolished after 1955; drill station for 'A' Company, 1st Battalion, Hertfordshire Regiment (TF), 1908; #Old Rectory Drive and Woods Avenue, land let by Hertfordshire County Council to TAVR, 2020

Hemel Hempstead, #Bury Road (1898), drill hall for 'F' Company (half), Hertfordshire Regiment (TF), demolished. #St Albans/Lower Adeyfield Road, TAC, 1955; redeveloped

Hertford, #28 St Andrew Street, Yeomanry House, HQ 4th East Anglian Brigade, RFA (TF); and ammunition column; HQ and 'B' Squadron, Hertfordshire Yeomanry, in 1914. #24 Raynham Road/Street, HQ and 'B' Squadron, Hertfordshire Yeomanry in 1908. #London Road, militia barracks built in 1883–84 for 4th Battalion, Bedfordshire Regiment (ex-Hertfordshire Militia), in use 1884–1914; Hertford area HQ, Eastern Command, 1939–45; demolished. #Port Hill, drill hall and armoury built 1898, for HQ and 'A' Company, 1st Battalion, Hertfordshire Regiment; 342 Battery, 86th (East Anglian), (Hertfordshire Yeomanry) Brigade, RFA (TA) in 1921; demolished

Hitchin, #Bridge Street, armoury of 'G' Company, 1st (Hertfordshire) Volunteer Battalion, Bedfordshire Regiment; in 1902; #Verulam Road, armoury of 'G' Company, 1st Battalion, Hertfordshire Regiment (TF), in 1908; #Bearton Camp, 344 (Howitzer) Battery, 86 (East Anglian), (Hertfordshire Yeomanry) Brigade, RFA (TA) in 1921; #Bedford Road 1930s TAC, included part of Bearton/Hitchin First World War camp. Refurbished 2023 and in current use by 3rd Battalion, Royal Anglian Regiment, and 162 Medical Squadron, 254 Medical Regiment

Hoddesdon, #Century Road, drill hall, 'H' Company, 1st Battalion, Hertfordshire Regiment (TF), opened in 1907 and destroyed by fire in 1975. Currently a cadet hut occupies the site.

Letchworth, #drill station for 'E' Company, 1st Battalion, Hertfordshire Regiment (TF), in 1908; #Icknield Way, TAC built 1930s for Hertfordshire Regiment; converted to a dwelling

Little Berkhamsted, drill station for 'A' Company, 1st Battalion Hertfordshire Regiment (TF), in 1908; no dedicated building identified, but village hall opened in 1888

London Colney, drill station, 'B' Company, 1st Battalion, Hertfordshire Regiment, in 1908; no dedicated building identified

Royston, #Melbourn Street, drill hall for 'E' Company, Hertfordshire Regiment, 1902 and 1908; #rifle range on Therfield Heath; #armoury in Mill Road by 1914, now Royal British Legion Club. #Tannery Drift School, ACF hut, 2020

St Albans, #Hatfield Road (opposite Marlborough's Almshouses), volunteer drill hall (1898) in use by 'B' Company, 1st Battalion, Hertfordshire Regiment (TF); 'C' Squadron, Hertfordshire Yeomanry; 1st (Hertfordshire) Battery, 4th East Anglian Brigade, RFA (TF) and 1 Section Ammunition Column, in 1914; #23 Prospect Road, HQ 'C' Squadron, Hertfordshire Yeomanry, by 1908; #Ramsbury Road; HQ 'C' Squadron, Hertfordshire Yeomanry, 1910–14; #Artillery Buildings, Harpenden Road, RFA gun park and riding school: 1st (Hertfordshire) Battery, 4th East Anglian Brigade, RFA (TF), in 1910; 341 Battery 86 (East Anglian), (Hertfordshire Yeomanry) Brigade, RFA (TA) in 1921; #Holywell Hill, TAC, 1939–47, Hertfordshire Yeomanry Field Regiment RA (TA); demolished in 1987 for Sports Centre; #99 Camp Road, TAC in converted bakery opened 1976, 201 Hertfordshire and Bedfordshire Yeomanry Medium Battery, 100th (Yeomanry) Field Regiment RA (TA); closed 2000, site re-developed for housing. #Holywell Hill, ACF and Sea Cadets huts in current use

Sawbridgeworth, drill station for 'C' Company, 1st Battalion, Hertfordshire Regiment (TF), in 1908; no dedicated building identified

Stevenage, #Southgate, drill station for 'G' Company, Hertfordshire Regiment (TF); no dedicated building identified, but public hall and assembly rooms on 1896 OS map

Tring, #Western Road, 'E' Company, 2nd (Hertfordshire) Volunteer Battalion, Bedfordshire Regiment, in 1890, 'F' Company in 1902; armoury in occupation, 1908; Tring Rifle Club, 1914. #Victoria Hall, Akeman Street, built 1886, reported as base in Kelly's Hertfordshire Directory for 1890, in use 1914

Wadesmill, drill station for 'C' Company, 1st Battalion, Hertfordshire Regiment (TF), in 1908; no dedicated building identified

Waltham Cross, #34 Station Road, drill hall for 'H' Company, Hertfordshire Regiment (TF), in 1914

Ware, #17 Amwell End, drill hall, built 1899 for 'D' Company of 1st (Hertfordshire) Volunteer Battalion, Bedfordshire Regiment, and after 1908, as a drill station for 'C' Company, Hertfordshire Regiment (TF)

Watford, #Clarendon Road, Clarendon (Agricultural) Hall, 'A' and 'G' Companies, 2nd (Hertfordshire) Volunteer Battalion, Bedfordshire Regiment, in 1902–08; #32 Market Street, 'A' Squadron, Hertfordshire Yeomanry, in 1908 and 1914; #19 and 20 E(a)stcourt Road, 'D' Company, 1st Battalion, Hertfordshire Regiment (TF) with drill hall in Clarendon Hall, in 1914; 2nd(Hertfordshire) Battery, 4th East Anglian Brigade RFA (TF), in 1914; 343 Battery, 86 (East Anglian), (Hertfordshire Yeomanry) Brigade, RFA (TA) in 1921; #Croxley Green, Tolpits Lane, 479 (Mobile) (Hertfordshire Yeomanry) HAA Regiment (TA), in 1951; ACF current (2023); #Brackenhill House, Oxhey Drive South, served the RNR as HMS *Wildfire*, 1988–2011

Watton-at-Stone, drill station for 'A' Company, 1st Battalion, Hertfordshire Regiment (TF), in 1908; no dedicated building identified,

Welwyn, #Becket Hall, 28 London Road, 'F' Company, 1st (Hertfordshire) Volunteer Battalion, Bedfordshire Regiment, in 1902; drill station for 'G' Company, 1st Battalion, Hertfordshire Regiment (TF), in 1908; #Lemsford Lane drill hall, 1939, for 79 (Hertfordshire Yeomanry) HAA Regiment; re-developed as housing

Whitwell, drill station for 'G' Company, 1st Battalion, Hertfordshire Regiment, in 1908; no dedicated building identified

Widford, Bell Lane, #Village Hall, built 1910 as drill station for 'C' Company, 1st Battalion, Hertfordshire Regiment (TF) (Bishops Stortford)

Wormley, drill station for 'H' Company, 1st Battalion, Hertfordshire Regiment, in 1908; no dedicated building identified

Appendix VI

Army Camps, Depots and Billets

First World War

Abbots Langley: 13th and 14th Battalions, London Regiment, 4th London Brigade, 1914

Apsley, Salmon Meadow: HQ 8th (Howitzer) Brigade, RFA, TF, 1914

Bedmond: 15th Battalion, London Regiment, 4th London Brigade, 1914

Berkhamsted Camp: Northumberland Fusiliers, 1914; then Inns of Court OTC/14 Officer Cadet Battalion, 1914–18. (See also Tring, below.)

Bishop's Stortford: assembly area for 137 (Staffordshire) Brigade, 1914 and for King Edward's Horse, 1915; concentration area for 3rd (Home Defence) Army, 1914–15; 2/17th and 2/18th Battalions, London Regiment, 180th Brigade, 60th Division, 1916. #Wheatsheaf Hotel, HQ North Midland Mounted Brigade, 1914

Chipperfield Common: 2nd London Divisional Army Service Corps (TF), 1915

Gorhambury Park: 21st–24th Battalions, London Regiment, 6th London Brigade, 2nd (London) Division (TF), 1914–15; divisional res, 1915

Harpenden: Notts and Derby (139) Brigade, 46 (North Midland) Division (TF), 1914; HQ 31st (Alien Labour) Battalion, Middlesex Regiment, 1918

Hemel Hempstead, #Gadebridge Camp: hutted camp for RFA units of 2nd (London) Division; then for infantry and artillery of 54th (East Anglian) Division; then reserve RFA units; then became VD hospital, 1917; High Street: #Corn Exchange, #Brotherhood Hall, #Old Recreation Ground, etc: 2nd London Division artillery, 1915; High Street, #Town Hall: HQ 5th Brigade RFA (Gadebridge Park); #St Pauls Sunday School: HQ 6th Brigade RFA (Hand Post Farm); #Boxmoor Hall: HQ 7th Brigade RFA, 1914

Hertford, 2/19th and 2/20th Battalions, London Regiment, 180th Brigade, 60th Division, 1916

Hitchin, Bearton Camp: RE signal draft depot, First World War; 11 Auxiliary MT Company, ASC, 1915–20

Kings Langley, Hunton Bridge: King Edward's Horse mobilised 1914; #Langley Lodge; 2nd London (Heavy) Battery, RGA, 1915

Leavesden Lunatic Asylum: 8th Battalion, London Regiment, 47th Division, 1915

Leverstock Green: 16th Battalion, London Regiment, 4th London Infantry Brigade, 1915

Much Hadham, #Wynches Camp, concentration area 3rd (Home Defence) Army, 1914–15

New Barnet, 2/4th Battalion, London Regiment, 2/1st London Brigade (TF), 1914

Piccotts End: #RAMC camp serving West Herts Hospital, 1915

Redbourn: 25th (Cyclist) Battalion, London Regiment (divisional cyclists, soon detached and sent to India as infantry), 1915

Royston, Therfield Heath, #militia camp, 5th Battalion, Royal Welsh Fusiliers and 4th Battalion, Cheshire Regiment, 1914; battalion HQ in #Church House, Kneesworth Street

St Albans, #Peahen Hotel: HQ 2nd (London) Division (TF), 1915; London District Signals, OC and three companies, 1914; 17th–20th Battalions, London Regiment, 5th London Brigade, 2nd London Division (TF), 1914; 28th Battalion, London Regiment, attached 2nd London Division (TF), 1914; St Peters St, #Donnington House: HQ 54th (East Anglian) Division (TF), 1915 and HQ 2nd (Reserve) London Division (TF), 1915; 4th, 5th, 6th and 7th Battalions, Essex Regiment, Essex Brigade, 54th Division, 1915; 35 Reserve Park Army Service Corps, 1915; 2/21st, 2/22nd and 2/24th Battalions, London Regiment, 181st Brigade, 60th Division (TF), 1915; assembly area for 176 Brigade, 59 (2nd North Midland) Division (TF), 1915–16

Sawbridgeworth, concentration area for 3rd (Home Defence) Army, 1914–15

Shafford Camp, #Childwickbury, RAMC hutted camp and military hospital, 1915–19

Shenfield, 4th Battalion, Suffolk Regiment, detached from 54th Division, 1914

Tring, HQ 21st Division; 12th and 14th Battalions, Northumberland Fusiliers, 14th and 15th Battalions, Durham Light Infantry, and 9th and 10th Battalions, King's Own Yorkshire Light Infantry (K3) billeted in Tring and Berkhamsted, 1914–15; 24th and 25th (Reserve) Battalions, Middlesex Regiment formed, 1915

Watford, 4th and 5th Battalions, Norfolk Regiment and 5th Battalion, Suffolk Regiment, Norfolk and Suffolk Brigade, 54th (East Anglian) Division (TF), 1914. (see Shenfield); Notts and Derby Brigade, 59 (2nd North Midland) Division (TF), 1915–16

Second World War

Albury Hall, Bishops Stortford was HQ XI Corps District, Eastern Command, 1941
Ashridge, 11th Hussars, attached XXX Corps, 21st Army Group, pre-D-Day, 1944
Barnet, Dyrham Park: 21st Army Tank Brigade workshops to 1942
Bishop's Stortford: Royal Artillery School of Aircraft Recognition moved to Deepcut 1944; US Military Police, 887 Aviation Company, Detachment 'B', 1944–45
Cheshunt, Theobalds Park, RA, AA Operations Room and AA gunners' camp
Colliers End, Militia Camp, 1938; S/L units 1940; US army post-war
Elstree/Boreham Wood, Eastern Command ordnance depot, 1943
Garston Manor, No. 4 War Office Selection Board, 1942
Harpenden, 'Pynders', Grange Court Road, HQ 136 Infantry Brigade, GHQ Reserve, 1941
Hemel Hempstead, Cupid Green, 1st AA Division ordnance workshop; REME basic training, post-1941, and command depot
Hitchin, 91 Bancroft Road: HQ 135 Field Regiment, 1939; US Military Police, 887 Aviation Company, Detachment 'D', Second World War
Hitch Wood Battle Camp, Second World War infantry/artillery training camp
Royston, Therfield Heath, militia camp, 1938
St Albans, St Peter's Institute, Hatfield Road, army recruitment office
St Albans, US military police, 887 Aviation Company, Detachment 'D', Second World War
Wall Hall, No. 4 War Office Selection Board, 1942
Watford, HQ US army Eastern Base Section, COMMZ, ETOUSA
Welwyn Garden City: Eastern Command intelligence centre

Appendix VII

Second World War Anti-Invasion Defences

Outer London Defence Line 'A'

Examples of structural components:

Type DFW3/22 pillboxes @ TQ074942, 129994, 139999; TL321049, 332048, 320049, 314048, 351044, 355045 and 363053

Type DFW3/24 pillboxes @ TQ190999 and 192999; TL148011, 180003, 187002, 197001, 201002, 249024, 254027, 277038, 289035, 298043 and 304041

Type DFW3/27 octagonal pillboxes @ TQ076942, 080941, 083942, 085944, 102947 and 123981; TL326048, 333046, 337046, 339045, 347047 and 376053

Heightened pillboxes @ TL332049 and 368052. Open-roofed, 5-sided pillbox @ TQ098940. Pillboxes built against buildings @ TQ107951 and 119955. Fortified bunker @ TL324050. Pillbox over porch at Merchant Taylors' School @ TQ092941. A/T Wall @ TL367052. A/T cubes (3′6″ or 4′): 27 at Ridgeway/Well Road (TL271035); 25 straddling the railway embankment @ TL249024; 85 @ TL307046; 15 @ TL333047; and 19 @ TL363053. Roadblocks @ TQ082942, 129991 and 136997; TL172004, 299043 and 302042

Vulnerable point defences (west to east)

A/T cones at Little Heath (TL015082); loopholed wall at Hexton (TL105304). Four pillboxes at Garston (High Elms) Manor (TL109017, 110020, 110022 and 114016); A/T Caltrop on B556 at South Mimms (TL218015);pillbox at Dancers Hill (TQ239981); A/T cones at the junction of Bradmore Lane and Station Road, Brookmans Park (TL240043); Tett Turret at (TL25398 05508) and A/T cones on the SE side of Woodside Lane, Bell Bar; Spigot

Mortar position at Brookmans Park (TL2616 0518); A/T cones at junction of Swanley Bar Lane and Great North Road (TL26143 03166); Spigot Mortar position at Hertford (TL316130); loopholes in the bridge parapet at Broxbourne on the B194 (TL373070)

AIRFIELD DEFENCES

Hunsdon: AM design shellproof Type DFW3/22 pillboxes @ TL424143, 423144,426145, 429144,428134, 417134, 418135 and 416139; BHQ @ TL425133; AM design splinter-proof Type DFW3/22 pillbox @ TL420142; F. C. Construction 'mushroom' pillbox @ TL425142

Leavesden: square pillbox @ TL086002; hexagonal non-standard pillbox @ TQ086998; five-sided pillbox @ TL103023

Panshanger: possible BHQ @ TL274126; formerly two Allan Williams turrets

Patchetts Green (TQ143973) Type DFW3/22 pillbox defending Elstree airfield

Radlett: Allan Williams Turret @ TL157047; Type DFW3/23 pillboxes @ TL154019

Sawbridgeworth: AM-design shellproof Type DFW3/22 pillboxes @ TL454184, 462184, 459186,458178 and 464183; BHQ @ TL464183

Appendix VIII

Hertfordshire Home Guard Units

Battalions: 1 Much Hadham; 2 Hitchin; 3 Hertford; 4 Welwyn; 5 Harpenden; 6 Oxhey; 7 Chipperfield; 8 Croxley Green; 9 Bricket Wood; 10 Watford; 11 Bishop's Stortford; 12 Letchworth; 13 de Havilland; 14 Hatfield; 15 St Albans

7th Battalion, Hertfordshire Home Guard dispositions (Francis and Crisp)

HQ 7th Battalion, 41 High Street, Tring; Tring Home Guard Battle School

No. 16 ('A') Company: HQ 47 High Street, Hemel Hempstead with platoons in Hemel Hempstead, Boxmoor, Felden, Apsley, Great Gaddesden, Brocks Fireworks factory and Dickinson's factory

No. 17 ('B') Company: platoons at Berkhamsted, Keys Yard; Northchurch Hall; Nettleden with HQ at New Lodge, Berkhamsted; Potten End village hall; Little Gaddesden, HQ Red House

No. 18 ('C') Company: with platoons at Icknield Way, Brock; Bunkers Hill, HQ Pendley Farm; Aldbury, HQ in The Old Rectory; Wilstone, HQ in Great Farm; Champneys House

No. 20 ('D') Company: HQ platoon; Bovingdon; Chipperfield House as platoon HQ; Old Vicarage and 32 Rucklers Lane, HQs of the two Kings Langley platoons

Other Home Guard units based in Hertfordshire

Bishops Stortford platoon of 13th Essex (35 GPO) Battalion

Boxmoor, Berkhamsted and Tring stations, railway sections under 10th Hertfordshire Battalion, with HQ at Watford Station. LMS platoon, The Grove, Chandlers Cross

Boxmoor, Tring Bus Garage and Two Waters Bus Garage at Durrants Hill, Hemel Hempstead, two sections of a London Passenger Transport Board Home Guard platoon
Bushey, 2043 (London) Home Guard Taxi Company
Hatfield, de Havilland works ('A' and 'C' LAA Troops of 13th Battalion); Radlett, Handley Page works ('A' LAA Troop of 15th Battalion); and Watford, Leavesden de Havilland works ('B' LAA Troop of 13th Battalion)
Hemel Hempstead, Berkhamsted and Tring, three sections of 19 Platoon, 'E' (Luton) Company, 6th (34 GPO) Cambridgeshire Battalion

Home Guard locations

Barnet, Dyrham Park, post office HG training school
Bishop's Stortford, 11th (Bishops Stortford) Battalion HQ, Market Square Drill Hall; Thorley, HQ Oxford House, White Posts, with a platoon in Twyford Mill
Harpenden, 'Ferndale', 50 Luton Road: zone HQ, No. 1 (West) Group HG; Victoria Road schools
Hertford, zone HQ, 19 North Crescent, then Port Hill, drill hall
Ringshall, HQ behind the Bridgewater Arms and a rifle range in the local parkland

Appendix IX

Air Defence in the Second World War and the Cold War

First World War: guns and searchlights

Cheshunt: 1×6-pounder Hotchkiss in early 1916; 1×3in. in summer 1917
Hoddesdon: 1×3in. in summer 1917. Ridgeway: 1×3in. in summer 1917
Tylers Causeway: 1×3in. in summer 1917. Watford: 1×75mm in summer 1917
Ware; 1×6-pounder Nordenfeldt in early 1916; 1×3in. in summer 1917
St Albans, HQ of the north-western sector of the London Gun Barrier equipped with sixteen 3in. 20cwt guns, seven 18-pounders in fixed positions and twenty 24in. searchlights

Second World War: guns, searchlights, and decoy sites

Cheshunt, Theobalds Park, TL345006, AA operations room and camp
Cheshunt, TL334006, possible HAA practice battery; now Gunsite Stud Farm
Cheshunt, Waltham explosives works, LAA position, TL365030, January 1940
ZE11 Cheshunt, Albury Farm, TL350017, unarmed but manned by 302 Battery, 99 HAA Regiment in August 1940
ZW3 Burnt Farm, Goffs Oak, TL321021, four 3in. mobile AA guns in 1940; unarmed in 1942, but manned by 469 Battery, 132 (Mixed) HAA Regiment in 1943. Recorded on site as subsequently being armed with four 3.7in. and four 4.5in. HAA guns
Hatfield airfield and de Havilland Works in May 1940 were defended by four 40mm Bofors guns, TL213088; June 1942, HM1 Lemsford HAA Battery, TL214116, armed with four 3.7in. static HAA guns; then 'A' and 'C' Home Guard troops (13th Battalion), 1943

RAF Hunsdon (VP611): four 40mm Bofors mounted on static platforms: TL429144, 431139, 423131 and 419136
Radlett Handley Page works, TL157023, four 40mm Bofors and 2 Lewis guns in May 1940; then 'A' Home Guard Troop (15th Battalion), 1943
Watford, Leavesden de Havilland shadow factory: 'B' Home Guard Troop (13th Battalion)

BOMBING DECOYS IN HERTFORDSHIRE

Barley (TL396399) 'Q' decoy for RAF Bassingbourn (Cambridgeshire)
Barnet (TQ234980) 'Q/K' decoy for RAF Northolt (Middlesex)
Braughing (TL411261) 'Q' decoy for RAF Hunsdon
Puttenham (SP883135) 'Q/QF' decoy for RAF Halton (Buckinghamshire)
Holwell Hyde (TL269132) 'Q/F' 'M' series decoy for de Havilland, Hatfield
Bendish (TL163205) and Flamstead (TL085127) 'Q/L'; permanent Starfish and marshalling yards (MY) and factory lights (FL) for Luton (Bedfordshire)
Essendon (TL264094) 'C' Series decoy for Hatfield, then factory blackout effects

ROYAL OBSERVER CORPS

Watford, GPO Buildings, Market Street: HQ No. 17 Group 1931–43
Watford, Cassiobury Drive, HQ No. 17 Group, 1943–53; No. 5 Group, 1953–68
Watford, Cassiobury Drive, Metropolitan Area Training Centre, 1968–73

POST-SECOND WORLD WAR AA

Chenies R8 ROTOR bunker (TQ015997) demolished

POSTS

Ashwell TL272392, 1931; TL268385, 1954; u/g 1960; in use until 1990
Berkhamsted TL001087, 1931; SP998091, 1958; u/g 1960; closed 1968
Brent Pelham TL433306, 1937; TL425315, 1955; u/g 1961 + ORLIT 'B'; in use until 1990
Cuffley TL288017, 1936; closed 1968
Elstree TQ181948, 1932; u/g 1959; in use until 1990
Great Offley TL136274, 1938; u/g 1959; in use until 1990
Hatfield TL242143, 1931; Welwyn 1934; 207111, 1957; u/g 1958; in use until 1990
Hertford TL339127, 1931; 314131, 1934; 324118, 1956; 293145, 1960; u/g 1961; in use until 1990
Kimpton TL173179, 1931; 181178, 1958; u/g 1958; closed 1968
Kings Langley TL068001, 1931; 067019, 1949; u/g 1959; in use until 1990

Letchworth TL215328, 1931; 202325, 1949; u/g 1960; in use until 1990

Markyate Street TL065166, 1931; 058155, 1935; u/g 1960; in use until 1990

Much Hadham TL436198, 1937; u/g 1962; in use until 1990

Park Street TL149036, 1931; 141043, 1935; 154042, 1960; u/g 1961; closed 1968

Rickmansworth TQ053945, 1931; 043948, 1935; Chorleywood, 1953; u/g 1959; closed 1968

Walkern TL282263, 1931; 303261, 1949; u/g 1953; closed 1968

Appendix X

Military and Auxiliary Hospitals

First World War

Aldbury (Isolation) Hospital treated typhoid cases
Aldenham, Wall Hall, VAD Hospital
Ashridge House, auxiliary hospital and rehabilitation centre for St Albans Hospital
Ayot St Lawrence, Ayot House, officers' hospital
Baldock, Ashwellbury, Red Cross auxiliary hospital;
Barnet, Ewen Hall, auxiliary hospital; ten-bed military hospital in militia barracks, 1914–18
Berkhamsted, The Beeches, Red Cross auxiliary hospital
Bishop's Stortford, Clare House and Dane Hall, Red Cross auxiliary hospitals
Boxmoor House, Hemel Hempstead, Red Cross auxiliary hospital
Broxbourne, Wormleybury, Red Cross auxiliary hospital
Childwickbury, village institute run by YMCA for RAMC at Shafford Farm (qv)
Chorleywood, drill hall, Red Cross auxiliary hospital, 1915–18
Croxley Green, The Dickinson Institute, VAD convalescent hospital, 1915–18
Federated Malay States Hospital, Blackmore End, Gustard Wood
Hadley, The Mount and Ken Cottage, Red Cross auxiliary hospitals
Harpenden, Rosemary (St John's), Red Cross auxiliary hospital
Hatfield, Northcotts, Red Cross auxiliary hospital
Hertford, Woodhall Park and Goldings, Red Cross auxiliary hospitals; Wallfields Hospital
Hitchin, The Maples and Kings Waldenbury, Red Cross auxiliary hospitals
Hoddesdon, Rose Hill, Red Cross auxiliary hospital
Knebworth, Golf Clubhouse, Red Cross auxiliary hospital
Monken Hadley, The Mount and St Martha's Convent School, auxiliary hospitals
Much Hadham, Woodham House, 54 High Street, Red Cross auxiliary hospital
Napsbury, the Middlesex County Asylum became the County of Middlesex War Hospital, with 1,600 beds, plus a further 250 for mentally ill troops, 1915–19

New Barnet, St James's, Red Cross auxiliary hospital
Potters Bar, Little Heath, Red Cross auxiliary hospital
Rickmansworth, St Augustine's and The Studio, Rectory Lane, Red Cross Hospitals
Rothamsted Park, twenty-four-bed tented military hospital, then Harpenden Common Golf Clubhouse
Royston, Queens Road, The Schools, Red Cross auxiliary hospital
St Alban's, Bricket House, Red Cross auxiliary hospital
St Pauls Walden Bury, Red Cross convalescent hospital
Shafford Camp military hospital, on Childwickbury Estate, 106-bed VD hospital
Stevenage, Bragbury End, auxiliary hospital
Totteridge, Park House, Red Cross auxiliary hospital
Tring (Isolation) Hospital treated scarlet fever, measles and diphtheria cases; Victoria Hall RAMC and VAD auxiliary hospital (1914–16); schools in the High Street and in Henry Street were taken over by the War Office as medical centres
Ware, The Priory, Red Cross auxiliary hospital
Watford, Wall Hall and Lady's Close, Red Cross auxiliary hospitals
Welwyn, Codicote Hospital; Digswell House convalescent home for Australian soldiers
Wheathampstead, Lamer Park, Red Cross auxiliary hospital

Second World War

SCHEDULE OF BRITISH GENERAL HOSPITALS IN HATFIELD HOUSE (FROM TNA WO222/1568)

September 1939: 24th British General Hospital (RAMC) to Belfast, August 1940
October 1940: 34th British General Hospital (RAMC) to Sierra Leone, December 1940
November 1940: 7th British General Hospital (RAMC) to Cairo, January 1941
November 1940: 17th British General Hospital (RAMC) to India, February 1942
February 1941: 38th British General Hospital (RAMC) to Iraq, February 1942
January 1942: 91st British General Hospital (RAMC) to Nathanya, Palestine, July 1942
April 1942: 68th British General Hospital (RAMC) to Lagos, May 1942
May 1942: 83rd British General Hospital (RAMC) to North Africa, November 1942
June 1942: 31st British General Hospital (RAMC) to Algiers, November 1942
November 1942: 73rd British General Hospital (RAMC) to Bayeux, July 1944
January 1943: 87th British General Hospital (RAMC) to Nairobi, April 1943

June 1943: 150th British General Hospital (RAMC) to Nairobi, July 1943
June 1943: 151st British General Hospital (RAMC) to Mombasa, July 1943
September 1944: 109th British General Hospital (RAMC) to Duffel, October 1944
November 1944: 23rd British General Hospital (RAMC) to Lille, December 1944
April 1945: 33rd British General Hospital (RAMC) to Goodwood, May 1945

MILITARY HOSPITALS

Abbots Langley/Leavesden Hospital, annexe EMS hospital
Hatfield House, RAMC, military hospital
North Mymms, 7th US General Hospital; 16th, 17th and 55th Hospital Trains
Panshanger Hospital, military hospital
Shenley Hospital, military psychiatric hospital
Watford General, EMS hospital
Watford, Reed's School, RAMC, military hospital

AUXILIARY HOSPITALS AND CONVALESCENT HOMES

Aldenham, Church Farm, convalescent home / auxiliary hospital
Ashridge House, EMS annexe to Charing Cross Hospital
Bishops Stortford, Hassobury Park, convalescent home / auxiliary hospital
Bishops Stortford, Haymeads Hospital, annexe of the London Hospital
Broxbourne, Wormleybury, convalescent home / auxiliary hospital
Hatfield, Bush Hall, convalescent home / auxiliary hospital
Hemel Hempstead Union Workhouse, huts added c. 1939 as temporary EMS wards
Hemel Hempstead Institute, military hospital
Hitchin, St Paul's Walden Bury, convalescent home / auxiliary hospital
Little Berkhamsted, Culverwood, convalescent home / auxiliary hospital
North Mymms Park, convalescent home / auxiliary hospital
St Pauls, Walden Bury, military convalescent hospital
Tring, Drayton Manor, convalescent home / auxiliary hospital
Ware, St Margaretsbury, convalescent home / auxiliary hospital
Watford, Munden House, Red Cross resthouse for Civil Defence workers

Appendix XI

POW Camps

First World War

Baldock, The Maltings House; Berkhamsted Common, Frith House; Bishops Stortford, Oak Hall; Braughing, Mount Hill; Buntingford, Bradbury House, Hare Street; Bygrave; Great Munden, Libury Hall Farm Colony; Hatfield: Chantry House, Church Army Rest, Marshmoor Sidings, Newtown House, The Workhouse; Hemel Hempstead, The Old House Camp; Hitchin Migratory Gangs and Holes Mansion, Great Offley; Knebworth, Migratory Gang; Standon, New Street Farm; Wallington (near Baldock)

Second World War

Gorhambury Park Camp 235; Harpenden, Batford Camp 95; Hemel Hempstead, The Arches, Felden Camp 235; Meesdon Camp 128; Much Hadham, The Wynches Camp 411; Royston Heath Camp 29; South Mimms, Dancers Hill Camp 33, two tented compounds

Appendix XII

The Secret War

Albury Hall was used by SOE for training agents.

Aldenham, Wall Hall, SOE Special Training School (STS) 39 from 1943; finishing school for SOE agents and for training Political Warfare Executive (PWE) operatives

Aldenham Country Club, requisitioned for BBC overseas broadcasts; standby RAF Fighter Command operations room

Ardeley, Gardeners End, Stevenage, SOE Station XIX Operation Periwig

Aston House, Stevenage, SOE Station XII research and development: weapons/tactics

Ayot St Lawrence, Bride Hall, SOE Station VI, weapons acquisition department

Barnet, Arkley View, HQ Radio Security Service (RSS), Radio Analysis Bureau, V(w); The Lawns, Scotswood, Rowley Lodge and Meadowbank were taken over for training, transmitting, intercept work, messes and billets.

Boxmoor House: reported as an SOE 'listening post'

Borehamwood, The Thatched Barn SOE Station XV camouflage

Brickendonbury Hall, SOE Station XVII, weapons development and sabotage training; initially Section 'D' of SIS for sabotage planning and training

Brockett Hall: SOE Station 20, possible accommodation for Polish operatives

Brookmans Park, BBC transmitter

Elstree, GPO repeater station linking research department transmitters and receivers

Elstree, RAF No. 80 (Signals) Wing meacon-jammer station paired with Harpenden

Elstree, Lister Institute, research into biological warfare from 1940

Garston Manor (High Elms Manor since 2010) Road Research Laboratory, RAF No. 80 (Signals) Wing first HQ of radio counter measures (RCM), Autumn 1940; standby RAF Fighter Command operations room in garage

Harpenden, Rothampstead Manor, No. 1 Special Wireless Group, army 'Y' service station

Harpenden, Home Office 'Y' service station

Harpenden, Kennels Farm, Kinsbourne Green near Luton Hoo entrance, meacon jammer set up by RAF No. 80 [Signals] Wing, paired with Elstree, one of fifteen such pairings countrywide

Hemel Hempstead, The Arches, Felden, Polish Radio Intelligence Section

Hexton, Section D, Political Intelligence Department, PWE

High Barnet, Ravenscroft Park, RSS intercept training centre

Letchworth, Icknield Way, British Tabulating Machine Company made Bombes for GC&CS at Bletchley Park

Letchworth, Pixmore Lane: parts for GC&CS Bletchley Park Bombes made in factory, in 1982 a government training centre

Letchworth, Spirella factory made wiring for GC&CS Bletchley Park Bombes

Little Berkhamsted, the Manor House housed SOE personnel before and after secret missions

Markyate: army 'Y' service listening post

Moor Park, Rickmansworth: 1 SAS Brigade tactical HQ, 1944, deception exercise

Old Welwyn, North Road Garage: store for SOE Station IX, then to The Frythe

Old Welwyn, North Road Garage: SOE MT section repair depot

Old Welwyn, The Frythe: Station IX SOE; research and development; engineering section ultimately used 20,000ft^2 of workshops and hangars

Park Royal, 487 Western Avenue, W3, United Dairies, storage for SOE submersibles

Potters Bar, outstation of radio counter measures (RCM) RAF No. 80 (Signals) Wing

Radlett, Aldenham Lodge Hotel, RAF No. 80 (Signals) Wing RCM HQ moved from Garston Manor in October 1940 with operations room at 'Newberries' on Radlett golf course from late 1941

Radlett, RCM HQ billets in 'Tintern' with NAAFI next door and 'Lamorna'; WAAF hostel at 'Heathwood' in The Avenue; sick quarters in 2 Beech Avenue with Shenley Military Hospital as backup; Howards Garage, on Watling Street, as RCM HQ MT section

Radlett Hall, Watling Street, RCM HQ services canteen

Radlett RCM HQ, The Houseboat, Watling Street, base for jamming unit from March 1943, monitoring three coastal anti-jamming sites set up in February 1942

Radlett RCM HQ, operations room for information from watchers, 'Y' stations, etc.

Radlett: MI5 safe house

RAF Sawbridgeworth, aircrew selection and flying training for SOE operations

St Albans, Glenalmond, Central Registry, Section V, V(d), MI6/SIS, until 1943
St Albans, Old Gorhambury House: SOE Station XI, accommodation for operatives
Sandridge, Woodcock Hill, Radio Security Service (RSS) / MI6 DF Station from 1937
Stanstead Abbots, Briggens, SOE STS 38
Shenley, army 'Y' service listening post
Watford, Yeast-Vite factory, Whippendell Road: Station VIIb SOE radio training
Watford, King George's Avenue, Allensor's joinery factory, SOE Station VIIc, wireless section research
Watton-at-Stone, Frogmore Hall and Farm: SOE Station 18, accommodation

Bibliography

Airfield Research Group News, 'Hatfield', in *Airfield Review* 63 (Ware: August 1993)

Anderson, I., 'Radlett Airfield History & Handley Page' in *Airfield Review* 115 (Thetford: ARG, 2007)

Barker, J., *England, Arise: The People, The King & The Great Revolt of 1381* (London: Abacus, 2014)

Benfield, D., 'Broxbourne' in *Airfield Review* 4.4 (Market Deeping: ARG, 1981)

Betts, A., *RAF Airfield Construction Service 1939–46* (Ware: Airfield Research Publishing, 1995)

Biddle, M., et al., *The Excavation of the Manor of the More, Rickmansworth, Hertfordshire* (Rickmansworth: Three Rivers Museum Trust, nd; accessed February 2023)

Brown, I., *Ravensburgh Castle Hillfort Project Interim Report No. 1* (Oxford: Institute of Archaeology, 2015)

Bryant, S., *Settlement and Landscape in the Late Iron Age of Hertfordshire and the Northern Chilterns* (unpublished Ph.D. thesis, University of Sheffield, 1999)

Busby, J., 'Local Military Forces in Hertfordshire 1793–1814' in *Journal of the Society for Army Historical Research*, 1953

Campbell, D., *War Plan UK: The Truth about Civil Defence in Britain* (London: Burnett Books, 1982)

Child, G., 'Pillboxes on the London side of the River Colne and the Grand Union Canal in south-west Hertfordshire' in *Loopholes* 11 (Dover: Pillbox Study Group, 1995)

Clapham, A, and Godfrey, W., *Some Famous Buildings and their Story* (London: Technical Journals Ltd., 1929)

Colvin, H. (ed.), et al., *The History of the King's Works Volumes 1 & 2 The Middle Ages* (London: Her Majesty's Stationery Office, 1963)

Corley, D., 'Bovingdon' in *Airfield Review* 65 (Ware: Airfield Research Group, 1994)

Davies, K., *The Deserted Medieval Villages of Hertfordshire* (Chichester: Phillimore, 1973)

Doyle, P., 'De Havillands, Salisbury Hall' in *Airfield Review* 9.1 (Reading: ARG, 1987)

Fitzpatrick-Matthews, K., pirtonhistory.org.uk (North Hertfordshire Museum, 2020)

Fitzpatrick-Matthews, K., *Caldecote: a deserted village in North Hertfordshire* (North Hertfordshire Museum, 2020)

Foot, W., *Beaches, fields, streets, and hills: the anti-invasion landscapes of England, 1940* (York: CBA, 2006)

Foot, W., 'AD 60, Boudica: Unlocated battle' in *British Archaeology* 165 (York: CBA, 2019)

Francis, P., and Crisp, G., *UK Military Command & Control Organisation* (London: English Heritage, 2008), on CD and Internet.

Francis, P., et al., *20th Century ARP Railway Control Centres* (Airfield Research Group, 2014) on CD.

Francis, P., 'RAF Panshanger: History and Context' in *Airfield Review* 147 (Sheffield: Airfield Research Group, 2015)

Halpenny, B., *Action Stations 8: Military Airfields of Greater London* (Sparkford, Yeovil: Patrick Stephens, 1984 and 1993)

hertfordshire-genealogy.co.uk/Military Matters

Hicks, C., *The Wars of the Roses* (New Haven and London: Yale University Press, 2010)

Hoskins, W., *The Making of the English Landscape* (London: BCA, 1955 and 1977)

irvingq.com/our/story

Kaye, S., 'Can computerised terrain analysis find Boudica's last battlefield?' in *British Archaeology* 114 (York: CBA, 2010)

Kent, J., et al., *Excavations at South Mimms Castle, Hertfordshire 1960–91* (London: London and Middlesex Archaeological Society, 2013)

Kingston, A., *Hertfordshire in the Great Civil War and the Long Parliament* (London: E Stock, 1894)

Jones, A., *'Commotion Time' The English Risings of 1549* (unpublished Ph.D. Thesis, University of Warwick, 2003)

Lewis, C., 'Plague Pits, Potsherds and the Shock of the Black Death' in *British Archaeology* 150 (York: CBA, 2016)

Liddiard, R., *Castles in Context* (Macclesfield: Windgather Press, 2005)

McCamley, N., *Cold War Secret Nuclear Bunkers* (Barnsley: Leo Cooper, 2002)

Morrison, W., et al., 'The Discovered Hillfort, the Chiltern Hills' in *British Archaeology* 176 (York: CBA, 2021)

Nash, F., *Spigot Mortar Pit at St Albans* (Stratford E15: After the Battle No. 81, 1993)

O'Connor, B., *Churchill's School for Saboteurs Station 17* (Stroud: Amberley, 2013)

Osborn, M., and Symons, G., *Airfield Focus 82: Nuthampstead* (Peterborough: GMS, 2010)

Osborne, M., *Defending Britain* (Stroud: Tempus, 2004); *Always Ready, the drill halls of Britain's volunteer forces* (Leigh-on-Sea: Partizan Press, 2006); *Pillboxes of Britain and Ireland* (Stroud: Tempus, 2008); *Grandad's Army: Volunteers Defending the British Isles in the First World War* (Stroud: Fonthill Media, 2020)

Peerless, G., 'A History of Elstree Aerodrome' in *Airfield Review 90* (Stockport: ARG, 2001)

Penn, T., *The Brothers York: An English Tragedy* (London: Penguin Books, 2020)

Pevsner, N., *The Buildings of England—Hertfordshire* (London: Penguin Books, 1953)

Pullen, R., and Omish, D., *Brickkiln Wood: Analytical Earthwork Survey 62-2010* (Eastney: English Heritage Research Department, 2010)

RCHME: *Pillbox at Merchant Taylors' School; Request Survey* (London: English Heritage, 1995)

Renn, D., *Medieval Castles in Hertfordshire* (Chichester: Phillimore, 1971)

Russell, M., *Arthur and the Kings of Britain* (Stroud: Amberley, 2018)

Sainsbury, Col. J., *The Hertfordshire Batteries, Royal Field Artillery 1908–20* (Welwyn: Hart Books, 1996)

Sainsbury, Col. J., *HERTS VR An account of the Hertfordshire Volunteer Regiment and other units of the Volunteer Training Corps and the Volunteer Force raised in Hertfordshire, 1914–21* (Welwyn: Hart Books, 2005)

Seymour, W., *Battles in Britain 1066–1746* (Ware: Wordsworth, 1997)

shenleyww1.wordpress.com

subbrit.org.uk/locations/hertfordshire/chenies: images of Chenies ROTOR station

Thurley, S., *The Royal Palaces of Tudor England* (London: 1993)

Index